Charging the Net

Charging the Net

• • • • • • • • • • •

A HISTORY OF BLACKS IN TENNIS
FROM ALTHEA GIBSON AND ARTHUR ASHE
TO THE WILLIAMS SISTERS

Cecil Harris

AND

Larryette Kyle-DeBose

*With a Foreword by James Blake
and an Afterword by Robert Ryland*

Ivan R. Dee

CHICAGO

www.ivanrdee.com

Library of Congress Cataloging-in-Publication Data:
Harris, Cecil, 1960–
Charging the net : a history of blacks in tennis from Althea Gibson and Arthur Ashe to the Williams sisters / Cecil Harris and Larryette Kyle-DeBose with a Foreword by James Blake and an Afterword by Robert Ryland.
p. cm.
Includes bibliographical references and index.
ISBN-13: 978-1-56663-714-5 (cloth : alk. paper)
ISBN-10: 1-56663-714-7 (cloth : alk. paper)
1. Tennis—History. 2. Tennis players—United States—Biography. 3. African American tennis players—History. I. Kyle-DeBose, Larryette, 1945– II. Title.
GV992.H37 2007
796.3420922—dc22
[5]
2007002747

This book is dedicated to the memory of Althea Gibson, one of the unsung heroes of her time in the struggle against racism. Although she suffered numerous humiliations, beginning in the 1940s she successfully fought to bridge the gap that prevented African Americans from playing in professional tennis. Ms. Gibson accomplished this feat with the quiet dignity of a true trailblazing visionary. Thank you, Althea Gibson, for your contribution to African-American history.

Foreword

I BEGAN playing tennis at the age of five with my older brother, Thomas, and our parents, Thomas Sr. and Betty. My parents met through tennis, so it was never unusual for us to play. I was really inspired by Arthur Ashe—the only black man to win Wimbledon and the U.S. Open. I was inspired by what he accomplished in tennis and the kind of humanitarian he was.

When I was a boy, Arthur came to speak to us at the Harlem Junior Tennis Program in New York City. I was in the program from the time I was five until I was ten years old. I can't say I remember what he said that day, but I knew he was famous, and it meant a lot that he took the time to speak to a group of kids. He became my role model. I speak to youth groups myself because you never know if someone listening will be inspired, the way Arthur's life inspired me.

Arthur often talked to black youth about the importance of education. My parents did the same thing. Because of them, my brother and I studied hard, got excellent grades, and went to Harvard University. Both of us played tennis there. Thomas was an All-American and graduated with a degree in economics. I was the No. 1 college player in the country before leaving in 1999, after my sophomore year, to turn pro.

During the 2006 season I became one of the Top 10 players in the world. I definitely overcame a lot to get where I am today. When I was thirteen I was diagnosed with severe scoliosis (curvature of the spine). I had to wear a brace eighteen hours a day. Thank goodness, I grew to be a pretty healthy and athletic guy at 6-foot-1.

I hope my success in tennis will spur a few more black players to pick up a racquet. I know it's helped in raising the awareness of the Harlem Junior Tennis Program. It means a lot to me to have learned to play tennis in Harlem because Althea Gibson—the first black person to win Wimbledon and the U.S. Open and to be ranked No. 1 in the world in the 1950s—grew up in Harlem. A few years ago some people were trying to get rid of the Harlem program and turn it into just an all-purpose boys' and girls' club with basketball and everything else, and get rid of the tennis altogether. Luckily that's been stopped. It's still all tennis.

I saw what happened with the Williams sisters when they were dominating tennis. I saw how many kids, especially African-American girls, wanted to be like Venus and Serena. When I was first starting out on tour, every time I'd go through a security check-in or something similar, someone would ask me, "Do you know Venus and Serena?" The Williams sisters were out there so much that people just wanted to be like them.

I hope I can have that kind of success and that kind of effect where people may ask other players if they know James Blake, if they can beat James Blake, or if they can hit a forehand like him. It makes me proud to be part of the legacy of black players in tennis, along with Althea and Arthur, Venus and Serena, Yannick Noah, MaliVai Washington, Zina Garrison, Lori McNeil, and so many others.

Kids today see that, as an athlete, you're part of something, and they see that other people look up to you, and they want to be like you. I think that's just natural for kids, to see role models and want to be like them. I want to show kids that there is a lot of athleticism and a lot of fun in tennis, with many fans. I've been lucky to have plenty of fans. I want to show kids that there is a way to do it without being in the National Basketball Association or the National Football League. I hope I can have that kind of lasting effect.

JAMES BLAKE

Contents

Foreword by James Blake   vii

Introduction   3

1   "There is no African-American culture in tennis"   9

2   "I'm not going to be who you want me to be"   25

3   "I'm not giving anything else away"   46

4   "He was exactly who we needed at the time"   76

5   "We were the only show in town"   106

6   "You tell me what the similarity is"   124

7   "It was as if God handed these two young girls to me"   140

8   "Tennis is a family sport"   155

9   "You niggers gotta get off the court"   169

10   "Nobody called me names on the court, but nobody rooted for me either"   182

11   "You could play the French Open and never really see Paris"   199

12   "It's nice not to have to be a fly in milk"   211

13   "We need you out here"   224

Afterword   237

Appendix A: ATA Singles Champions   239

Appendix B: World-Ranked Black Tennis Players   244

Bibliography   247

Index   257

Charging the Net

Introduction

STRANGE, isn't it, how societal mores have made certain occur-
rences in the sports world seem odd to us? We would do a double
take today at the sight of a black jockey, though at the turn of the
twentieth century, before large purses became familiar in thorough-
bred racing, most of the top jockeys—including Isaac Murphy, Jimmy
Winkfield, and Oliver Lewis—were black.

Similarly, people of all hues used to look askance at a black person on a tennis court, racquet in hand. "Are you trying to be white?"
the player would hear. "Why do you want to play that sissy sport?"
Yet despite tennis's country-club roots, blacks in America have played
"the gentlemanly game" since the late nineteenth century.

So, no, Richard Williams is not the Father of Black Tennis, and
black involvement in the sport did not begin in the mid-1990s with
his braids-and-beads-wearing daughters, Venus and Serena. Yes, the
sisters were the first black tennis superstars of the hip-hop generation, and they are the most celebrated sister act in sports history. But
others came before them.

Ninety-one years ago blacks started a tennis organization of their
own that exists to this day. But because the gates to tennis's premier
events were closed to blacks for generations, the history of the American Tennis Association and its earliest champions remain virtually un-
known, even to the most eager consumers of sports. Names like Tally
Holmes, Reginald Weir, Ora Washington, Margaret and Roumania

Peters, Jimmie McDaniel you did not hear unless you went out of your way to listen. That's one oversight this book will attempt to correct.

The ATA, which consists of member clubs throughout the United States and the Caribbean, used to be the only place where blacks could play tennis and become champions. The ATA was not to tennis what the Negro Leagues were to baseball, because the ATA is still here. Not as celebrated in the black community as it once was, but still here.

The relatively simple act of blacks playing tennis together, encouraging one another, pushing one another, keeping their egos in check, may be just what American tennis needs in 2007 to reverse its decline in the sport. What decline, you ask? Well, in 2006 no American man or woman won a Grand Slam event. That had not happened since 1937—a year in which blacks were segregated from big-league tennis.

During most of the twentieth century, when the United States Lawn Tennis Association was not interested in prospecting for talent in the nation's black communities, the ATA did the work. Even after the gatekeepers of American tennis dropped "Lawn" from the name of their organization and then allowed a few blacks to play, the ATA continued to develop players. Players who became champions. And champions who became teachers of world-class champions.

John Wilkerson belongs to the latter group. The 1971 ATA singles champion established a public park program in the shadow of predominantly black Texas Southern University in Houston, Texas—the kind of program that could exist in any largely black community in America if the people running the sport really wanted it to happen. And from Wilkerson's program in the 1970s sprouted a pair of world Top 10 talents, Zina Garrison and Lori McNeil, and several other successful pros. Black tennis is a concept Wilkerson endorses with a passion.

"Being a USTA champion could be too hard, too big a step," he said. "But being an ATA champion was one of the little steps you could take. That's where you learned about yourself and could grow. You found out you weren't alone. There were other black players in the same struggle as you.

"Nowadays black players think they're alone because they're put into environments like these tennis academies, where they are the only black players, and they're made to feel like they're doing something wrong because they play tennis. There's nothing wrong about doing something you have the God-given ability to do."

Althea Gibson had the ability. Black tennis's answer to Jackie Robinson was a South Carolina–born, Harlem-reared, self-described tomboy who excelled in basketball, football, baseball, stickball, and any other activity with the word "ball" in it before her introduction to tennis. Power and speed in a nearly six-foot frame and a steely resolve made Gibson the most celebrated female athlete of her time—twice an Associated Press Athlete of the Year—even though tennis's gatekeepers kept her out of the sport's major tournaments until she was twenty-three. It was a terribly late start for a world-class player. Come to think of it, Robinson was named the National League Rookie of the Year as a Brooklyn Dodger at age twenty-seven, once the major leagues finally opened to him. Both pioneers knew how to make up for stolen time.

But if you are among the 35,000-plus who attend a day or evening session of the U.S. Open tennis championships in New York City during a fortnight from late August to early September, try to find the name Althea Gibson anywhere. She grew up less than an hour from the Billie Jean King National Tennis Center, where the Open takes place. She won the singles tournament twice and the mixed doubles event once. She was No. 1 in the world—the first black tennis player given the chance to reach that status. Aside from her name being listed on the board of champions as the 1957 and 1958 title holder, she is missing.

Blacks at the highest level in tennis struggle for recognition and respect, whether they are players, coaches, administrators, or umpires. That reality has always been part of the challenge.

At least the main stadium at the U.S. Open bears the name of Arthur Ashe, as transcendent an athlete as tennis has ever seen—another black champion with roots in the ATA. A native of Richmond, Virginia, Ashe once said, "What infuriated me most was having a white Richmond type come up to me somewhere in the world and say, 'I saw you play at Byrd Park when you were a kid.' Nobody saw me play at Byrd Park, because when I was a kid it was for whites only."

Considering how Arthur Ashe distinguished himself as a human-itarian, goodwill ambassador, cultural idol, author, journalist, and social activist, it may be easy to forget what a great player he was. On July 5, 1975, Ashe played the perfect match, dismantling the seemingly invincible, world No. 1 Jimmy Connors to become the first black man to win tennis's premier event, Wimbledon. Ashe also was a collegiate star at UCLA, the 1968 U.S. Open champion and U.S. Nationals champion (another first for African-American men), and a Davis Cup winner as player and captain for the United States. Intro-spective and shy, Ashe nevertheless accepted the burden of playing not only for himself but for all African Americans while raising our collective consciousness and teaching us how to live, and die, with dignity.

There is a bridge in black tennis from Gibson and Ashe to the Williams sisters that will be traveled in these pages, including stops at Washington, as in the Washington family, which has produced four black tennis pros with one becoming a Wimbledon finalist; and Aus-tralia, for Evonne Goolagong, the first Aborigine tennis star who did not give voice to her cultural pride until later in life; and Lynchburg, Virginia, for Dr. Robert Walter Johnson, who for twenty years opened his home and backyard clay court to teenage and preteen black players every summer to nurture and teach, and produce ath-letes. Many excelled in the ATA, others became pro stars. And his most accomplished pupils, Althea and Arthur, became legends once the racial barriers came down.

Chicago is also part of the journey. It's the birthplace of former tour champion Katrina Adams and the trumpeted teenager Donald Young, who may prove in 2007 that he is, as advertised, "the future of American tennis," or a plum plucked too soon. And Chicago is where Bob Ryland, still active in tennis at age eighty-seven, first found success in the sport. Before he was born to an African-American mother and an Irish-American father who taught tennis, his parents fled Mobile, Alabama, to avoid being killed for loving each other.

When Ryland's mother died, he was sent to Mobile to live with a grandmother. Several years later he found a cousin hanging from a tree. Once his father remarried, he moved to Chicago. He defeated Chris Evert's father and became the first black to win the Illinois high school tournament. He was one of the first blacks to compete in the NCAA championships, and in 1959 he was the first black tennis pro, touring with Pancho Gonzales, Don Budge, and Bobby Riggs. But in his greatest victory, ten years ago, he defeated cancer in straight sets.

So many stories, so many names of those linked by virtue of being black and in tennis. Scores of black men have achieved success in amateur tennis and early in their pro careers only to be burdened with the label "the next Arthur Ashe." Black women intent on finding their game and their place in the sport were labeled "the next Althea Gibson." Pressure came with such high expectations and the mistaken assumption by others that a black tennis professional, pre–Williams sisters, was a walking oxymoron.

Yet here we are in the second century of blacks competing in tennis. Those who make it on the pro tour, if only fleetingly, are the clearest success stories. Phil Williamson, an Ivy League Player of the Year at Columbia University, lacked the financial wherewithal to sustain a pro career. Dr. Diane Morrison Shropshire shot to the world Top 50 in her rookie year only to find that a tennis life held less appeal than a medical career. Both succeeded. So did many others. (A list appears at the back of this book.) Not every black person who has contributed to tennis will appear in these pages. Fortunately, the names are too numerous to mention. But those who represent a larger sample of the black experience in tennis are featured here.

Blacks will continue to come to tennis because of a sheer love of the game. Some will make tennis their life's work. Others will leave, having never felt comfortable at the highest level of a predominantly white and elitist sport.

How elitist is tennis? An instant-replay rule implemented in 2006 at selected tournaments, including the U.S. Open, allows players to challenge a limited number of line calls through the use of video technology. But the vast majority of tour professionals will never have a chance to use it. The technology exists only on the two main courts at the Open, where the "stars" play.

The chance to become a star, to be somebody, keeps blacks coming to tennis from around the world. Younes El Aynaoui, a lanky 6-foot-4 Moroccan, continues although he will soon turn thirty-six in a young person's sport. Eighteen years ago he arrived unannounced at the Nick Bolletieri Tennis Academy in Florida and strung racquets, drove the bus, and baby-sat for younger players so he could afford the fees to develop his game. He became a quarterfinalist at the U.S. Open and the Australian Open, two of the sport's premier events.

Yannick Noah also came from Africa. Ashe spotted him as an eleven-year-old in Cameroon, playing tennis with a wooden plank. Noah became a spectacular shot-maker, a French Open champion, a Davis Cup champion for France, a Hall of Famer. Today Gael Monfils, a black Frenchman who chose tennis over basketball, seeks his own path to stardom.

James Blake has found stardom. He began 2007 as tennis's top-ranked American and the No. 4 player in the world. He is America's best hope in the major tournaments this year. But in terms of achievement, he still lags behind the Williams sisters.

Venus Williams made a spectacular debut at the 1997 U.S. Open, showing an impressive combination of power, speed, and athleticism. But the women's tour was not ready for the seventeen-year-old. That's why her Romanian opponent in the semifinals delivered "the bump heard 'round the tennis world," a deliberate attempt to intimidate that failed. Venus triumphed and laid the groundwork for herself and Serena to become cultural phenomena that forever altered the landscape of tennis. Entering the 2007 season, Venus had won five singles titles in the sport's Grand Slam events (U.S. Open, Wimbledon, French Open, Australian Open). Serena had won seven—more than any black player in tennis history.

Venus missed the 2006 U.S. Open because of a right wrist injury. But Serena was there, sans the beads and braids she sported as a first-time Open champion in 1999. But she came as much as a curiosity as a contender. Many wondered would she be there sans intensity, sans hunger to regain the stature she once held in the sport. Just how would Serena look?

CHAPTER ONE

"There is no African-American culture in tennis"

• • • • • • • • • • •

Serena Williams looked better. Not better than she ever had. But when the 2006 United States Open began at the newly renamed Billie Jean King National Tennis Center in New York City, Serena looked better than she had in at least two years. That happened to be the last time she was the best female tennis player in the world. Although the sport has no commissioner to give voice to the sentiment, tennis sorely needed Serena to look better, and play better, than her health and outside interests had allowed. Professional tennis is infinitely more interesting when Serena is interested, when she is truly engaged in the competition—pumping her fists and emoting after a timely ace or a lethal passing shot, covering every nook and cranny of the court and preying upon opponents like an embodiment of the feline logo that adorned her wardrobe until 2003, the year she switched from Puma to Nike.

What neither tennis nor her legion of fans needed at the 2006 U.S. Open was the supersized Serena, the overweight and undertrained player who huffed and puffed and got blown off the court in the third round of the 2005 Wimbledon tournament by a journeywoman named Jill Craybas and in the third round of the Australian Open by a beanstalk-thin Daniela Hantuchova of Slovakia. Hantuchova had not won more than four games in any set against Serena in their three previous encounters. Yet against the supersized Serena, Hantuchova dictated every point and dismissed her in straight sets. Serena evoked images of tennis journalist Bud Collins's description of 1970s Czech defector Martina Navratilova: "The Great Wide Hope."

As America's premier tennis tournament began on August 28, 2006, Serena's fans hoped the most successful African-American player in the history of the sport—a player with seven Grand Slam singles titles before her twenty-fifth birthday—was again ready to perform like a champion. In part because of a balky left knee but largely because of an assortment of other interests, Serena appeared much closer to the end of her tennis career than the beginning.

Before her promotional appearance in May 2006 at a Ronald McDonald House in New York City, in support of stuffing teddy bears for ailing children, the Manhattan-based public relations firm representing Serena sent out a press release touting her accomplishments in every field other than tennis: She acts in movies. She acts on television. She has appeared on a reality show on cable television. (Hasn't everyone?) She designs clothes. She has her own perfume. She's a guest color creator for Estee Lauder cosmetics, distributed exclusively at Kohl's Stores.

But was she still Serena the tennis player? Or had she become Serena the brand? The fervent hope of those who were not ready to choose between Serena's lip gloss and Maybelline's, or between Serena's evening wear and Vera Wang's, or between Serena's cameo appearance on a sitcom and Salma Hayek's, was that the three weeks she spent at the Nick Bolletieri Tennis Academy in Bradenton, Florida (two weeks during the Wimbledon tournament and one week before the U.S. Open) would be enough to produce a fortnight of Serena at her best.

Serena at her best had the muscle definition of a superwoman—feminine yet powerful, the way women are drawn by Marvel or DC Comics. Only Serena's combination of strength and beauty was real, something to marvel from up close. Not too long ago, the mere act of Serena unpeeling her warm-up jacket to reveal the kind of finely sculpted arms and shoulders that other women—and most men—could only dream of brought gasps from a tennis crowd. The closer you sat to watch Serena play in those days, the better. Those who keep statistics at the Women's Tennis Association, of which Serena is a member, albeit a rather infrequent participant, list her at 5 feet 9 inches tall and 135 pounds. Actually, she stands 5-10. As for those 135 pounds? Well, maybe that was true in her teens. But that only goes to prove what veteran watchers of professional sports learned long ago: when it comes to athletes' physical dimensions, women lie to appear shorter and slimmer; men lie to appear taller and heftier.

When Serena looked her best—in the years 2002 and 2003, when she could place every major award in tennis on her kitchen table at the same time—she was truly something to see. As if to emphasize the point, Serena decided during the 2002 U.S. Open to pour herself into a skin-hugging black spandex number she called the "Cat Suit." It remains the only piece of wardrobe in tennis history that should have required a warning label: DANGEROUS CURVES AHEAD. The actress Michelle Pfeiffer, who played Catwoman in *Batman Returns*, had absolutely nothing on our girl Serena. That Serena won the 2002 U.S. Open in a breeze was of great benefit to the international photographers who crammed themselves into every available courtside location at the National Tennis Center. The shutterbugs got to click away at Serena in all her voluptuousness for two solid weeks, for seven matches, for the entire length of the tournament.

This was an untouchable period for Serena: she could be neither defeated nor outshined on a tennis court. From June 2002 to January 2003 she earned the Suzanne Lenglen Cup for winning the French Open on the slow red clay of the Stade Roland Garros in Paris. She captured the Venus Rosewater Dish for winning the championships at Wimbledon on the lush green grass of the All England Lawn Tennis and Croquet Club outside London. In her bodacious Cat Suit she clutched the silver trophy from Tiffany's that is awarded to the champion of the U.S. Open on the asphalt courts of New York. And she seized the Daphne Akhurst Cup as the winner of the Australian Open on the rubberized hard courts of Melbourne.

Normally, anyone who holds all four of these coveted titles simultaneously is credited with a Grand Slam, something that only five players in tennis history have accomplished: the Australians Rod Laver (twice) and Margaret Court; Oakland, California, native Don Budge; San Diego native Maureen ("Little Mo") Connolly; and Steffi Graf of Germany. But Serena, the finest player in the world in 2002 and 2003, and arguably the finest female player in the history of the sport, was not credited with a Grand Slam because of an outdated rule that a player must win all four titles in the *same* calendar year. (The same trivial distinction prevented Navratilova from being credited with a Grand Slam even though the Czech-born American won six consecutive Grand Slam tournaments, from Wimbledon in 1983 to the U.S. Open in 1984.) Clearly tennis needs to institute the kitchen-table rule: any player talented enough to put all four major tennis trophies on his or her kitchen table at the same time shall henceforth be awarded a Grand Slam.

No Grand Slam from the established order of tennis? No problem, Serena said. "I call it the Serena Slam," she told reporters. "I'm starting a new tradition." If not a tradition, the colorful monicker has become a lasting symbol of her preeminence on the distaff side of tennis. Billie Jean King never won all four major tournaments consecutively. Neither did Chris Evert. Neither did Althea Gibson, a multi-talented athlete barred from major tournaments until 1950 because of racism, who nonetheless became the first African American to win a Grand Slam event and achieve the world's No. 1 ranking. And neither did Evonne Goolagong, the second black woman—or, more precisely, the first Aborigine tennis player from the Australian outback—to win a Grand Slam title and become No. 1 in the world and a member of the International Tennis Hall of Fame.

While Serena dominated women's tennis, for her there was a significant downside: she dominated her sister, Venus, as well. Her older sister. A great player in her own right, when healthy and sufficiently motivated. The older sister who smoothed the potholes, who cleared away the brush and broken glass that could have tripped and injured Serena, who parried the blows more stinging than those Serena would later face.

Were it not for Venus, the elder sister by one year, three months, and nine days, Serena would not have been, could not have been, nearly as successful. To use an analogy from American football, if Serena, with her seven Grand Slam singles titles, six Grand Slam doubles titles, one Olympic gold medal, two Grand Slam mixed doubles titles, and designation as the world's No. 1 player for fifty-seven weeks, was the dynamic and speedy halfback who excelled whenever she touched the ball, Venus, with her five Grand Slam singles titles, two Olympic gold medals, six Grand Slam doubles titles, two Grand Slam mixed doubles titles, and designation as the world's No. 1 player for eleven weeks, was the powerful lead blocker, versatile enough to punish opponents and score entirely on her own.

Venus began clearing a path for Serena when she made her pro debut in 1994. Three years later, in her first U.S. Open, Venus began to deflect criticism of her father's decision to withhold her from junior tennis matches, the traditional prerequisite for success on the women's tour. Was Venus "scared" to play against other teens? That was the charge leveled by Martina Hingis—the Swiss player who in 1997 became the youngest ever to be ranked world No. 1 at age sixteen—and by Anna Kournikova, then a promising Russian player who would go on to win as many pro tournaments as any woman who ever held a racquet.

While Venus parried such verbal thrusts, Serena made her way up the world rankings, slowly. In her pro debut in September 1995, having just turned fourteen, she lost 6-1, 6-1 in the first round of a qualifying tournament in Quebec City to Anne Miller, a physician's daughter from Midland, Michigan. Afterward Miller said, "Maybe Venus will be an O.K. tennis player, but her sister sucks!"

Serena got into the qualifying tournament in Quebec City—which meant she would have had to win three matches to reach the main draw of the event—as a wild card because Big Sis had already beaten some women ranked in the Top 100, names like Amy Frazier and

Shaun Stafford, and because her father had already brokered deals with the sports management company IMG and the sportswear company Reebok that got his girls more exposure than the typical promising tennis teen.

Venus strode the same path as Serena, bypassing matches against other teens and taking on the women. For her coming-out party at the 1997 U.S. Open, Venus was seventeen with braided hair that looked like beaded tentacles because of the white beads that clicked and clacked with every stride and sometimes fell onto the court as a stark reminder that a heretofore unseen type of African-American tennis player had arrived. As Serena watched from the stands, Venus—all 6 feet 1-1/2 inches of her—displayed remarkable speed, power, and tenacity en route to the tournament final. But not without a vivid indication in the semifinals that an African-American player, especially one as talented and proud as Venus, would not be embraced or welcomed by the sport's Old World Order.

Representing the Old World on that first Friday afternoon in September 1997 was Irina Spirlea, a 28-year-old Romanian, a pro since 1990 with three tournament wins on her resumé. Representing change—lasting, forceful change in a country-club sport—was Venus Ebony Starr Williams, an unseeded player, meaning that she was not considered one of the top 16 players in the field of 128 women. Her world ranking was No. 66. Spirlea was the tournament's No. 11 seed.

The women's locker room at the U.S. Open was already a frosty place for Venus, the white players viewing the talented newcomer with an unmistakable contempt. "I smiled at her and she didn't smile back," was the publicly voiced criticism from Lindsay Davenport, then a twenty-one-year-old star from Southern California, who made Venus's perpetual game face sound like a punishable offense. Earlier in the tournament, Spirlea told reporters that Venus was not friendly in the locker room and acted like she was better than the other players. Soon they would find out she was.

These were familiar criticisms of a black outsider in sports: "uppity," too unaware of "her place" in the sport's hierarchy, which of course meant anyplace beneath the white players. But Venus's parents raised her and Serena to be proud and not to defer to anyone. After all, how can you beat a player who you believe to be superior? Zina Garrison, a black woman who reached the 1990 Wimbledon final, said Venus not making nicey-nice with the other girls in the locker room was hardly unprecedented. "All this criticism for Venus not talking to people?" Garrison wondered. "Monica [Seles] and Steffi [Graf] didn't talk to people either. Why are the standards different?" Because Graf and Seles, superstars in the 1980s and 1990s, are white. "That's America," Garrison said. "That's the reality."

Venus, and later Serena, would inspire fear in white players on the circuit because of their superior ability. Other black females had performed at the U.S. Open since 1968, the advent of the "open" era, when players competed for actual prize money like true professionals instead of receiving only under-the-table appearance fees. Garrison and Lori McNeil, black women from the same public park program in Houston, played with distinction on the women's tour. So had quite a few others, including Kim Sands of Miami, Katrina Adams of Chicago, Leslie Allen of Ohio, Renee Blount of St. Louis, and Diane Morrison and Andrea Buchanan, both of Los Angeles. Venus in 1997 was different. Venus was an African-American teenager talented enough and confident enough to win the tournament. And then win every other tournament. And not be so Joe Louis–humble about it ("I'm just glad I won"). Said Roger Smith, a black pro from the Bahamas who retired from the tour in 1997, "I remember seeing Venus in the players' lounge, always with her head high, looking like a queen, looking like she knew she belonged, because she did. She wasn't going to take a back seat to anybody, and when Serena came on tour, Serena acted the same way."

A black person who is not deferential can be intimidating to those who expect black people to act intimidated. That helps explain the actions of Irina Spirlea in the 1997 U.S. Open semifinals. She noticed that Venus never looked at her when walking to the chair during a changeover, which is the rest period that occurs after odd-numbered games or at the end of a set. So Spirlea, en route to her chair during the third set, intentionally walked into Venus and bumped her in full view of 23,000 spectators and millions of viewers on worldwide television. Spirlea reacted with spiteful glee. Venus said not a word and continued on to her chair to read the notes prepared by her parents and coach—notes on where to serve and what shots to play, and reminders to maintain her poise, which she needed to do now more than ever.

Reflecting on the "Bump Heard 'Round the Tennis World," Venus said, "A reporter informed me that while I was reading my notes, Irina was smirking and laughing and gesturing to her coach and friends in the stands." Clearly Spirlea tried to intimidate Venus, tried to make her remember that a seventeen-year-old black girl, a few years removed from living in hardscrabble Compton, California—"a ghetto Cinderella," according to her father—was not supposed to be at the U.S. Open, and certainly was not supposed to be beating a more experienced, higher-ranked white woman in the semifinal round. Yet there was Venus across the net, focused and resolute, determined to establish her own place in the U.S. Open final. After Venus showed enough speed, athleticism, and grit to fight off two match points and win the match, 7-6, 4-6, 7-6, Spirlea whined to the international media when asked about the bump. "I'm not going to move," she said defiantly. "She never tries to turn. She thinks she's the fucking Venus Williams."

A feeling of white skin privilege is what convinced Spirlea, an Eastern European, that she could deliberately bump Venus, an American, at America's annual Grand Slam tournament and then curse the American before the international media and get away with it. The American in this case was black, as much of a distinct minority in tennis in 1997 as she would have been in 1957, as she still is in 2007. Spirlea did her best to try to redirect the winds of change, to keep the elder of two supremely talented black sisters from ever having a major impact upon the sport. She tried and failed. So where is Spirlea now? In that unique place reserved for hula hoops, pet rocks, and New Coke: oblivion. "She's a tall white turkey," Venus's father told the sporting press about Spirlea. "She's lucky she didn't bump Serena like that. Serena would have knocked that girl out."

That Venus would lose the U.S. Open final to Martina Hingis, then ranked No. 1, was almost inconsequential. Venus had shown Serena, indeed every black person, what the possibilities were, even in a sport as unwelcoming as tennis. "Venus is out there playing for the African-American race," said Garrison, a guest in the Williams family box during the 1997 final. "It's an all-white sport. You feel it, are made to feel it, like you don't belong."

A profound change had come to women's tennis, to women's sports, and to international sports thanks to two sisters and the parents who raised them: the mother Oracene Price, a nurse by trade, and the father Richard Williams, a rascal by design. A bearish man of raspy voice, Richard Williams was given to outrageous boasts and wacky pronouncements, such as his supposedly forming a group to purchase Rockefeller Center in New York, or his acquiring the air space over France so that all owners of aircraft would have to compensate him for flying rights. But to many in the 1990s his craziest utterance was that his two daughters from a southern California ghetto would not merely become professionals in tennis but would someday be the two best tennis players in the world. Yet he turned out to be absolutely right.

Mr. Williams's seeming madness had a method. "When Richard would do crazy stuff like say outrageous things and hold up signs at tournaments ['IT'S THE WILLIAMS PARTY AND YOU'RE NOT INVITED'], he would be taking pressure off the girls," said Dave Rineberg, who as the hitting coach for both sisters from 1992 to 1999 helped refine their strokes and sharpen their games technically and strategically. "The press would focus on Richard instead of saying, 'Wait a minute. Venus just reached the semifinals of the U.S. Open at seventeen. Or Serena just won the [1999] U.S. Open at seventeen. Maybe we should be putting some pressure on these girls.'"

The parents understood that their daughters already faced more than enough pressure as black women in a predominantly white sport. Anything the parents, especially Mr. Williams, could do publicly to lighten the load was welcome. So he danced atop the broadcast booths on Wimbledon's Centre Court when Venus won her first of three titles there in 2000. And he danced on the court at the National Tennis Center three months later when Venus won her first U.S. Open title. He would do anything to try to take the bull's-eye off his daughters' backs and place it on his own. And if he did not completely succeed in removing Venus and Serena from the crosshairs of their detractors, he did diminish the pressure. Blacks who have played on the pro tour, particularly since the open era, know what those pressures are: the feeling that it's harder for you than your opponent to focus solely on your match because you have been subjected to racial slights—not finding a family in the tournament city to house you during the event; or being eyed with suspicion by security types on the event grounds; or being mistaken for another black player at the tournament if there is another one; or being referred to as "the brown one" if you are the only one; or having to win qualifying matches to get into the main draw of tournaments when less talented white players (perceived by tournament directors as "more marketable") get wild cards into the main draw; or not getting product endorsements that white players of lesser ranking receive; or being viewed by spectators as more of a curiosity than a competitor; or being asked *ad infinitum* by media types why you, a black tennis player, are even there!

"The game itself is not really an inviting place for people of color," said Kim Sands, a former women's head coach at the University of Miami. "There just aren't enough people of color who are successful in tennis where it becomes like the National Basketball Association or the National Football League. Tennis isn't like those sports in that you might not all be from the same background or you might not all be highly educated, but there are enough people in the sport who look like you and are successful. That makes the NBA and the NFL comfortable places to be for a black athlete, even though the players are not all of the same status. There's an African-American culture in the NBA and the NFL. There is no African-American culture in tennis. There's not a variety of our race represented in tennis. So it's not really an inviting place to hang around. It's as if they keep trying to find a way to block us out instead of including us more. In tennis the color line is what separates us. Players can be from Sweden, Russia, Belgium, wherever, but they're all white and they all gravitate toward one another. They don't feel like they're alone. Their color is the common denominator."

Approximately two dozen blacks are ranked among the top thousand men and women in tennis's world computer rankings today. Being a distinct minority as part of a relative handful of black players on the pro circuit helps explain why Serena and Venus Williams have always spent more time away from the circuit than other top players. The sisters rarely enter the same non–Grand Slam event, as was the case during their most dominant phase, because they do not wish to compete against each other. In the early years of Venus's and Serena's development, Richard Williams removed them from amateur tournaments. Lack of success was not the reason: by age twelve Venus had a 63-0 record in regional events sanctioned by the United States Tennis Association in southern California. But Richard Williams did not care to overexpose budding star Venus and stealth weapon Serena.

"Mr. Williams knew he had a couple of thoroughbreds, and he wasn't going to let the system, and by that I mean the USTA, ruin his girls," said William Washington, a black man and the father of Mali-Vai Washington, a 1996 Wimbledon men's finalist. "All the USTA would have tried to do was change the way those girls were playing, which would have been the worst thing for them."

The Williamses lived at that time in Compton, a place immortalized in rhythmically notorious terms by the 1980s gangsta rap group N.W.A. (Niggaz Wit Attitude). In a 2005 national study of America's most dangerous cities based on six crime categories, Compton finished fourth (behind St. Louis, Detroit, and Flint, Michigan). "I wanted to live in the worst ghetto in the world so [my daughters] could see all the bad that can happen to you if you don't get an education," Mr. Williams said. Whether or not Mr. Williams, a man given to expressions of hyperbole and braggadocio, was serious about his reason for living in Compton, he and his family would find out in 2003 just how dangerous that neighborhood can be. When he reflected on life in the 'hood in the 1990s, he almost boasted of having to sweep broken glass and crack vials off the tennis court before he could coach his daughters. He's understandably proud of his role in producing two world-class superstars in a sport in which his family had no previous history, a sport he neither played nor watched much as a boy raised by a single mother. Julia Williams supported her son and four daughters by picking cotton in Shreveport, Louisiana. "My mother was my dad, my psychiatrist, my hero, the greatest person who ever lived," Richard Williams said in a 1997 interview. "She taught me pride, decency, religion, and that civilization would disappear when the family went bad. The only mistake she ever made was to marry my father."

In the 1970s Richard Williams met Oracene Price, a woman with three daughters, Yetunde, Isha, and Lyndrea, from a previous relationship. Richard already had children from an earlier union who lived with their mother. Richard and Oracene married and had two children together: Venus born June 17, 1980, in Lynwood, California, and Serena born September 26, 1981, in Saginaw, Michigan. By the time the family of seven settled in Compton, Mr. Williams ran a small business, Samson Security, and held on to a big dream. He saw in the 1970s that it was now possible for women to make big money playing tennis, thanks to the efforts of crusading athletes like Billie Jean King, who in 1971 became the first female athlete to earn $100,000 in prize money in one year. Mr. Williams wanted all five daughters with whom he now lived to play tennis, but he knew the two youngest would have the best chance to succeed.

Watching a women's tennis final on television one Sunday afternoon, he saw Natasha Zvereva, a good but not great player from Belarus, pocket $75,000 for one week's work. Mr. Williams became convinced that he was on the right track. He now viewed the sport the way a mid-nineteenth-century prospector viewed gold on the trip west. With tennis books and videocassette tapes, Richard and Oracene taught themselves enough about the game to get the girls started. Venus and Serena hit with power and tenacity—Venus more upright and precise with her strokes, Serena more powerful, compact, and daring in her choice of shots. Both covered the court like baby lionesses. And both loved the game. The metronomic ritual of hitting forehand after forehand, backhand after backhand, serve after serve, did not seem to bore them. Not yet, anyway.

Neither Venus nor Serena is a natural tennis player, for there is no such thing. The unique strokes required to play the game with proficiency must be learned, as does the footwork, as does the pursuit of proper angles from which to strike the ball for a desired effect, as does a temperance of the desire to try to crush the ball with every swing. Although Mr. and Mrs. Williams laid the foundation on which two future champions were built, they list themselves as the coaches of record for Venus and Serena for the same reason that people buy vanity license plates: because they can. The truth is, a pair of amateur coaches, no matter how much they adored their daughters, could not have turned them into world-class players, indeed world champions, without helping hands. Truly experienced coaches were sought to provide schooling in the more technical aspects of the game. First, Rick Macci (pronounced MAY-cee), who runs a tennis academy in Florida, worked with the girls for a year and a half during their adolescence. But the relationship soured.

Word of developing talent travels fast in the tennis community. It was not long before representatives from sneaker companies such as Reebok, Nike, adidas, and Fila, who prowl the junior tournaments and tennis academies in search of the Next Big Thing, had taken note of the Williams girls. Always savvy in his business dealings, Mr. Williams extracted from Reebok an under-the-table deal worth $1 million, allowing the company the first opportunity to sign Venus to an endorsement deal. Not an actual deal, mind you, only the *chance* to sign Venus once she turned pro. And the deal did not guarantee that Reebok would be able to sign Serena. With Reebok money in tow, the Williamses bid adieu to Compton, the land of drive-by shootings and the ceremonial emptying of forty-ounce bottles of malt liquor in tribute to dead homies, and moved into a house with a tennis court in Palm Beach Gardens, Florida.

The parents of Venus and Serena deserve kudos for shielding their girls from the world of junior tennis, where cronyism, favoritism, and nepotism, not to mention racism, can crush the spirit of a talented athlete who comes from outside the mainstream. But the shielding became much easier because of the Reebok deal, which allowed the girls to have separate hitting partners when they were not hitting with each other. During the embryonic stages of their development, the sisters were observed by such respected coaches as Macci, Rineberg, Bolletieri, John Wilkerson, and Bob Ryland. "You could see they were going to be special players even then," said Ryland, a 1950s champion in the American Tennis Association. "You could see their personalities too. Venus was always the very polite young lady: 'Yes, Mr. Ryland. Thank you, Mr. Ryland.' Serena, she was mean: 'I don't wanna do that anymore. I wanna do what Venus is doing.' When Serena was ready to stop practicing, she'd just walk off that court. That's it."

Venus made her professional debut at the Bank of the West Classic at the Oakland Coliseum in California, on Halloween Night, 1994. Hardly spooked by the occasion, the fourteen-year-old Venus eliminated Shaun Stafford, No. 58 in the world, in the first round, and led world No. 2 Arantxa Sanchez-Vicario of Spain 6-2, 3-1 in the second round before inexperience and fatigue led to a three-set defeat. "Finally we got a chance to see this girl we had been hearing so much about, and we found out that Venus was going to be a very, very good player," said Bud Collins, the dean of tennis journalists.

While Mr. Williams, who took to calling himself "King Richard," accepted plaudits from those who acknowledged Venus's considerable talent, he made an even bolder prediction. "Serena will be even better than Venus," he said, "because she understands angles better and she's meaner."

Neither sister bows or half-steps around the court, or displays the slightest hint of subservience off the court, which is one thing that black people in particular love about them. Role models, however trite the phrase, are solely needed but in short supply for black youth. The Williams girls have filled some of the breach. In their formative years, when either sister appeared flustered after an errant shot on a practice court, Oracene could be heard to demand, "You pick that head up right now. You keep that head up. Those other girls are going to try to knock you down. You gotta be strong."

Strong they are. That doesn't make them perfect, just vitally necessary. As the sisters ascended to No. 1 and No. 2 in the world, their popularity, particularly in the demographics labeled Blacks and Young Females, skyrocketed. But at the same time their father became an increasingly polarizing figure. Tournament directors, media members, and coaches felt manipulated by him. Once Venus and Serena became the two most marketable players in the sport, Mr. Williams told reporters that his daughters should receive some of the TV revenue from coverage of their matches. On several occasions he threatened to pull Venus and Serena out of an event unless the tournament director placed them in separate halves of the draw, thus preventing them from having to play each other until the final, according to someone who worked for the family. Of course, a Venus vs. Serena final meant that the prize money for the champion and runner-up all went to the family.

Evidence of Mr. Williams's sometimes adverse effect on his daughters' public image surfaced in 2006 when a multi-million-dollar breach-of-contract lawsuit filed by sports promoters Carol Clarke and Keith Rhodes against Mr. Williams, Venus, and Serena went to trial. The promoters argued that Mr. Williams had committed his daughters to a "Battle of the Sexes" exhibition doubles match against a team of male players. The promoters had not yet reached an agreement with any male players, their lawyer said. In December 2005 the promoters' initial case against the Williams family ended in a mistrial. The following September a Palm Beach County (Florida) circuit judge ordered Venus and Serena to submit their tax returns to prosecutors, who claimed the documents would prove that the tennis players lied in sworn depositions about the extent of their father's involvement in their careers. An attorney for the Williams family, F. Michael Cunningham, argued unsuccessfully that the sisters' tax returns were irrelevant to the case. "There is nothing unusual about two successful daughters paying their father for coaching and for creating them," Cunningham said. "Those payments have nothing to do with whether or not the dad had the authority to commit them to play in a battle of the sexes." Venus and Serena themselves never agreed to take part in the proposed doubles match. There has not been a high-profile "Battle of the Sexes" doubles match since August 1987, when Martina Navratilova and Pam Shriver defeated Vitas Gerulaitis and Bobby Riggs at the Atlantic City Convention Center in an event promoted by Donald Trump. In December 2006 a jury found that Mr. Williams had indeed breached a contract and committed fraud, but it did not award money to the promoters. That Mr. Williams took ill during the trial seemed indicative of how stressful the episode had been.

Because it seemed that people could not get enough of Venus and Serena, they managed to tolerate the actions and utterances of Mr. Williams. That is, until the semifinal round of the Pacific Life Open in Indian Wells, California, on March 15, 2001. Serena and Venus entered and were placed in the same half of the draw in the two-week event in southern California, one of only four American-based tournaments in which the top men and women compete at the same site. (The others are the Sony Ericsson Open in Key Biscayne, Florida, in late March/early April; the Pilot Pen tournament in New Haven, Connecticut, in August; and the U.S. Open in late August/early September.) Fans eagerly anticipated a semifinal match between the sisters, particularly after Serena overpowered world No. 2 Lindsay Davenport 6-1, 6-2 in the quarterfinals. Venus, ranked No. 1 in the world at the time, moved easily through her early-round opponents. As soon as the Venus vs. Serena match was set, the cable network ESPN2 heavily promoted the event, set to begin at 6 p.m. local time, 9 p.m. Eastern time. No, it was not a Grand Slam event like Wimbledon, where Serena's defeat of Venus in 2002 was the first final contested by sisters at the All-England Club since 1884, when Maud Watson defeated Lillian Watson in three sets. But on the tennis calendar the Pacific Life Open is a big deal. So what happened a mere twenty seconds before the clock struck six at Indian Wells Tennis Garden will not soon be forgotten.

CHAPTER TWO

"I'm not going to be who you want me to be"

• • • • • • • • • • •

Pam Shriver, a Hall of Fame player for her doubles prowess in the 1970s and 1980s, was doing play-by-play commentary that night for ESPN2. "I got word in my earpiece twenty seconds before we were going on the air, 'Venus is not playing tonight. She's pulling out with right knee tendonitis.' We immediately had to scrap everything we planned to do, and I became a reporter to tell the audience what was happening."

Apparently no member of the Williams family, not Venus, not Serena, not Richard or Oracene, not anyone working for the family, had mentioned to any tournament official, Women's Tennis Association trainer, or media member that Venus's knee was bothering her enough to possibly cause her to withdraw. Everyone from the capacity crowd of 16,100 to the worldwide TV audience to the tournament officials were completely taken aback. "It was very unprofessional by Venus," said Bud Collins, who would have broadcast the match on international television. "If she was hurting, she should have let them know in the morning. And I thought she could have gone on court, as [Spanish star] Rafael Nadal did at Shanghai [in 2005], and said, 'I'm sorry, folks, but I'm injured and I can't play.' Instead she gave a very sullen press conference, which turned a lot of people against her."

If Venus was sullen in her press conference, perhaps it was because she could not play. Unfortunately for her and Serena at the time, they did not get the benefit of the doubt from the international media. While it is easy to suggest that prominent black athletes never do, that's not always accurate. Venus withdrew at the eleventh hour from a match against her sister, someone she clearly does not enjoy competing against, but the withdrawal would not have raised eyebrows had it been the first time she had withdrawn citing an injury. In 2000 Venus missed the first four months of the year, citing wrist tendonitis, and missed the year-ending WTA championships, citing anemia. Her withdrawal from Indian Wells would not have caused a tempest had there been some advance warning and had Mr. Williams not been telling everyone that his daughters were now bigger than tennis. His boasts fueled a perception that Venus, who had not withdrawn from any Grand Slam event because of injury until the 2000 Australian Open, and Serena, who had not missed a major because of injury until Wimbledon 1999 (the flu), did not care about non–Grand Slam events. Rightly or wrongly, the media were skeptical toward Venus in the interview room after the withdrawal.

"Will you need surgery?"

"No, I'm not going to get surgery. I'm going to pray."

"Why do you think there's a perception amongst some of the other players that when you play Serena you guys aren't always giving a hundred percent against each other?"

"I have no idea."

"What do you say to them? Do you say, 'That's not the truth. We play as hard as we can. Whoever wins was the best woman on that day'?"

"I don't say anything to them. For me it's not an issue at all. I don't even think for them it's an issue. I just think they come in here and you guys ask them a question."

"The crowd in the grandstand was pretty vocal when they made the announcement you weren't playing. Pretty angry response. If you

never pulled out of any tournaments before, I don't think there would be that kind of response. Do you think you're getting a reputation with the fans as somebody who doesn't always show up?"

"No, I don't think so. It's very disappointing for me and most of all for the fans. I'm scheduled to be there, and I can't. What more can I do? I can't send Venus No. 2."

"I understand some are down at the ticket office asking for their money back."

"I don't have any money to give them back."

Refunds were demanded, and granted. Yet spectators were still angry when Serena and Kim Clijsters met in the women's final on St. Patrick's Day. Fans did what is considered unthinkable for a usually laid-back California tennis crowd: they booed, loud and long, when Venus and Richard Williams entered the stadium to take their seats in the family box. In Europe, tennis fans never boo; they whistle to express their disapproval. In America, tennis fans sometimes boo at the U.S. Open in raucous New York City. But New York sports fans boo at any event. No one in tennis could ever remember family members being booed merely for showing up. "The booing was certainly regretful," said Shriver, who was Venus's mentor in a WTA-sanctioned Partner for Success program. "In other sports, like baseball and football, booing is part of an audience's right. If they buy a ticket, they can boo. But in tennis, booing seems out of place. But people were upset. This was another incident where the race question was brought into it. But I think if another athlete [who was white] had surprised a crowd by pulling out of a match they were looking forward to, the reaction would have been the same."

Who is to say whether that's true or not? Tennis had never seen anything quite like the booing of Venus and Richard Williams before the Indian Wells final. Or the booing of Serena—who grew up less than an hour away from the Tennis Garden—when she was introduced. Or the crowd's cheers when Serena hit a faulty serve or an errant shot. Or the near-total crowd support given Serena's opponent, from Belgium, in a final-round match played on American soil. Yet through it all Serena performed like a champion. If the booing

intimidated her, she did not show it. What surely would have un-
nerved a lesser athlete seemed to motivate her. Before another capacity crowd of 16,100, of which 16,098 stood firmly against her, Serena
handled her business with poise and aplomb, rallying from one set
down to defeat Clijsters, 4-6, 6-4, 6-2, for her second straight Pacific
Life Open title. But she did not win over the crowd. She was booed
while receiving her championship trophy. Afterward she met the
press:

*"When they clapped when you missed a shot, were you an-
noyed?"*

*"I mean, in the beginning, I was a little shocked, but it never re-
ally annoyed me. It eventually got old. I was like, 'Wow, this is getting old. Move on to something new.'"*

*"Even if the crowd booed you today, do you wish to come back
next year?"*

*"I have a championship to defend next year. You'll probably see
me here."*

Serena has yet to return to Indian Wells. Nor has Venus. Nor has
any member of the Williams family. If Richard Williams's postmatch
statements were accurate, their prolonged absence is understandable.
After the match, Mr. Williams told Bud Collins that he was called
"nigger" as he walked to his seat. No one else in the stadium that day
has come forward to say he or she heard the slur, but that alone does
not mean it was not said.

"I have a lot of respect for Richard, actually, but I never heard
anyone else say they heard it," Collins said. "It might have been said.
Even so, it's a terrible thing if it was said. But I think if you're a professional and this is your job, you belong wherever the game is
played."

"I don't believe what Richard said because I know how many lies
he used to tell," said Dave Rineberg, who alleges Mr. Williams owes
him six months' pay after his dismissal as the Williams sisters' hitting
coach in 1999. "If he had really been called that word, he would have
blown that out of proportion to the press in a heartbeat. He wouldn't
have told just one writer."

"Well, I don't know," Pam Shriver said, when asked about the possibility of Mr. Williams being slurred. "It's important for those of us who are not racial minorities to know that that word is still used and it shouldn't be."

"There were no winners in this situation; everybody was a loser in this," said Ray Moore, the president of PM Sports, which runs the Indian Wells tournament. "The Williams sisters are boycotting the tournament. They're two tremendous athletes and great girls and we'd love to have them again, so we're certainly not winners. I don't think they've come off very well, because we've extended an olive branch to them."

In this issue of black and white there is plenty of grey. If one believes Mr. Williams's accusation, one might also believe that racism was a problem at Indian Wells on St. Patrick's Day 2001. But the city's mayor at the time, Percy Byrd, is black. The slur could still have been uttered, but the predominantly white city had a black mayor. Byrd made overtures to the Williams family, urging them to return to the Pacific Life Open, but those efforts failed. (Byrd is no longer Indian Wells's mayor, having retired to Arizona.)

"I can't say for sure that [nigger] was not said," Moore said. "But I find it unlikely. And I don't think you can hold management responsible for what some bigoted fan might have yelled out. If basketball players were going to hold management accountable for things said by spectators, they wouldn't be playing basketball anywhere. We have tried to sit down with the Williams sisters and their parents to talk it out. We had an arrangement to speak with Oracene at a hotel in Los Angeles, but when we arrived for the meeting, they called us and canceled the meeting. We still have an open-door policy, but we can't seem to get to first base. Even if they wanted to sit down with us and scold us . . ."

Moore's voice trailed off, and he forced a laugh. But he is none too pleased about having to promote an annual two-week event that does not feature the two biggest names in the sport. In the lucrative world of tennis, where top performers like Venus and Serena become multi-millionaires before reaching adulthood, players can easily skip a non–Grand Slam event without doing much harm to their ranking. But the sisters' prolonged absence from a California event in a sport that has become increasingly global means Americans have fewer chances to watch Venus and Serena play in person.

"They had one bad year there," Collins said, "and they took a lot of money out of the place, and that's one of America's two biggest tournaments other than the U.S. Open. But that's the Williamses going their own way. They bother other people more than they bother me. I think that's because I covered a lot of Muhammad Ali. His credo to all of us was, 'I'm not going to be who you want me to be.' And that's essentially their outlook: we are different, not just our skin color. We are different, and we're going to do things our own way. It gets a lot of people mad because they don't play as many tournaments as we'd like them to play. But their way hasn't been too bad a way."

It's hard to argue with success. Two young black women who first swung racquets in a ghetto twenty miles from Los Angeles have in the past decade rewritten tennis's record book. On February 28, 1999, Serena prevailed in the Paris Indoors tournament and Venus captured the Oklahoma City title, marking the first time in history that sisters won professional tennis championships on the same day. Exactly one month later, Venus beat Serena, 6-1, 4-6, 6-4, in Key Biscayne, Florida, the first time two sisters met in a tour final in the open era. Richard Williams did not spend that night anxiously biting his nails from a courtside seat. Instead he walked the grounds of the Crandon Park Tennis Center, shaking hands and accepting plaudits from spectators as if he had been anointed the Father of Tennis.

"Well, what I thought would go through my mind was not what was going through my mind," he said about the match. "I thought I would be happy to see both my girls being out there. What was really going through my mind was all the problems we've had in tennis, bringing the girls up, how difficult it was, all the gang members, all the people out there. I guess I was just thinking about those things. I was saying, 'Look where you are today.' It was so difficult for me to believe it. I think I was going to cry, so I left and went out."

Any proud parent could relate to that, but perhaps only Richard Williams could have uttered what follows, in a press conference after the history-making match in Key Biscayne: "We paid a guy. His name is Michael J. Goldstein. He's a psychiatrist. I wanted him to find out what happens when brothers and sisters play each other. Well, in the study we found out more than what we needed to know. But it was very helpful. We learned that tennis is the only game that's extremely rough on a family. . . . So we employed two more doctors to do the same thing. And I learned that it wouldn't be good to enter Venus in this tournament and Serena in this tournament because we wanted two girls to grow up with a bunch of love for each other. And that love needed to be cultivated and developed, and it needed time to do so. So Venus was going to play Long Beach, Serena was going to play someplace else. So Venus might be in one place, and Serena might be in another. Today it works the same way. And they are really happy to do it that way."

In fact Mr. Williams commissioned no such psychological studies. But what the heck, his girls sure play a mean game of tennis, don't they?

On April 22, 1999, Serena cracked the world Top 10, making her and Venus the first sisters to be ranked in the Top 10 since Manuela and Katerina Maleeva of Bulgaria in 1991. When Venus ascended to the No. 1 perch in the world rankings she was the first African-American pro to do so in the open era. (Arthur Ashe's highest world ranking was No. 2 in 1976.) Venus and Serena, in that order, became Nos. 1 and 2 in the world for the first time on June 10, 2002. No other siblings, male or female, have ever accomplished that. Without a doubt, the Sister Act is the yardstick by which every other African-American tennis player will be measured.

"The Williams sisters will definitely leave a footprint," said James Blake. "They did it in the hip-hop era. It's still very easy for kids to say, 'I don't want to play tennis. I want to be like [NBA stars] Allen Iverson and Tracy McGrady.' But the Williams sisters played tennis and made it cool."

Added Angela Haynes, a pro who grew up with the Williams sisters in Compton, "My friends in the neighborhood didn't understand why I'd spend so much time practicing tennis or playing in junior tournaments when they were going to movies and parties. But when Venus and Serena hit it big, they all said, 'Now we know why Angela's been working so hard the last fifteen years.' A lot of black folks get it now."

"The Williams sisters definitely have influenced me," said Ahsha Rolle, a twenty-one-year-old from Miami who made her Grand Slam debut at the 2006 U.S. Open. "I grew up watching them on TV. Just to be playing in the same tournament with them now is a privilege."

"Venus and Serena, oh, they're an inspiration to me," said Brittany Augustine, a fourteen-year-old from Carson, California, who played junior doubles at the 2006 U.S. Open. "They are just so cool."

The Williams sisters made tennis cool because they were so different—bolder, more aggressive, more athletic, more style-conscious than their tennis peers. Venus is the introvert with an almost regal sense of style, as reflected in the on-court attire she designs for Reebok. Never would Big Sis play in a Cat Suit. She is the angular, long-limbed power hitter with the fastest recorded serve in women's tennis history (127 mph in Zurich in 1998). Serena is the curvaceous, sometimes tempestuous extrovert, with the better all-around game and a laudable capacity for creating angles for her lethal ground strokes. Serena is the one who pushes the fashion envelope off the table with attire like her "tennis boots" (actually knee-high leather accessories removed after her on-court warm-up) at the 2004 U.S. Open. "Nobody else would have the guts to wear something like that," Angela Haynes said. "As a tennis player myself, I'm thinking, 'I wonder what Serena is going to wear at this Grand Slam.' She's got such a sense of style to her game and her fashion. That's exciting. The fans want to see that. Even people who don't care about tennis are interested in what Serena is wearing."

Even if tennis fans did not like everything they saw from a Venus vs. Serena match, they found it hard to avert their eyes. From the 1999 U.S. Open through the 2003 U.S. Open, a span of thirteen

Grand Slam events, the sisters combined to win ten of those tournaments:

Grand Slam titles by Serena, 1999–2003: U.S. Open in 1999 and 2003; Wimbledon in 2002 and 2003; French Open in 2002; Australian Open in 2003.

Grand Slam titles by Venus, 1999–2003: U.S. Open in 2000 and 2001; Wimbledon in 1999 and 2000.

Venus's consecutive championships in both majors stirred memories of Althea Gibson, the first black player to be ranked No. 1 in the world, who achieved the rare Wimbledon–U.S. Open double in 1957 and 1958.

At the 2000 Olympics in Sydney, Australia, Venus won the gold medal in singles and partnered with Serena to win the doubles gold medal. They also played against each other in six of the ten Grand Slam tournament finals from 1999 to 2003. Venus vs. Serena became the Sister Act series to which the media gave roman numerals, like pro football does for its Super Bowl. Serena won five of the six, including the four tournaments that comprised her "Serena Slam." The only one she did not win was Sister Act I, the 2001 U.S. Open final. CBS, the network that has televised every U.S. Open since 1968, shrewdly capitalized on the Williams sisters' burgeoning popularity by moving the women's final to prime time, starting with the 2001 finale.

Never before had a Grand Slam tournament final, for men or women, been televised in the host country during prime-time viewing hours. Because of CBS's decision, the U.S. Open women's final immediately went from having the worst time slot of any Grand Slam final—sandwiched between the men's semifinal matches on Saturday afternoon, without a definite start time—to having the best national exposure. Venus won 6-2, 6-4 in a match best remembered for the TV ratings it generated. An audience of 22.7 million people tuned in, making Sister Act I the most-watched major tournament tennis match in U.S. history. An athletic contest involving two black sisters went head-to-head against a college football game between perennial powers Notre Dame and Nebraska, televised by ABC, and the sisters won in ratings points, 6.8 to 4.8, and in ratings share (the percentage of television sets tuned to the event), 13 to 9.

Since Venus had just turned twenty-one and Serena was three weeks shy of her twentieth birthday, CBS had every reason to believe Sister Act I would be the start of an annual ratings bonanza for the rest of the decade. Unfortunately for the onetime "Tiffany Network," legitimate sports events cannot be scripted. Without the involvement of either or both of the Williams sisters since 2003, CBS's ratings for the U.S. Open women's final have gone into the tank:

YEAR	U.S. OPEN FINALISTS (winner first)	VIEWING AUDIENCE (in millions)
2001	Venus Williams, Serena Williams	22.7
2002	Serena Williams, Venus Williams	20.1
2003	Justine Henin, Kim Clijsters	9.1
2004	Svetlana Kuznetsova, Elena Dementieva	9.7
2005	Kim Clijsters, Mary Pierce	9.8
2006	Maria Sharapova, Justine Henin	10.8

The 2003 final featured a pair of Belgians, the 2004 final a pair of Russians, the 2005 final a Belgian and a Canadian-born, Florida-reared player of French ancestry, and the 2006 final a Russian and a Belgian. Having Sharapova, the Siberian-born, Florida-reared "it girl" of tennis in the 2006 final created a slight ratings bump.

Even if an American player or players other than Venus and Serena had been involved in a U.S. Open women's final since 2003, the TV ratings would have been far below the twenty million-plus who tuned in for Sister Acts I and II. Nothing compares to watching history in the making. "We'll never see anything like that in tennis again, maybe not in any sport," said Cliff Drysdale, a tennis commentator for ESPN. "What if Tiger Woods had a brother and they competed for all the major golf titles? What if Roger Federer had a brother and they played each other in all the Grand Slam tennis finals? That's what it would be like. Something incredible. It's hard enough to compete against your friend in a big match, or against somebody from your own country. I can't imagine what it's like to compete against your own sister."

Venus ascended to the world No. 1 ranking on February 25, 2002, and Serena replaced her as world No. 1 on July 8, 2002. A Williams sister stood atop the world rankings until Clijsters assumed the top spot on August 11, 2003. One month earlier, Serena had defeated Venus in three sets to win her second straight Wimbledon championship. But neither would appear in another tournament that year because of injuries—Serena to her left knee, Venus an abdominal strain.

However intriguing the specter of watching Sister vs. Sister, rarely has a Serena-Venus match produced truly memorable tennis. This prompted ESPN.com columnist Darren Rovell in February 2003 to wonder, "Are Venus and Serena bad for tennis?"

Fans at the U.S. Open semifinals on September 6, 2002, acted as if they thought so. In the first semifinal, defending champion Venus led 5-4 in the third set and served for the match. When she lost the first three points, giving Amelie Mauresmo triple break point, the New York City crowd roared . . . for the Frenchwoman, against the American. Venus tuned out the cacophony and won 6-3, 5-7, 6-4. In the second semifinal, Serena faced a fellow American, Lindsay Davenport, and a startling lack of crowd support. Still, she prevailed 6-3, 7-5. Afterward, Ms. Price told *New York Times* columnist William C. Rhoden she believed the negative crowd reaction to her daughters had racial overtones. "I've been thinking about it and I think that's it. I guess women can't have power, no matter what race it is," she said. "That's a problem in America. It's ridiculous."

Surely that is a difficult charge to levy because it is so difficult to prove. One would have to spike the spectators' beverages of choice with truth serum to find out what they really thought of Venus and Serena. Or perhaps tennis fans, the overwhelming majority of whom are white, rooted so openly against the Williams sisters in the 2002 U.S. Open semifinals because they don't find Venus vs. Serena matches aesthetically pleasing. MaliVai Washington, a black former pro, suggested in 2003 that their matches lacked passion. "In any great rivalry, fans want there to be bad blood," he said. "They want the opponents to give you the feeling that they want to shove a ball down the other's throat and kick the daylights out of them. But Serena isn't as emotional when she's playing Venus, and Venus gives the appearance that she doesn't mind losing, saying she's happy that Serena is No. 1. Do you think she would say that about Jennifer Capriati?"

What's hate got to do with it, anyway? In women's tennis's most storied rivalry, Chris Evert and Martina Navratilova faced each other in fourteen Grand Slam finals. A major reason those matches were cherished by fans was the obvious respect the women had for each other. Each wanted to beat the other, but not kill the other. The same held true for the friendly rivalry between Pete Sampras and Andre Agassi, last staged in Sampras's epic 6-7, 7-6, 7-6, 7-6 victory in the 2001 U.S. Open quarterfinals.

After a Sister Act, the meetings at the net are marked by commiseration for the loser rather than expressions of unbridled joy from the winner. Because of the sisters' obvious discomfort when competing against each other, many thought Venus would hang up her racquet after losing to Serena in five straight Grand Slam finals. "People seemed to think I was going to be devastated," she said. "I guess they assumed that jealousy would eat away at me and that our relationship would change for the worse. . . . Whatever happens on the tennis court, it's not going to change my love for Serena or my pride in her accomplishments." Observers at the 2002 French Open final won by Serena over Venus were stunned when Venus pulled a camera out of her tennis bag to join courtside photographers for shots of Serena posing with the Suzanne Lenglen Cup.

"Long before fans and reporters knew us," said Serena, "our parents taught us that our relationship is much more important than being successful in tennis or getting ahead in the world."

For those who crave cutthroat competition on court, the Williams sisters have responded better to a designated villainess across the net, one like Hingis, the Swiss star who returned to tennis in 2006 after a three-year retirement and reclaimed her world Top 10 status. After

Hingis beat the teenage Venus in a 1997 match in Key Biscayne, she jauntily entered the interview room and flicked one of Venus's wayward hair beads to reporters, saying, "Here, a souvenir for you." Hingis also was among several women pros to accuse Mr. Williams of manipulating the outcome of Venus vs. Serena matches—a charge no longer levied, at least not publicly. In response, Serena told reporters that comments made by Hingis, a former teen prodigy, should not be taken seriously because "she has little formal education." Neither Serena nor Venus has ever needed extra incentive to defeat "the Swiss Miss."

Whether as individuals or as an entry, the Williams sisters have reached a level of stardom previously unattained by anyone in tennis, especially anyone black. We know each of them by one name. The surname need not be added, evidence of their having transcended tennis. In 2000 Venus was named Sportswoman of the Year by *Sports Illustrated*. Also that year, the *Forbes* magazine Power 100 in Fame and Fortune listed Venus No. 62 and Serena No. 68. In the spring of 2006 the Internet site *www.geniusinsight.com* ranked the world's Top 10 female athletes based on likeability. Serena finished No. 1. Venus placed third, behind boxer Laila Ali, the youngest daughter of Muhammad Ali. (Maria Sharapova came in fourth.) That Serena and Venus would rank first and third, respectively, was all the more impressive because both women have played so little tennis since 2005. Serena has competed only sporadically the past three years after surgery to repair a torn ligament in her left knee. Still, she won the Australian Open in January 2005 for the second time. Venus has battled an abdominal strain and an ailing right wrist, though she pulled herself together for the Wimbledon fortnight in 2005 and won the event for the third time. Venus received an ESPY (Excellence in Sports Performance Yearly) Award from ESPN for her Wimbledon triumph. She rallied after being one point from defeat in the championship match to beat Lindsay Davenport 9-7 in the third set. (Actually, the ESPY is more a measurement of one's popularity than of sustained athletic excellence. The Women's Tennis Association Player of the Year in 2005 was Kim Clijsters, who defeated Venus in the quarter-finals en route to the U.S. Open title.)

But as their competition has worked harder at getting better in tennis, Serena and Venus have pursued other goals. Tennis isn't everything, nor is it the only thing, the sisters have said, even while ranked Nos. 1 and 2 in the world. Success in tennis put them in the spotlight, and they have luxuriated in it. Both have appeared as models in *Sports Illustrated*'s annual swimsuit issue. Venus is pursuing a bachelor's degree in interior design at the Art Institute of Fort Lauderdale. Serena used to take courses in fashion design there. Venus runs an interior design business, V Starr Interiors, which created the set for *The Tavis Smiley Show* on PBS. She designs women's clothes for Wilson's Leather and plans to publish a book of poetry. Serena has a clothing line, aneres (Serena spelled backward), which has had a showing in Miami. She acted in the Showtime television mini-series *Street Time* and the motion picture *Hair Show*. Although she won good reviews in the former, she barely drew notice in the latter, largely because of an implausible role as a federal agent moonlighting as a stripper. She also took a comedic turn as a school-teacher in the since-canceled ABC sitcom *My Wife and Kids*. She voiced a character on the Disney Network's animated series *Higgleytown Heroes*. She and Venus have voiced animated versions of themselves on the Fox Network's cartoon series *The Simpsons*. They starred in the short-running (one season) reality series on ABC Family Channel, *Venus and Serena: For Real*. And it is safe to say that no other tennis player has made as many appearances as Venus or Serena on award shows and talk shows, including David Letterman, Jay Leno, and Oprah Winfrey.

"Serena and I [have gone] to college for the same reason that everyone else does—so that we have more options in life," Venus wrote in their 2005 book of advice to young women and girls. "There is life after tennis, and we don't plan to be sitting on the sidelines." It's hard to argue with young women who seek to become well-rounded by going to college. Still, many wonder why they chose to pursue so many other interests so soon. At the end of 2006, Venus was only twenty-six and Serena twenty-five. Couldn't they have waited? Couldn't they have devoted more time and energy to their tennis until they turned at least thirty, to see how many more major championships and records they could acquire?

Chris Evert wondered. Tennis's American idol in the 1970s and 1980s now serves as publisher of *Tennis* magazine. She wondered mainly about Serena, the more athletically gifted of the sisters. In the May 2006 issue, Evert wrote an open letter—from one Hall of Famer to a future member—expressing regret about Serena's choices:

Dear Serena,

I've been thinking about your career, and something is troubling me. I appreciate that becoming a well-rounded person is important to you, as you've made that desire very clear. Still, a question lingers— do you ever consider your place in history? Is it something you care about? In the short term you may be happy with the various things going on in your life, but I wonder whether 20 years from now you might reflect on your career and regret not putting 100 percent of yourself into tennis. Because whether you want to admit it or not, these distractions are tarnishing your legacy.

Just a couple of years ago, when you were fully committed to the game, you showed the athleticism, shot-making, and competitive desire to become the greatest player ever. Many besides myself shared the same sentiment. You won five of the Grand Slams you entered over the 2002 and 2003 seasons and looked utterly dominant in the process. Then you got sidetracked with injuries, pet projects, and indifference and have won only one major in the last seven you've played. I find those results hard to fathom. You're simply too good not to be winning two Grand Slam titles a year. You're still only 24, well within your prime. These are crucial years that you'll never get back. Why not dedicate yourself entirely for the next five years and see what you can achieve?

Perhaps the reason I feel so strongly about this is because I wasn't blessed with the physical gifts you possess. I know that the lifespan of an athlete's greatness is brief and should be exploited. Once you get to No. 1 in the world and start winning major titles, you should see how far you can take it. You've become very good at many things, but how many people would trade that to be *great* at just one thing? I don't see how acting and designing clothes can compare with the pride of being the best tennis player in the world. Your other accomplishments just can't measure up to what you can do with a racquet in your hand.

Ironically, I believe that if you fulfill your potential on the tennis court, all your other endeavors will become that much easier to pursue. You could become the most famous athlete in the world. Every magazine will want you on its cover and any door you wish to walk through will be wide open. When I was playing, I always knew there would be time to get married, have children, do TV commentating, and even coach if I wanted. I assure you there will be time for you to chase all your dreams once you're through with tennis.

I offer this only as advice, not criticism, from someone with experience. If you're completely happy with the way your life is, then crumple up this letter and throw it away. I wish you nothing but luck and success in all your pursuits. Just remember that you have in front of you an opportunity of the rarest kind—to become the greatest ever at something.

I hope you make the most of it.

Chris Evert, Publisher

Through 2006, Venus has received more than $16 million in career prize money with thirty-three singles titles and ten doubles titles. Serena has won $16 million in career prize money with twenty-six singles titles and eleven doubles titles. And that doesn't take into account their endorsement money. In 2001 Venus signed a five-year, $40 million contract with Reebok that was the most lucrative ever for a female athlete until Serena signed a five-year, $50 million deal with Nike in 2003. Serena pitches for Nike, Wilson racquets, Estee Lauder, Wrigley, McDonald's, and Unilever. Venus has deals with Reebok, Wilson racquets, American Express, Avon, Wrigley, McDonald's, and Wilson Leather.

On the eve of the 2006 U.S. Open it was much easier to find Serena and Venus on the gossip page, their names in bold type, than on the sports page, their names in agate type. Who's Serena dating now, the guy who directed *Rush Hour*? That linebacker from the Giants? The actor from *Idlewild*? And what about Venus posing with minstrel-rapper Flavor Flav at a party on South Beach? Is she going to do a cameo on his show? Do these girls ever practice their tennis anymore?

Perhaps Serena and Venus are closer to the end of their careers than the beginning. What if they're tired of practicing their tennis for four hours before lunch and four hours afterward? If they're ready to rest on their tennis laurels—and both adamantly say they are not—whose business is that except their own? Maybe Benny Sims, the coach of black pro Chanda Rubin, is right when he says, "It's hard to stay motivated when you've got $30 million in the bank." Although the $30 million figure may be a conservative estimate for either sister, what if Sims is correct? What if for Venus and Serena the thrill of athletic competition is gone? What if the desire to pay the heavy price off the court to maintain their proficiency is gone too?

Some tennis people insist, perhaps hopefully, that Venus and Serena are still hungry, just not healthy. "If they can stay healthy enough to get through a whole season, Venus and Serena can play great tennis again," black former pro Rodney Harmon said. "I don't want to predict No. 1 and No. 2 in the world for them again, but to me their outside interests are not as big a problem as the injuries. I think they're still hungry. Fame and fortune are like drugs, and the adrenaline rush you get from winning Grand Slam tournaments and being a celebrity has great allure. And they both have a lot of pride. They don't like losing to players they shouldn't lose to."

The year 2006 was the first since 1997 in which neither sister won a tournament, in singles or doubles. A year in which neither survived the first week of the Australian Open. A year in which Venus did not survive the first week of Wimbledon—she lost as the defending champion to Jelena Jankovic of Serbia in the third round. A year in which Serena entered the U.S. Open with only twelve tournament matches under her belt, losing in the third round of the Australian Open, and in the semifinals at Cincinnati (to Vera Zvonareva of Russia) and at Carson, California (to Jankovic).

In all, 10 black players appeared in the main draw of the 2006 U.S. Open, of a possible 256 players: five men and five women. Of the men, only James Blake, the No. 5 seed, was projected to reach the quarterfinals. The others were Gael Monfils of France, the No. 27 seed, and American teenagers Donald Young, Jr., Scoville Jenkins, and Phillip Simmonds. The American trio all received wild cards, or an automatic entry, into the main draw. The black women in the main draw were Chanda Rubin, a 30-year-old on the comeback trial after an assortment of injuries; Jamea Jackson of Atlanta, the 19-year-old daughter of a former pro football player; Shenay Perry, who learned the game in a public parks program in Washington, D.C.; Miami's Ahsha Rolle, a U.S. Open rookie; and Serena, the winner of more Grand Slam titles than any black tennis pro in history.

Serena entered the event with a world ranking of No. 91. She received a wild card based on her status as a two-time Open champion. Her unheralded first-round opponent was Lourdes Dominguez Lino, No. 41 in the world. The Spaniard has a baseline game better suited for clay, a much slower surface. The New York hard courts would almost assuredly expose her lack of foot speed and power.

Hearty applause, the kind Serena did not receive when she ruled the sport, greeted her as she walked onto Arthur Ashe Stadium, the Open's main court named for the humanitarian and only African-American man to win the U.S. Open (1968), Australian Open (1970), and Wimbledon (1975). Serena, now wearing an ill-fitting No. 91 instead of No. 1, had assumed an underdog role. White fans were more inclined to root for her. African-American fans, of course, always did. That is because there have been so few African-American Grand Slam champions in the sport's history: Ashe; Gibson; Venus; and Serena.

Resplendent in a deep purple, Asian-influenced dress of her own design, trimmed in red and gold with a golden tree on the back, a red headband, gold hoop earnings, gold necklace, and white Nikes trimmed in red, black, and orange, Serena looked ready to administer a quick and color-coordinated beating. "I love you, Serena," a young woman yelled before the first ball had been struck. Her fans went home happy after a routine victory, 6-2, 6-1. Lino provided no test. Lino asked Serena no hard questions about her level of fitness or the depth of her commitment to the sport. Such questions would come later.

After the victory, Serena entered an interview room, adjacent to the stadium court, that had raised, theater-style seating, bright lighting to accommodate the photographers who perched behind the last row, and a backdrop filled with U.S. Open logos behind a desk that stood bare except for a name card that read SERENA WILLIAMS and an unopened bottle of Evian water. The water was not to be drunk but to satisfy a sponsor that had paid millions of dollars for two weeks of product placement. A thin boom microphone loomed above Serena as she took queries from reporters. When asked about tennis, she kept her answers brief and conveyed a level of enthusiasm better suited for a recitation on how to brush your teeth. She gave her longest, most enthusiastic response when asked about her on-court attire:

"We wanted to do something that has the Asian influence because we see a lot of that. Going into this fashion season, purple is a really hot color this fall. I just bought a purple dress from Herve Leger, one of my favorite designers. . . . I wanted to keep the silhouette of the dress really simple because of the design that was on it. It would have been too much, I thought, if we had had a flashy dress or anything. We needed to keep the silhouette really simple and just have the fabric and the pattern do all the talking."

"Do you feel you've regained your physical condition the way you want it to be, and how difficult was it?"

"I'm definitely more physically fit than I've been in the past. I am always looking to get more fitter [sic]. I think no matter how fit I am, I feel like I can go a little bit better."

"Are you working out hours and hours?"

"Unfortunately, yeah."

"In the gym, out of the gym? What are you doing?"

"In the gym, I was doing—I would never tell you everything I do. . . ."

"When you talked about the dress, the nuances, you seemed real animated about it. Do you find fashion, truth be told, more intriguing than tennis these days?"

"Oh, God, no. Fashion is so hard. It's like you just—you never know what's going to happen. I love wearing things that I sat down and had a part of and came up with the concepts for. It's exciting. But you know, it's a hard business to be in. Like Heidi Klum says, 'Some days you're in, the next you're out.'"

A tennis tournament can be for a distracted champion as the fashion world is for a supermodel like Klum—in one day, out the next. Serena breezed through the first round at the Open, got a measure of revenge in the second round with a victory over Hantuchova—the Slovakian who beat a supersized Serena at the Australian Open in January—and outslugged Ana Ivanovic, a six-foot Serbian teenager, to win her third match. Still, Serena had not yet been tested by an athletic opponent, someone who could make her prove she was truly fit enough and hungry enough to win a major title again.

Mauresmo provided that test in a fourth-round match played after the sun had set on Labor Day. Except for the second set, when Serena again displayed the most potent and versatile serve in the women's game, and cracked winners off the forehand and backhand wings, and moved crisply and authoritatively about the court and won 6-0, she was not her old tennis self. Serena at her best would have followed a 6-0 set with another set of near-equal dominance, regardless of the opponent, and walked away the victor. Not on this night. The fist-pumping and intensity that used to characterize her matches, particularly in the Grand Slam events, made only cameo appearances against Mauresmo. The muscular Frenchwoman wisely redirected most of Serena's power shots in the ultimate set rather than take full cuts. The tactic frustrated Serena, who fell behind 4-2 after having her serve broken, and she could not draw even. A physically and mentally grueling thirty-five-stroke rally won by Mauresmo in that sixth game proved to be Serena's undoing. Serena at her best would have summoned the strength and will to bounce back and win the next point, the next game, the match itself. But her lack of conditioning had been exposed. She lost the next game on three forehand errors and one errant backhand. And she lost her place in the tournament after hitting a forehand drop shot, more out of desperation than conviction, which Mauresmo quickly tracked down and used to set up a winning backhand volley on match point. Afterward Serena told reporters that she would play "a few" tournaments in Europe to end the year. Instead she did not play another match in 2006, except on the Williams sisters exhibition tour.

Still, Serena looked better in New York. She had given her fans reason to hope that she would take her fitness and conditioning to a higher level and become her dominating self again. But in the end, that was Serena's call and no one else's. Already she has won more Grand Slam singles titles than any black player in the history of tennis. The number at the end of 2006 stood at seven. Did she want to add to it? Did it really matter to her anymore? Tennis player, fashion designer, aspiring actress, celebrity, pop diva, Serena had cause to leave New York pondering a question that performers have asked since the invention of drama: What's my motivation?

CHAPTER THREE

"I'm not giving anything else away"

• • • • • • • • • • •

Althea Gibson did not lack motivation. Just let her know what time the competition began and there she would be, ready to do her utmost to win. Losing never suited her. Family members recall the card tables she destroyed after losing in a game of pinochle. Sam Jones, a Hall of Fame basketball player with the Boston Celtics, remembers playing hoops as a boy in a Wilmington, North Carolina, community center with a nearly six-foot-tall girl who did not hesitate at all to shove him aside in pursuit of a rebound. Althea. Gardnar Mulloy experienced the thrill of competing for a Wimbledon championship in 1956 in mixed doubles, a brand of tennis in which the time-honored though chauvinistic strategy is to attack the woman. Although his team reached the final match in tennis's premier event, Mulloy never got used to the habits of his partner, who always insisted on serving first and responded to every lob sent their way by yelling, "Mine!" Althea.

Serena Williams, an aspiring actress, has played a drug dealer's girlfriend in a cable television mini-series, a grade-school teacher in a network television situation comedy, and a federal agent in a motion picture. But one day, after she completed work at her day job with a second-round victory at the 2006 U.S. Open, she talked about the woman she really wants to portray: Althea.

"I would like to do anything that would let people know about her and what a tremendous person she was, definitely," said Serena, whose 1999 U.S. Open title was the first by an African-American woman in a major tournament since Althea won the Open forty-one years earlier. "I once wrote a paper about her for school. I know that it was so hard for her. There were tournaments that wouldn't let her play because they weren't accepting blacks. That went on for years. And when she could get into tournaments, she wasn't always allowed to use the locker room like the other players, or eat in the dining room like the others. She had to sleep in cars at tournaments when everybody else was sleeping in hotels. She would wake up, play her match, and then she'd go back to the car."

Serena, at twenty-five, walks a far easier path to tennis immortality because of the trail blazed by Althea. Reflecting on the indignities Althea faced on and off the court, Serena said, "I don't know if I could have done that." Perhaps she would have if, like Althea, life had presented her with no other choice. A half-century ago Serena would have been called Negro, or colored, or something much worse. In Althea's day anyone of her color who achieved anything of significance did so through enormous sacrifices. It is precisely because of those sacrifices that Serena, and every other black tennis player, will never have to find out if they could have done the same.

Because of Althea, blacks in tennis today have the freedom just to play the game. They have the opportunity to make $16 million in prize money in less than a decade, as both Serena and Venus have— the kind of income about which Althea, an amateur during the prime of her tennis career, could only dream. Players now have the option, exercised assertively by Serena and Venus, to work at tennis only when they feel like it, because money is no longer an issue. And the degree of public adulation afforded the Williams sisters today did not exist for Althea. She experienced only a fraction of it, infinitely less of it than an athlete of her stature deserved.

After years of painful and humiliating rejection, Althea gained entry into tennis's premier tournaments and became the first black player to win three of the four Grand Slam events: the French Open in 1956, Wimbledon in 1957 and 1958, and the U.S. Open in 1957 and 1958. She grew to be a robust 5 feet 10-1/2 inches and 145 pounds, which helped her bring down the walls erected by the tennis establishment to keep black people out. Otherwise shy and insular, she summoned the inner strength to prove that she not only belonged in big-league tennis but also belonged at the head table. Yet praise for Althea's efforts, even from other blacks, was far from unanimous. The sometimes curt manner in which she asserted her right to define herself in any way she pleased ruffled many. That was Althea's way. She wrote in a 1958 autobiography, *I Always Wanted to Be Somebody*, "Someone once wrote that the difference between me and Jackie Robinson is that he thrived on his role as a Negro battling for equality whereas I shy away from it. That man read me correctly."

Althea was not Rosa Parks with a tennis racquet, despite some attempts by contemporary African Americans to reinvent her as a civil rights pioneer. Protest marches and rallies went on without her. Althea once wrote, "I have no lofty, overpowering ambition. All I want is to be able to play tennis, sing, sleep peacefully, have three square meals a day, a regular income, and no worries." The burden Althea carried as the lone black presence in major international tennis tournaments in the 1950s was difficult enough without others trying to force her to speak for an entire ethnicity. She always wanted her tennis to speak for her, and in that regard Althea spoke eloquently, and in volumes. Her tennis success is what inspired countless other blacks to take up the racquet and battle for what she most believed in: proving oneself equal to, if not superior to others, in athletic competition.

A partial list of the honors bestowed upon Gibson includes:
- International Tennis Hall of Fame
- Associated Press Woman Athlete of the Year in 1957 and 1958
- Babe Zaharias Outstanding Woman Athlete in 1957 and 1958

- Sports Illustrated Top 100 Greatest Female Athletes
- International Scholar-Athletes Hall of Fame

If you never saw Althea play, either in person or on grainy black-and-white film, picture Venus as a consistent net-rusher instead of a baseliner, with a racquet made of wood instead of graphite, with a classic one-handed backhand instead of the two-fisted backhander in vogue today, and wearing a shirt, vest, and shorts instead of a tennis dress. You would have a fairly good image of Althea in action. Come to think of it, if Venus, 6 feet 1-1/2 inches and long-limbed with rich brown skin, were the Williams sister with the acting bug instead of Serena, the casting would be almost perfect.

The cable network HBO showed interest recently in producing a TV movie about Althea and Angela Buxton, a Jewish woman from England with whom she won the 1956 Wimbledon doubles title. Negotiations ended, according to Frances Gray, who runs the Althea Gibson Foundation, because HBO Sports would not give Althea top billing in the proposed film, insisting that Gibson and Buxton have equal billing. Hence Althea's story remains underpublicized and underappreciated.

Althea's story began August 25, 1927, the day she was born into poverty and squalor on a cotton plantation in Silver, South Carolina. Like many Southern blacks of the day, her parents, Daniel and Annie, decided to migrate North in search of a less circumscribed life. When Althea was three, the family moved to the unofficial capital of Black America, Harlem in New York City. The Gibsons moved into an apartment on 135 West 143rd Street, and Daniel found work as a night mechanic at a garage. He noticed Althea's athletic prowess early on, but tennis was not on his mind. "I taught her how to box," he said. "There were a lot of women boxers then, and I thought that would be a good career for her. She was fine with that."

Mainstream America would not have embraced a black woman boxer in the 1940s the way it accepts a Laila Ali today. Still, Althea's boxing skills would be apt metaphors for the battles she later faced in and out of tennis. The eldest of five siblings, she took seriously the role of defender of sisters Millie, Annie, and Lillian, and brother

Daniel Jr. "Nobody dared pick on us when we were kids," Daniel said. "Althea could beat up anyone. When she was only thirteen years old, she reached up and gave a black eye to a six-footer who had said something about me she didn't like."

Daniel Gibson, Sr.'s job at the garage didn't pay enough to keep the family from struggling financially. A job may have been easier to come by in the North, but the prevalence of racism limited employment avenues for blacks. Housing in Harlem also was extremely tight. The Gibsons' block of 143rd Street between Lenox Avenue and Seventh Avenue was marked by six-story buildings where black people lived right on top of one another. Hundreds of people crammed into one narrow city block. And the situation repeated itself on avenue after avenue. Park land, where children could roam and play and be oblivious to the discrimination against which their parents struggled daily, was also in short supply. In an effort to provide a semblance of relief, the city's Police Athletic League designated some blocks as play streets, closed to vehicular traffic during the summer. Car owners had to move their vehicles elsewhere so that black children could run on black asphalt and pretend it was grass. Althea's block was a play street, and that's where she became acquainted with tennis, or at least an offshoot of the game.

"One summer morning, I came down from my parents' apartment and saw two bats and a sponge rubber ball lying on the ground," Althea recalled. "So this friend of mine, who I called in those days my 'boon coon' because we played together, we started hitting the ball back and forth and it got good to us. So we would anticipate every summer morning, being the first on the paddle tennis court—practicing, hitting balls, enjoying it. As a matter of fact, it got to where we owned the paddle tennis court. Nobody could get on the court but us."

Not yet a teenager, Althea's paddle-tennis prowess caught the eye of Buddy Walker, a Harlem bandleader who worked as a supervisor on the play street to earn money between gigs. Walker got Althea her first racquet, a secondhand model with real strings, for five dollars. After having Althea hit sponge balls against the wall of a handball court, Walker became enamored with her raw talent. "He later introduced me to a member of the Cosmopolitan Tennis Club," she said. "And in those days the Cosmopolitan Tennis Club was the elite black tennis club in New York City."

In those days institutional racism prevented blacks from living wherever they wanted, so Harlem was home to the socioeconomic elite, the middle class, and the poor. Harlem was a place where a poor girl like Althea could get to know a star prizefighter like middleweight king Sugar Ray Robinson. And the black elite—doctors, lawyers, educators, businesspeople, and other professionals—played tennis at the Cosmopolitan, on 149th Street and Convent Avenue, less than a mile walk from Althea's apartment. The Cosmopolitan was a member club of the American Tennis Association, a predominantly black organization founded in 1916 that gave those who were barred from white clubs an opportunity to play the game. When Althea was fifteen, her family could not afford the seven-dollar annual membership fee, so the Cosmopolitan Club made her an honorary member. At the time the Gibson family was on welfare. "I was supposed to be looking for a job," she said, "but I didn't look very hard because I was too busy playing tennis in the daytime and having fun at night. The hardest work I did, aside from practicing tennis, was to report to the welfare ladies once a week, tell them how I was getting along, and pick up my allowance."

Althea met her first tennis coach, a one-armed man named Fred Johnson, through contacts at the Cosmopolitan. Johnson tutored Althea at the club and at the Harlem River Courts, on 150th Street and Seventh Avenue, courts that today bear his name. In one smooth but highly unusual service motion, Johnson would toss the ball with his right hand while holding the racquet. Owing to his missing appendage, he used a Continental grip: he held the racquet the same way whether he hit a forehand or a backhand. He taught Althea to use the same grip.

At the age of fifteen Althea won her first tournament, the ATA New York State junior championship at the Cosmopolitan, defeating Nina Irwin, a Jewish girl from Manhattan, in the final. Club members then took up a collection to send Althea to the 1942 ATA national girls' tournament at Lincoln University, a black institution in Pennsylvania. Nana Davis defeated her in the final.

Those who watched Althea knew she had a special talent for tennis. They also knew she flirted regularly with trouble. She played hooky from school to play sports or hang around pool halls and bowling alleys. She excelled on a basketball team of Harlem girls, the Mysterious Five, which would have been fine if she had gone to school now and then and arrived home on time. "We used to have to drag her back into the house," said Althea's sister, Millie. "When other girls were putting on lipstick, she was playing stickball. When she got a whipping, she never cried. She just stood there and took it." Or she fought back. Her father punched her one night for coming home late, and she punched him back, in the jaw.

Tennis was still an amateur sport, and a racist one at that. Blacks were barred from all events sanctioned by the United States Lawn Tennis Association (now the USTA). And without playing in USLTA tournaments, no black could ever acquire the credentials to compete in the major events such as Wimbledon, the French Open, and the U.S. Nationals (now the U.S. Open). So for Althea Gibson the ATA represented what Negro League baseball did for her namesake Josh Gibson—a place to excel athletically but without any chance to test your skills against the best white players of the era and gain recognition as one of the best in the world. Althea, a burgeoning talent in tennis, and Josh, a poorly paid catcher, were not related by blood. But they seemed related by fate. Few ever saw a game played by Josh Gibson, who was nicknamed "the black Babe Ruth." In the mid-1940s it may have seemed to Althea that few outside the ATA would ever see her perform. But that all changed because of the efforts of two physicians, both ATA members, who followed the Frederick Douglass credo—"agitate, agitate, agitate"—to try to get qualified blacks into tennis's premier tournaments, and a white female champion who struck a blow for fairness.

At the 1946 ATA tournament in Wilberforce, Ohio, Althea lost in the final to Roumania Peters, a student at Tuskegee Institute in Alabama and one-half of an ATA champion doubles team. Never again would another black woman defeat Althea on a tennis court. She had no clue that day she was being observed by Dr. Robert Walter Johnson of Lynchburg, Virginia, and Dr. Hubert Eaton of Wilmington, North Carolina. Both were enamored with her speed, athleticism, and sheer power. Her game lacked technical proficiency, but the doctors raved about her potential. When they found out Althea was eighteen, had not attended high school in years, and lacked social graces, she became their pet project—someone who could, if given the opportunity, change the face of tennis.

Althea in the 1940s was formidable in a variety of sports and not at all reluctant to let people know about it. "I saw a lot of Althea back then, and she was tough," said Bob Ryland, a two-time ATA champion. "The way Muhammad Ali used to call himself 'The Greatest,' Althea used to talk about herself that way. You didn't hear any other women talking about themselves the way Althea did." David Dinkins, who would become New York City's first black mayor in 1989, first met Althea at a social club in Scotch Plains, New Jersey, in the mid-1940s. "Ever since that day, I called her 'Champ,'" he said. "She was excellent in tennis, paddle tennis, basketball, softball, pool, any sport she played."

But Althea's braggadocio concealed a more vulnerable side seen only by a few. Edna Mae Robinson, the wife of boxer Sugar Ray, recalled, "She was unhappy. She had a great build, and she felt she was the least good-looking girl she knew. She had insecurity and went into herself. She used to talk wild. I tried to make her feel she could be something."

Drs. Johnson and Eaton also thought she could be something, and Althea accepted their offer. She went to live with the Eatons in Wilmington during the academic year to finish high school, and spent the summer with Dr. Johnson in Lynchburg, where she could play on his backyard clay court and train with other players as part of the Junior Development Program he founded for the ATA. She became the most dominant female player in ATA history, winning a record ten consecutive singles titles from 1947 to 1956. But outside the narrow prism of black tennis, no one noticed. "Winning the [ATA] championship got me three or four lines of type at the bottom of the page in the *New York Times*," she wrote in her 1958 autobiography. "The *New York Daily News*, which has less space, didn't mention it at all."

Althea still had no money, but now she had a support system in the form of the ATA and its member families. When traveling to tournaments she stayed in the homes of ATA members, and she learned there were others, thousands of other blacks in America, who played tennis. Nevertheless the efforts of Drs. Johnson and Eaton to get their most promising players such as Althea into white-run national events continued to meet resistance from the USLTA. It conveniently "lost" applications mailed by Dr. Johnson to state and regional tournaments, or he would be told the applications "arrived too late." When the ATA lobbied to have Althea play in the U.S. Nationals in Forest Hills, New York, in the mid-to-late 1940s, the cited reason for rejection was that she had not participated in enough USLTA tournaments, when of course the USLTA had not given her, or any other blacks, a chance to compete.

Nevertheless the ATA kept agitating, just as hard as the advocates of Negro League baseball stars kept agitating until Jackie Robinson signed his minor-league contract with the Brooklyn Dodgers' top affiliate, the Montreal Royals in October 1945, and made his debut as the first black man in Major League Baseball on April 15, 1947. The success of Robinson, the National League's Rookie of the Year in 1947, and those of other black players who followed him to the big leagues, convinced the ATA that their struggle would eventually be won. The breaking down of racial barriers in baseball, professional basketball—where Charles "Tarzan" Cooper, Nat "Sweetwater" Clifton, and Earl Lloyd debuted as the first blacks in the NBA in 1950—and professional football—where Woody Strode and Kenny Washington in 1946 became the first blacks in thirteen years to play in the NFL—also convinced fair-minded whites that those in charge of the major tennis tournaments needed to see the light.

Alice Marble, a four-time U.S. Nationals champion and the 1939 Wimbledon champion, stood firmly in the camp of the fair-minded.

In 1944 she and British tennis star Mary Hardwick played an unprecedented mixed doubles exhibition match with ATA stars Bob Ryland and Dr. Reginald Weir at the Cosmopolitan Tennis Club. Over
cocktails at the bar afterward, Marble and doubles partner Ryland
discussed the potential of Althea Gibson.

"Alice asked me if I thought Althea could make it in the major
tournaments, and I said she definitely had the talent to do it," Ryland
recalled. "I told her Althea was strong and had a good head for the
game. She just lacked the experience, that's all." In June 1950, in an
open letter in *American Lawn Tennis Magazine*, Marble, who had
not yet met Althea, nonetheless became her best-known lobbyist.

"If tennis is a sport for ladies and gentlemen, it's also time we
acted a little more like gentle people and less like sanctimonious hyp-
ocrites," she wrote. "If there is anything left in the name of sportsmanship, it's more than time to display what it means to us. If Althea
Gibson represents a challenge to the present crop of women players,
it's only fair that they should meet that challenge." Although Marble's view was decidedly unpopular with those who were running tennis, her stature in the game gave her words considerable weight. "The
entrance of Negroes into national tennis," she wrote, "is as inevitable
as it has proven to be in baseball, in football, or in boxing."

A combination of ATA advocacy, the Marble letter, and a percep-
tible shift in public sentiment compelled the USLTA to pry open the
wrought-iron gates of the sport just enough in 1950 to allow Althea
entry into an event at the Orange Lawn Tennis Club in East Orange,
New Jersey. During the tournament she stayed with the family of
Rosemary Darben, a young tennis player from the ATA whom she
first met at the Cosmopolitan Club in Harlem. "I really enjoyed having Althea around because we were about the same age," Darben
said, "and we enjoyed doing so many things together like tennis, golf,
and bowling. Every night after dinner we would play pinochle. We
were just like sisters."

Althea's creditable showing in USLTA-sanctioned tournaments
made it impossible for the organization to deny her one of the fifty-
two slots allotted for women at the U.S. Nationals, a Grand Slam

event, in August 1950. At the age of twenty-three, Althea finally had her chance to compete in the big leagues.

Tennis was a game devised for European royalty, and those who played it, even in the United States, acted as though they represented royalty, the "civilized" and "cultured" of American society, without ever stopping to think about how systemic discrimination based on race could be civilized or cultured. Still, the lords and ladies of the American court were in a snit, for a commoner from a South Carolina plantation and a Harlem ghetto was about to enter their hallowed grounds. It's easy to envision members of the West Side Tennis Club nailing down anything that could conceivably be carried off during the U.S. Nationals fortnight, but at least Althea, and black America, would no longer be denied the opportunity.

"In many ways it's even a tougher Jim Crow–busting assignment than was Jackie Robinson's when he first stepped out of the Brooklyn Dodgers' dugout," one New York newspaperman wrote. "It's always tougher for a woman." Without question, Althea faced enormous pressure while making the trek via subway to Forest Hills from the Harlem brownstone she shared during the fortnight with Rhoda Smith, another ATA friend, for a history-making debut at the grass-court tournament. Playing not only for herself but also for "the race" could make even the most solid player skittish. Yet Althea seized the moment, easily dismissing her first-round opponent, Barbara Knapp of England, 6-2, 6-2.

The victory set up an intriguing second-round match against Louise Brough, the three-time defending Wimbledon champion, the 1947 U.S. Nationals champion, and a three-time U.S. runner-up. Brough (as in rough) had also won every U.S. Nationals doubles title since 1942 and the three previous Wimbledon doubles trophies with her partner Margaret Osborne.

Those unfamiliar with Althea's serve-and-volley game undoubtedly believed she would have her lunch handed to her by the formidable Brough. But the match turned out to be fiercely contested. Only several thousand people could view the action live, and tennis was not a television sport in 1950. Even most spectators at the West Side

Tennis Club did not see the match because of the USLTA's curious decision to stage it on an outer court, well removed from the clubhouse. Indeed, more spectators could watch a doubles match involving Ginger Rogers, Fred Astaire's dance partner, than Gibson vs. Brough.

Play began under an ominous sky with the threat of a thunderstorm. After an understandably nervous Althea dropped the first set, 1-6, she harnessed her emotions and power to take the second set, 6-3. Althea's shots crackled from the forehand and backhand wings. With strong serves followed quickly by decisive volleys at the net, her style of play, particularly in 1950, had more in common with the men's game. Running forth and back and side to side, she covered the court better than any of the other women. But her strokes were not as technically proficient or consistent as those of Brough, Shirley Fry, Doris Hart, or Nancy Chaffee, the top white stars in the sport. Althea had a tendency to hit at three speeds: hard, harder, hardest. Hitting with slice to keep the ball low, or using topspin to elicit a higher bounce and confound an opponent were not yet part of her repertoire. Further, Althea did not yet have the advantage of regularly competing against the top white players to gain a measure of their games while improving her own. That Althea played Brough to a standstill after two sets and the first twelve games of the final set was an accomplishment in itself.

The sky above the West Side Tennis Club grew darker and the wind gained intensity as Althea held serve to take a 7-6 lead in the final set. She was one game away from a monumental victory when the sky opened and shook the foundation of the club. "I'll never forget that storm," said Bertram Baker, executive secretary of the ATA and a New York politician. "Fans were shouting from the stands for Althea's opponent to 'beat the nigger, beat the nigger.' I'll always remember it as the day the gods got angry. A flash of lightning came and knocked down one of the [stone] statues of the eagles on the court."

A violent thunderstorm postponed play until the following day. "Althea got a little nervous thinking about how close she was to winning," Ryland said. "It would have been much better for her if she could have finished the match on the day it started. She had some momentum going."

Momentum did not follow her to Forest Hills the next day. Spraying errors about the court, Althea lost all three games played and the match, 6-1, 3-6, 9-7. But she had made her presence known at the 1950 U.S. Nationals. Althea would become a force in tennis; it just took a while longer than anyone expected.

While Althea continued to make headlines in tennis, she couldn't eat them. She still had to make a living. She enrolled in Florida Agricultural & Mechanical University, a historically black school in Tallahassee, and in 1954 earned a degree in physical education. At Florida A&M she played recreational tennis, basketball, softball, pool, and the saxophone given to her by Sugar Ray Robinson. All the while she dominated the ATA tournament in singles, doubles, and mixed doubles.

The doors of tennis's premier events were no longer closed to her, but she was not winning the white-run tournaments. She became a highly ranked player in the USLTA: No. 9 in 1952, No. 7 in 1953, No. 13 in 1954. But black America was growing impatient. If Althea was "the Jackie Robinson of tennis," as others had named her, how come she was not beating the white folks in the big leagues the way Robinson did with the Dodgers?

Jet magazine, a black weekly, labeled her "the biggest disappointment in tennis." Before the 1955 U.S. Nationals, a New York City newspaper wrote, "Win or lose, this could be Miss Gibson's last whirl on the big-time circuit. She's teaching physical education at Lincoln University in Jefferson City, Missouri, and at 27 is more concerned with groceries than silver [trophies]."

Althea at twenty-six had had a romantic fling with a Jefferson City man who was in charge of the ROTC program at Lincoln, a man who encouraged her to quit tennis and join the Women's Auxiliary Air Corps. She filed an application, took the physical, and waited to be called. She was not winning championships against the likes of Maureen "Little Mo" Connolly—who in 1953 became the first woman to win the Grand Slam—Fry, Brough, and Hart.

Had she joined the WACs, Althea's story would have ended here. But in 1955 she reconnected with another old ATA friend who convinced her to give tennis one last shot. Sydney Llewellyn, a Jamaican-born New Yorker, became her coach and helped develop her tactical approach to the game. He changed her grip from the Continental to an Eastern grip, which is similar to a handshake and gave her more racquet control. Gradually she stopped hitting every shot with violent intentions. A little slice here, some topspin there. Subtlety, she learned, often worked better than sheer power. Her game improved, but still she had not won the big one. Not yet.

Despite the persuasiveness of Llewellyn, a former doubles partner from the ATA, Althea might have chosen military service after losing early at the U.S. Nationals. But after the tournament she received an offer too enticing to refuse. Renville McMann, an influential USLTA official and the president of the West Side Tennis Club, invited her to accompany three white tennis players, Karol Fageros (a blonde known as "the Golden Goddess of tennis"), Hamilton Richardson, and Bob Perry, on an international goodwill tour sponsored by the State Department.

The quartet entered tournaments, gave tennis exhibitions, conducted clinics, and attended social affairs in India, Ceylon, Pakistan, and Burma.

Being a black woman proved advantageous for Althea in this circumstance. In 1955 America had a serious image problem at home and abroad because of a burgeoning civil rights movement that had led to vicious attacks upon blacks in many cities, and because of a horrific murder in the South. Emmett Till, a fourteen-year-old Chicago boy visiting relatives in Mississippi, was mutilated and killed for whistling at a white woman. The tennis tour was part of an attempt to try to improve America's image around the world. Having a black woman alongside three whites created at least the appearance of a racially harmonious country.

While it is unlikely the journey of four tennis players to Southeast Asia did anything to improve America's image abroad, the trip did wonders for Althea. For starters, she did not have a steady source of

income after leaving her job at Lincoln University, so she enjoyed seeing the world on the State Department's tab. Further, her tennis game
matured because she got to hit regularly and talk tennis strategy with
the men. (Richardson, who along with Alex Olmedo won a U.S. Nationals doubles crown in 1958, was an especially good strategist.)
Fageros could not beat Althea, but she provided good competition.
She was a player against whom Althea could try out new things.

Now a more thoughtful power player, Althea shined on the international circuit, winning a remarkable nine consecutive tournaments
and fifteen of eighteen during an eight-month span. Critics pointed
out that she had not beaten any of the stars who won Grand Slam titles in the 1950s—Connolly, Hart, Fry, Brough, and Britain's Angela
Mortimer. An AP story put it bluntly: "Many of her titles were won
in tournaments where tennis nobodies and second-raters filled out
the field." Nevertheless Althea felt like a champion, which is the first
step toward becoming one, and she went into the 1956 French Open
with confidence. As it turned out, a *New York World Telegram* article on July 20, 1955, "This Could Be Althea's Year for New
Heights," had been written a year too soon.

Displaying her usual power and the patience required to prevail
on the red clay in Paris, Althea captured her first Grand Slam title
three months shy of her twenty-ninth birthday, in her seventh year of
competition against the world's best players. In the 1956 final she
scored her first win ever over Mortimer, the defending French Open
champion, 6-0, 12-10. Althea also won the doubles title with Angela
Buxton, a pairing of tennis outsiders who became lifelong friends.

"Neither of us had partners and we were very friendly, so we decided to try it together," Buxton said. "My coach, C. M. Jones, said,
'How would you feel about playing with Althea since you're already
buddies?' And I said, 'Yeah.' My [British] peers felt that something
was a little off. They didn't say anything. At the very most, they
raised their eyebrows because I was playing with an American, and
particularly a black American."

For several years Buxton had been an admirer of Althea's game,
particularly her kick serve, crisp volleys, and sliced backhand pat-

terned after that of Aussie star Ken Rosewall. "She didn't look like a young woman playing," Buxton said with a laugh, "particularly when I first saw her. She played with a vest and shorts. I thought it was a young man out there. She cracked that ball and ran up to the net. I thought, 'Oh, I'd like to do that.'"

Not a great mover, Buxton was a smart player who understood the geography of the court. She complemented Althea with her ability to hit well-angled volleys for winners. Most important, she was a friend to a black woman who really needed one amidst the loneliness of the tennis circuit. "We never talked about racism or anti-Semitism, or the times," Buxton said. "We just enjoyed each other—playing together, going to movies together, practicing together, eating together."

Together they wore down the American team of Darlene Hard and Dorothy Knode, 6-8, 8-6, 6-1, for the French championship. Althea then accepted an invitation to stay at Buxton's home during Wimbledon. In a tune-up event in Manchester, England, Althea defeated Fry in the semifinals and Brough in the final to mute the critics who had downplayed her other tournament titles.

Althea was flying. Yet there were members of the sporting press as well as paying customers at Wimbledon in 1956 who hoped she would crash and burn. Appalled by the racial climate on the famed Centre Court during one of Althea's early-round matches, journalist Scottie Hall of London's *Sunday Graphic* wrote, "Shame on the Centre Court. I accuse the Wimbledon crowd of showing bias against Miss Gibson. . . . It wasn't anything that was whispered. It wasn't anything that was shouted. . . . It was just an atmosphere, tight-lipped, cold."

Hall also attributed this quote to an unnamed American tennis writer at Wimbledon: "So Joe Louis became a champ. And what happened? Nigger boxers came out from under every stone. Same thing if Gibson walks away from here with a tennis pot."

As bizarre and ugly as that comment was, it was also stupefying. For one thing, Louis had excelled in *prize*fighting. Those inspired by the success of the Brown Bomber included many whites who laced on gloves in search of fame and fortune in the boxing ring. There was no money for black people in tennis in the mid-1950s. It would not be possible for any black person to make a living playing tennis for quite some time, as Althea herself would become painfully aware. Despite her on-court success, tennis remained an elitist activity, something still beyond the interest of most blacks, something that even male relatives of Althea's dismissed as "a sissy sport." Blacks were hardly about to storm the gates of tennis clubs to take up a new game because of the feats of one accomplished *amateur* athlete. At the time, only a handful of white male stars made a living from tennis from under-the-table appearance fees. The nascent pro circuit, which would not pay much money either, was still years away.

Regardless, Althea's detractors at Wimbledon were placated when she lost in the semifinals to Fry, who was nearly half a foot shorter but a strong competitor. Fry then defeated Buxton for her only Wimbledon title. But Althea did not leave Wimbledon empty-handed; she and Buxton won the doubles title, downing Britain's Fay Muller and Daphne Seeney, 6-1, 8-6. Never before had a black player won a championship at Wimbledon. Asked what the British press had to say about it, Buxton said, "Not a lot. Looking back on it, it was as if the press felt, 'Maybe she'll go away.' When we won the doubles title, there was in one of our major papers in England a small column in thin type, 'Minorities Win.' That was it."

The momentum from Wimbledon carried Althea to her first U.S. Open final at Forest Hills. But she fell again to Fry, 6-3, 6-4. "She was very nervous, it being New York," said journalist Bud Collins, attributing her defeat to hometown jitters. "She didn't play her game."

Nevertheless in 1955 and 1956 Althea silenced the critics who considered her incapable of winning a major title. No longer was she "the biggest disappointment in tennis." No longer did she consider enlisting in the army. She seemed to know she was on the verge of a breakthrough, one that would cement her place in tennis history. But perhaps unbeknownst to her, she was inspiring others.

"She had great presence, and I could tell the other women were intimidated by her," said Billie Jean King, who in 1956 was a thirteen-year-old Californian with the surname Moffitt when she first saw Althea. "With her wingspan, power, and shot production, she was awesome. She mixed power and spin and had great placement. She seemed to glide on the court. She had a big serve, and in those days you had to keep one foot on the ground when you served. Today's players don't realize that."

Althea strode confidently into Wimbledon in 1957, largely because of her successful Southeast Asian tour. "It was from this experience that my tennis rise had begun," she said. "Championship form was beginning."

In the July 6 final, with the temperature on Centre Court a scorching ninety-six degrees, Althea dominated like never before. She overpowered Darlene Hard, who made her living as a waitress in Montebello, California. One big serve after another from Althea was met with a weak reply. Althea stormed to the net and snapped off winning volleys. Within minutes she went ahead 4-0. After fifty minutes of work, the championship was hers, 6-3, 6-2.

"Althea Gibson fulfilled her destiny at Wimbledon today and became the first member of her race to rule the world of tennis," the *New York Times* story began. Queen Elizabeth, no tennis fan, was nonetheless brought out to hand Althea the Venus Rosewater Dish. "At last! At last!" Althea exulted as she clutched the champion's hardware to cordial applause from the Centre Court spectators.

Later that day the telephone rang in the home of Albert and Miriam Terry in Montclair, New Jersey. Family friends of Althea's through the ATA, the Terrys would eventually become her relatives after Althea married Miriam's brother, William Darben. "Althea called my mom to tell her she had just won Wimbledon; that's how we found out," said Roger Terry, who was seven at the time. "You didn't have TV coverage of tennis then, so I remember waiting around for the phone to ring to find out how she did."

Althea did just fine, teaming with Hard to win the doubles title, 6-2, 6-1, over Mary Hawton and Thelma Long of Australia. Althea would have achieved a rare Wimbledon triple, but she and partner Neale Fraser of Australia lost to Hard and Mervyn Rose in the mixed doubles final.

Because of the rich history and tradition of Wimbledon, no singles championship means more to a player. That Althea had become the first black player to win there, less than a decade after being barred because of racism from any major tournament, made her an American star.

"It would be even more to the credit of all of us," a *New York Times* editorial observed, "if there were no occasion even to mention her race. But there has to be a first time when barriers are broken down, and when this happens it is news in itself and the time for congratulation."

In keeping with one of Wimbledon's grand traditions, the ladies' and gentlemen's champions, Althea and Lew Hoad of Australia, were honored at the Wimbledon Ball. "I dressed Althea because she didn't have anything to wear to the Ball," said Buxton, a fashion designer whose tennis career ended in 1956 because of a wrist injury. "I always had a fashion show just before Wimbledon to get some publicity, and she was one of my models. That was one way of paying me back. She attracted a fair amount of attention."

Reading a handwritten acceptance speech at the ball, Althea began, "In the words of your own distinguished Mr. [Winston] Churchill, this is my finest hour. This is the hour I will remember always as the crowning conclusion to a long and wonderful journey." She thanked those chiefly responsible for her tennis career—Buddy Walker, Fred Johnson, Dr. R. Walter Johnson, Dr. Hubert Eaton, Sydney Llewellyn. She thanked Buxton, the ATA, and the USLTA. As a band played "April Showers," Althea took the ceremonial first dance with Hoad and also took a whirl with the Duke of Devonshire. She also broke precedent and sang two numbers, "If I Loved You" and "Around the World."

Having traveled the world, Althea returned to New York a conquering heroine with a welcoming committee, including her parents and siblings, and local politicians, waiting at Idlewild (now Kennedy) Airport. Having a world champion in the family elicited from her parents emotions ranging from "I told you so" to "You have got to be kidding."

"I didn't think she would do it," Annie Gibson told the *New York Post*. "I didn't think a Negro girl could go that high."

"I knew she would do it," Daniel Gibson told the *Post*. "She only wanted to try for the top, and she finally made it. I knew she had the strength to do it."

"What kind of strength?"

"Physical strength and any other kind of strength that's needed," he said.

Congratulatory telegrams came from President Eisenhower, New York governor Averell Harriman, and Sugar Ray Robinson. And on July 12, 1957, New York City gave Althea a ticker-tape parade along the Canyon of Heroes, up the streets of Broadway, against the usual flow of traffic, from Battery Park to City Hall. Seated atop the back seat of a convertible, Althea wore a red-and-blue-checkered silk dress with a white orchid pinned over her right breast. Riding with her was Manhattan borough president Hulan Jack, the first black person to hold a major elective office in New York.

Thousands cheered, waved, and blew kisses at a black woman who had truly fulfilled her highest ambition: to become somebody. "If we had more wonderful people like you, the world would be a better place," Mayor Robert Wagner told Althea in remarks broadcast live on the city-owned radio station. Althea told the crowd, "This victory was won through the help of all your encouragement and all you well-wishers."

When she returned home, to 135 West 143rd Street, the apartment buildings were adorned with streamers, a large WELCOME HOME sign extending across the street. A crowd of three hundred cheered, and Althea received a bouquet of red roses. Winning became Althea. She followed her Wimbledon title with a championship run at the U.S. Open, routing Louise Brough, 6-3, 6-2, in the final. This time the sky did not open, and not a single stone eagle fell from its perch.

In 1958 Althea successfully defended both her major titles. At Wimbledon she stormed past Angela Mortimer, 8-6, 6-2, to repeat as queen of Centre Court, and she partnered with Maria Bueno of Brazil to capture the doubles title. That made Althea the first woman in tennis history to win the Wimbledon doubles title three years running with three different partners. At Forest Hills she rallied from a set down in the title match to defeat Hard, 3-6, 6-1, 6-2, for a second U.S. Nationals title.

The young woman from Harlem had become the finest female tennis player in the world. But she was still black in America, which meant that many doors remained closed to her while others were only beginning to be pried open. For example, before the open era of tennis in 1968, the U.S. Nationals singles and doubles tournaments were staged in different cities: the singles at the West Side Tennis Club in New York, the doubles at the Longwood Cricket Club in Boston. Althea was not invited to play in the U.S. Nationals doubles championships until after she won the 1957 Wimbledon singles title. That Althea had been ranked in the Top 10 in America since 1952 was not good enough for the USLTA. She had to be No. 1 just to get into a major doubles tournament that the white stars routinely played. "It was a racist thing," said Collins, who covered the doubles event for the *Boston Herald*. "In those days, tournaments could exclude anybody they wanted."

Gibson and Hard lost in the final at the 1957 U.S. Nationals doubles. The Gibson-Bueno team took second-place honors the following year.

Now that Althea Gibson was a "name," she partied with other celebrities and met heads of state and business leaders. She graced the cover of *Time* magazine's August 26, 1957, issue with an accompanying story on "That Gibson Girl." She cut an album of blues and jazz standards for Dot Records, *Althea Gibson Sings*, released in May 1958. She sang "Around the World" on the CBS Sunday night staple, *The Ed Sullivan Show*, on May 25, 1958. She appeared as the mystery guest on another CBS hit show, *What's My Line?* on August 10, 1958. And she snagged a bit part as Lukey, a servant girl to an aristocratic Southern belle in John Ford's 1958 Civil War film *The Horse Soldiers*, starring John Wayne and William Holden. Tinseltown did not call on Althea again after her turn in a thankless, stereotypical role. *The Hollywood Reporter* wrote, "The tennis champion Althea Gibson makes her screen debut in this role. Miss Gibson should stick to her own racket."

Surely she would have, but tennis kept her struggling financially. The album, the TV appearances, and the John Wayne film were fun but hardly a steady source of income. And no matter how many amateur tournaments she won, she could not dine on trophies or headlines. She reached that painful conclusion in 1958, after two years of dominance in her sport. "After ten years of it, I am still a poor Negress," she told a New York newspaper, "as poor as when I was picked off the base streets of Harlem and given a chance to work myself up to stardom. I have traveled to many countries, in Europe, in Asia, in Africa, in comfort. I have stayed in the best hotels and met many rich people. I am much richer in knowledge and experience. But I have no money."

Having what some considered a gruff personality certainly did not help Althea's cause. She appeared at charity functions when her schedule allowed. But celebrities are sometimes maligned for not doing "enough" for charity, and it is never the celebrity who decides what constitutes enough. The black press, in particular, often stood at odds with her. Black journalists generally found her dismissive, and unwilling to equate her tennis triumphs and setbacks with the larger black struggle for autonomy in America.

Russ J. Cowans of the *Chicago Defender*, an influential black newspaper, wrote, "Instead of presenting Althea with a trophy, the Queen [of England] would have done the field of sports a real service if she had given her a few words of advice on graciousness."

Wendell Smith of the *Pittsburgh Courier*, whose forceful columns in the 1940s were pivotal in persuading Major League Baseball to integrate, condemned Althea in the 1950s for "her curt manner and insulting responses to friendly writers of all papers in Chicago."

Occasionally a white journalist would take Althea to task. Lee Fischer, writing for the *Chicago American*, wrote, "Someone ought to tell Althea that graciousness is as much a quality of a real champion as the ability to play the game well."

In her autobiography *I Always Wanted to Be Somebody*, Althea responded to her critics: "I have always enjoyed a good press among the regular American newspapers and magazines, but I am uncomfortably close to being Public Enemy No. 1 to some sections of the Negro press. I have, they have said, an unbecoming attitude. They say I'm bigheaded, uppity, ungrateful, and a few other uncomplimentary things. I don't think any white writer ever has said anything like that about me, but quite a few Negro writers have, and I think the deepdown reason for it is that they resent my refusal to turn my tennis achievements into a rousing crusade for racial equality, brass band, seventy-six trombones, and all. I won't do it. I feel strongly that I can do more good my way than I could by militant crusading. I want my success to speak for itself as an advertisement for my race."

In theory, any athlete, regardless of race, should be allowed to concentrate primarily, if not solely, on her sport and not have to be cast as a spokeswoman for her race—a role she may not have the education or insight or desire to fulfill. But given the racial turbulence in America in the 1950s, when in the South blacks were arrested or brutally attacked daily for such everyday acts as going to school, expecting service at a lunch counter, sitting in the front seat of a bus, or attempting to vote, a feeling prevailed in black America that anyone of prominence, in any field, should have readily identified herself as an integral part of the civil rights struggle, or at least as a supporter. Althea did not, and did not believe she should have had to. She was a tennis player first and foremost, and a great one. But tennis, especially in the 1950s, was an activity about which very few blacks cared. More blacks might have cared about Althea if they perceived her as being involved in the struggle or, to use a popular expression of the time, "down with the cause." But that was not the way she wished to be perceived.

From an article, "The Story of Althea Gibson," which ran in the *New York Post* on September 1, 1957, came the following: "When a woman reporter asked if she was proud to be compared to Jackie Robinson, she said, 'No. I don't consider myself to be a representative of my people. I am thinking of me and nobody else.'"

Althea retired from competitive tennis after the 1958 U.S. Open and accepted an offer from Abe Saperstein, owner of the Harlem Globetrotters, to travel the country as a warm-up act for the "clown princes of basketball." A makeshift tennis court, not of regulation size, was rolled onto the basketball floor, and Althea would play a set against Karol Fageros, tennis's "Golden Goddess" who caused a sensation at the 1958 French Open by wearing gold lamé underpants. The traveling party included Althea's coach, Llewellyn; her road manager, Bill Davis, an eleven-time ATA champion who grew up with Althea in Harlem; and Fageros, Althea's answer to the Washington Generals, the team the Globetrotters regularly defeated.

"Saperstein gave our group eight hundred dollars a performance," Davis said, "but I don't know how much Althea got out of that because that eight hundred was for all of us combined: Llewellyn, me, Karol, and Althea."

Spectators who bought tickets to be entertained by the Globetrotters merely tolerated the tennis. The first player to eight games won the set, and Althea prevailed in 114 of the 118 sets against Fageros. Davis filled in as the opponent whenever Fageros had to miss a performance.

To Fageros, who died in 1998, Althea was not the haughty woman others perceived her to be. "Althea was so nice to me," Fageros wrote. "She allowed me to stay in her one-bedroom apartment. She had an extra fold-up, and I slept on that at night. As a Miamian, I hadn't much affiliation with black people. But I had gotten to know Althea well and had seen so many cruel things happen to her on the circuit even though she was No. 1 and had proven herself. I had a lot of empathy and compassion for her, not to mention a healthy dose of respect."

As ego-deflating sports jobs go, being the opening act for a barnstorming basketball team is not quite as bad as running against thoroughbreds at a race track, as Jesse Owens once did to make ends meet after winning four gold medals for the United States at the 1936 Olympics in Berlin. After Althea's contract was not renewed by the Globetrotters, she left with her dignity intact. But she remained in search of enough income to live comfortably. Reporters asked Jack Kramer in the late 1950s about including women on his nascent pro tennis circuit, which featured Pancho Gonzales, Bobby Riggs, and Althea's old ATA friend, Bob Ryland—the first black professional tennis player—but Kramer balked. "There is no demand for the girls," he said. "They don't pull in enough gate to make it worthwhile. All they'd do is cut the take [reduce the money] for Pancho Gonzales and the boys. Besides, who could Althea play?"

Althea played Pauline Betz in 1960 at Cleveland Arena in an event billed as the "World Pro Tennis Championships." But the show failed at the box office. At the time Althea's sources of income were $75 a month from Henry C. Lee Sporting Goods, which manufactured her racquets, and $25,000 a year as an endorser of Tip-Top bread. Prodded by Llewellyn, she invested heavily in another traveling sports tour in which she played tennis and basketball. In the parlance of poker, she lost her shirt.

Her trailblazing spirit still strong, Althea made history in 1963 as the first black on the Ladies Professional Golf Association tour. A women's pro tennis circuit was still seven years away. "I had to make a living, I had to make money to live, so I decided to give professional golf a fling," she said in a 1979 interview. "It was played for purses, but the purses were very, very small."

Althea played in 171 LPGA events between 1963 and 1977 and won none. Her best result was a second-place finish to Mary Mills at the 1970 Immke Buick Open in Columbus, Ohio. "When I turned pro, I thought I'd set the world on fire," she said. "It didn't work out that way. I hit the ball a ton, 275, 285 yards, but I never knew where it was going."

Among those who helped finance Althea's golf career were David Dinkins, a childhood friend, and William Darben, Althea's first husband. The two dated off and on for several years before marrying in 1965. They divorced in 1976 amid allegations of infidelity by both parties. Years later Althea would marry and divorce Llewellyn, her former coach. But those close to Althea say Darben was the love of her life. As a married couple, the Darbens lived at 69 Pleasant Way in Montclair, New Jersey.

"Althea loved that house and the memories she shared with my uncle so much," said her nephew Roger Terry, now the deputy chief of the Montclair police department. "Even after they divorced, she used to sit in a car across the street and just look at the house. I would get calls sometimes from the new owners, 'Your aunt is outside staring at the house again.' There wasn't any question that Aunt Althea and Uncle William were better as friends than as lovers. They always got along great as friends. Years after they divorced and were older, they used to love to sit around and watch sports together."

In 1972 Althea made a tennis comeback, this time as a pro. The Women's Tennis Association was in its infancy, but the top women could finally make a living playing tennis. Unfortunately Althea Gibson Darben, at age forty-four, was well past her prime. Her final headline in competitive sports occurred at the 1973 U.S. Open. Her mixed doubles team lost a first-round match to Marita Redondo and Jean Chanfreau, 6-2, 6-2. Her partner at Forest Hills that day was a thirty-year-old former U.S. Open champion named Arthur Ashe.

"I have regrets about Althea," said Bud Collins, the Hall of Fame tennis journalist. "She was so late in being accepted by tennis—not being allowed to play in the U.S. Nationals until 1950—that she really didn't develop into the player she could have been. She didn't reach fulfillment. She did damned well, as we know. But had she been the typical teenager, and not had to play in segregated events, she would have come on the [major tennis] scene at seventeen or eighteen and built a much stronger record."

Althea's tennis resumé, which merited her induction into the International Tennis Hall of Fame in 1971, includes fifty-six singles and doubles titles. She won five Grand Slam singles titles (two at Wimbledon, two at the U.S. Nationals, one at the French Open), five Grand Slam doubles titles (three at Wimbledon, one at the French Open, one at the Australian Open), and one Grand Slam mixed doubles title (U.S. Nationals). And let's not forget that even after she was allowed to compete in major tournaments as a singles player, racism prevented her from participating in the U.S. Nationals women's doubles championships until 1957.

Althea became the New Jersey state athletic commissioner in 1975 but resigned two years later saying, "I don't wish to be a figurehead." Becoming one of the few women to serve as a state athletic commissioner placed Gibson back in the headlines temporarily. But the last time many sports fans saw and heard from her came at Wimbledon in 1990. She made a last-minute appearance at the ladies' singles final and sat in the Royal Box as Zina Garrison became the first black woman to compete for the championship since 1958—the second time Althea won on Centre Court.

"She looked smashing," said Collins, who interviewed Althea on the NBC telecast. "She was in a pantsuit, which was certainly forbidden in the Royal Box. But she had such aplomb, such presence. Everybody was glad to see her. And she was in such a good mood."

Althea faded from the public's consciousness after that. Despondency set in shortly after her position with the New Jersey Commission on Physical Fitness was eliminated in 1990 because of budget cuts. A woman so vital and purposeful became largely reclusive.

In 1992, however, Althea watched an early-round U.S. Open match at the National Tennis Center from the champion's box, an area of courtside end zone seats reserved for past Open winners. Virginia Wade, the 1968 U.S. Open champion from Britain, sat alongside her. A young reporter approached, hoping to interview Althea for an article that he thought could introduce her to a new generation of sports fans.

"How much do you pay?"

"We're not allowed to pay for stories. I just . . ."

"I'm just not doing any interviews then. I gave away too much early in my career. I'm not giving anything else away."

The reporter returned to the press box to write about the day's matches and never attempted to speak with her again.

"I thought Althea when she was on top didn't do what she could have," said Arthur Carrington, a former ATA champion and tour pro who owns a tennis academy in Massachusetts. "She never owned her own spot [academy]. She thought they were just going to give her some stuff, but you know it's not like that."

In 1995 came the jolting news that Althea, living in East Orange, New Jersey, had become so destitute, frail, and despondent that she called Angela Buxton, with whom she won the 1956 Wimbledon doubles crown, to say goodbye.

"She was struggling; she didn't have much at all in savings, and she went through that money rather quickly," said Buxton, who had relocated to Florida. "She was coming to the end. She could see the end, in fact. I told her to hold on. I asked her, 'How much does it cost for you to live? How much does it cost for you to pay the rent? Pay the electricity? Get food?' And we figured out fifteen hundred dollars a month. I said, 'Okay, I'll pay that for a while, and we'll see where we go from there.'"

Buxton contacted her tennis friends, including Collins, who wrote about Althea's plight, as did *Inside Tennis* writer Matt Cronin. The ATA also collected money to send to its most prolific champion. Money poured in, more than one million dollars all told, from around the world. Frances Gray, by that time Gibson's caretaker and confidant, said Althea told her, "I know now that people love me."

Despite these financial contributions, Althea's health continued to deteriorate. She suffered a stroke in 1995 and a heart attack in 2003. A venereal disease left untreated for too long also hastened her demise. She died on September 28, 2003, in East Orange, New Jersey. The official cause of death was respiratory failure. She was seventy-six.

Because Althea had requested the same funeral arrangements as her first husband, William Darben, the service took place before several hundred people at Trinity and St. Philip's Cathedral in Newark, New Jersey. Leslie Allen and Zina Garrison were among the black women in tennis who attended. In her eulogy Garrison told the mourners, "I, for so long, was supposed to be the next Althea Gibson. But I discovered my role was to fill the gap in a path for women of color. Thank you for the chance to be me. You broke down the doors for me and many others."

Gibson was laid to rest at Rosedale Cemetery in Montclair, next to William Darben, in a plot overlooking the house they shared on Pleasant Way. "On the way to the cemetery," said Terry, her nephew, "we saw groups of children along the route—black children, white children, Hispanic children. They were waiting for the procession to pass by, and when we did they would wave to us."

The tennis establishment has done virtually nothing to keep alive Althea's legacy. The Women's Tennis Association, established in 1970, has no award named for her, no tournament named for her, no championship trophy named for her. The U.S. Open, played in New York City where she was reared, has no court or any section of the National Tennis Center named for its first-ever African-American champion. The main stadium bears the name of Arthur Ashe, the only African-American male U.S. Open champion.

The No. 2 stadium bears the name of music legend Louis Armstrong, who lived in Queens, the borough of New York City where the Open takes place. Louis Armstrong Stadium already existed on the site before the U.S. Tennis Association moved from cramped Forest Hills and built a new tennis facility around the stadium in 1978. The No. 3 court at the Open is a six-thousand-seat venue called the Grandstand. There appears to be no good reason for the USTA not to rename that venue Althea Gibson Court. Failing that, why not rename the women's championship trophy, which currently has no name at all, the Althea Gibson Cup? Putting someone's name on a trophy, a court, a tournament, emphasizes the important contribution of that person to the sport. It may also encourage those unfamiliar with Althea to seek out information about her.

"I wish we in tennis were as good as golf about remembering our legends," Hall of Famer Pam Shriver said at Ashe Stadium during the 2006 U.S. Open. "Obviously, with someone like Arthur Ashe you get a stadium like this named after him and that helps a great deal. But Althea is such an historic figure as the first black champion in our sport, male or female."

Yet many African Americans who began watching tennis in the past decade think black success in the sport started with Venus and

Serena. They have neither seen film of Gibson nor heard of her. But in pockets of the country there are African Americans who don't play or watch tennis yet know about Althea. One such place is the Althea Gibson Community Education and Tennis Center in Philadelphia, which features academic instruction and computer training as well as guest appearances by people who talk about Althea's impact.

Much more could be done to raise awareness about Gibson. Even the historically black school of which she is an alumna, Florida A&M University, has done nothing substantial to keep Althea's name alive. There has been talk of renaming the tennis facility after her and erecting a bust or statue in her likeness. What is the delay? She graduated from the school more than a half-century ago.

At a tennis clinic in Nigeria in the 1980s, Leslie Allen, then on the pro circuit, found that the Gibson name and persona had resonance in the African country. "Althea and I played a mixed doubles match with a couple of African boys," she said. "People in Africa treated her like royalty, bowing to her, treating her like a queen. I said to myself, 'This is what she should get at home.' She knocked down the doors so people like me who came behind her could get more."

Perhaps Serena, another of Althea's tennis descendants, is correct when she says that making a feature film about Gibson may be the best way to revive her legacy. But the greatest challenge, one even greater than securing financing for the project, is to convince the public that Althea Gibson was as important to tennis history as an African-American man yet to be immortalized in a film whose name graces the largest stadium in the sport, Arthur Ashe.

CHAPTER FOUR

"He was exactly who we needed at the time"

• • • • • • • • • • •

Perhaps he would have been a better player, won more championships, reached No. 1 in the world in his professional tennis career had he not devoted himself to so many social causes. But then, Arthur Ashe likely would not have been as important a human being. And it is just as likely that we would not have been as enriched by all that we learned from him.

A true citizen of the world who could also play a mean game of tennis, Arthur combined grace, class, and intellectual curiosity with his status as an African-American sports star, to the lasting benefit of his sport, his people, and the human race. The burden he chose to carry—combining social activism at a time of virulent racial prejudice with a demanding athletic career—was as large as any assumed by an American athlete since Jackie Robinson. Both men, not unsurprisingly, died young: Robinson at age fifty-three in 1972, Arthur at age forty-nine in 1993.

Human rights abuses, in his home country or abroad, sparked the concern of Citizen Ashe to the very end. On September 9, 1992, fewer than five months before his death, he was arrested outside the White House as part of a protest march against America's treatment of Haitians seeking asylum to escape the violence in their country. Handcuffed and escorted into a police van, he wore a T-shirt that read, HAITIANS LOCKED OUT BECAUSE THEY'RE BLACK, with the word HAITIANS superimposed onto an American map.

In his final years he taught others how to live with vigor, spirit, and purpose despite carrying the disease that causes AIDS, contracted through a transfusion of tainted blood after his second heart attack. In the years after his playing career ended in 1979, he earned praise as an Emmy Award–winning writer and author of a three-volume historical series on black athletes in America, *A Hard Road to Glory*. Rather than join the chorus of those lamenting the absence of a comprehensive study of black sports history, Arthur rolled up his sleeves, assembled a team of researchers, and wrote the books himself.

"Arthur was exactly who we needed as black people at the time," said John Wilkerson, who like Arthur was a champion in the predominantly black American Tennis Association. "Arthur was like Jackie Robinson in that white society let him in because he acted a certain way—but when he got in you knew that he never forgot where he came from."

The city Arthur Robert Ashe, Jr., came from, Richmond, Virginia, was so crippled from segregation that he was not allowed to enter white-run amateur tennis tournaments there. Wounds he sustained in the years from his birth on July 10, 1943, to the day he left Richmond as a teenager never left him. Once Arthur broke through barriers erected by hate and secured the right to perform in the world's premier tennis venues, he earned lasting fame through a series of significant firsts, including but not limited to the following:

• First black man to win the United States Open.

• First black to win the U.S. Nationals and U.S. Open in the same year; though it should be pointed out that 1968, the first year of open professional tennis, and 1969 were the only years a player could have competed in both events.

- First black to compete on the U.S. Davis Cup team. (The Davis Cup is an annual competition among nations in men's tennis. The women's international tournament is called the Federation Cup.)
- First black to captain the U.S. Davis Cup team. In 1981 the United States defeated Argentina in the final. With Ashe again as captain in 1982, America won another Davis Cup, defeating France in the final.
- First black to win the Australian Open.
- First black man to win the Wimbledon championship.

Also a force in tennis behind the scenes, Arthur was instrumental in the formation of the Association of Tennis Professionals, which runs the men's pro tour, becoming the second ATP president (after Cliff Drysdale) in 1974. Combining a love of the game with a high regard for education, he founded the National Junior Tennis League; served as chairman of the Black Tennis and Sports Foundation; and teamed with tennis coach Nick Bolletieri to form the Ashe Bolletieri Cities program, which in 1990 was renamed the Arthur Ashe Safe Passage Foundation, a program designed to introduce inner-city youth to tennis while stressing discipline, academic instruction, and life-sustaining skills. The Safe Passage Foundation has branches in ten U.S. cities. California teenagers Brittany Augustine and Asia Muhammad from the Carson, California, program have become a world-ranked junior girls doubles team.

Arthur debuted on the world tennis stage at a time when the sight of a black person on television still prompted other blacks to pick up a telephone and spread the news. Word traveled fast that Arthur—handsome, intelligent, polite, poised, and well-spoken, yet fiercely independent in thought and action—exemplified black America at its best. Although even he tired at times of the smooth and polished image he cultivated in the genteel and segregated world of tennis, Arthur did what was necessary to create a climate that would allow other blacks—whose personalities differed markedly from his own—to come behind him.

"Sure, I get fed up being the nice guy," he told a reporter in 1985, "but back in the '60s if you were black and the first one, you simply had to behave yourself. I couldn't have gotten away with coming on like [Muhammad] Ali—it wouldn't have been tolerated. I genuinely believe that if [John] McEnroe were black, he wouldn't be allowed to do some of the things he does."

Tennis was not boxing, and a black man could not throw racquets and abuse tennis umpires and officials and remain in the sport, so Arthur behaved himself. He played with a quiet intensity and a stoicism neither seen in his sport before nor duplicated since. His demeanor on court rarely betrayed whether he was ahead by a set or behind by the same margin. His trancelike states of meditation during stoppages of play were primers on how to concentrate so as to get the maximum effort out of one's ability, which he readily admitted was not the equal of the game's top practitioners.

"I was not a great athlete," he once said, "but I was fast, had quick hands, good eye-hand coordination, and repertoire and attitude together at a time when the pro game was mushrooming with prize money and commercial endorsements."

Arthur's forehand could be unsteady, and his serve-and-volley game—something he was not encouraged to learn until he was sixteen—was never superior. But he had weapons, most notably a mastery of the cerebral and tactical side of tennis. "In my dictionary he was a great player; he could probe until he found an opponent's weakness and then attack it," said Drysdale, a former pro, who lost eight of ten career matches against Arthur. "He would not compare with a [Pete] Sampras, an [Andre] Agassi, a [Rod] Laver, because he never won that many Grand Slam titles and that's usually a barometer of greatness."

Arthur won three Grand Slam titles, a far cry from Agassi's eight, Laver's eleven, or Sampras's men's record of fourteen. Arthur's highest career singles ranking as a pro was No. 2 on May 10, 1976, though he did reach world No. 1 as an amateur in 1968. His career won-lost record against the chief rivals of his era was hardly dominant:

1-6 vs. Jimmy Connors

3-19 vs. Rod Laver

4-10 vs. John Newcombe

6-14 vs. Ken Rosewall

8-9 vs. Bjorn Borg

5-5 vs. Guillermo Vilas

6-5 vs. Ilie Nastase

11-6 vs. Stan Smith

14-2 vs. Roy Emerson

17-8 vs. Tom Okker

Certainly not for his on-court achievements alone does the name Arthur Ashe appear on the largest tennis stadium in the world, the 23,000-seat main court at the U.S. Open. Not merely for his tennis prowess does a bronze sculpture meant to represent him (though it more closely resembles a naked sumo wrestler) stand outside Ashe Stadium. As Bob Davis, a longtime friend and former doubles partner of Arthur's, puts it, "Arthur's name is on that stadium because of the exemplary life he led. He was a tennis champion who transcended the sport."

"Arthur fought against social injustice; he stood firmly in that regard," said Drysdale, who broadcast tennis matches with him on ABC in the 1980s and 1990s. "His activism was more of an intellectual kind. My sense about him was that he wanted to change things from within the system. But my sense also is that as a black athlete in the 1960s and 1970s, he realized that he had to present an image of being serious while also letting everyone know exactly how he felt about issues."

Dignified. Focused. Persuasive. Effective. Arthur Ashe Stadium stands in tribute to a quiet revolutionary who stood for fairness and against injustice, a trailblazer for African Americans in tennis who carried his competitive zeal into battles outside the sports arena, and outside the narrow parameters in which others expected a black man to operate.

It was a turbulent year, 1968. On April 4 Dr. Martin Luther King, Jr., was assassinated in Memphis, Tennessee, where he had gone to support a strike by local sanitation workers. On June 9 Robert F.

Kennedy was assassinated in Los Angeles, at the Ambassador Hotel, minutes after speaking to cheering supporters following a victory in the California primary that might have carried him to the Democratic party nomination for President of the United States. The civil rights movement raged on, with scenes of rioting, looting, police brutality, and major urban cities set ablaze by those who, in the words of Mississippi activist Fannie Lou Hamer, were "sick and tired of being sick and tired." And the Vietnam War continued apace with its disturbing visual images of death and inhumanity reaching into America's living rooms.

In August, after he emerged as champion of the U.S. Nationals amateur tournament and shortly before play began at the inaugural U.S. Open on the new professional circuit, Arthur had dinner with a friend and fellow tennis player, a white South African named Ray Moore. As they dined, they watched on television sickening scenes of rioting and police clubbing protesters and journalists on the streets of Chicago during the Democratic National Convention. The two men often discussed politics and social issues, including the human rights struggle in Ashe's homeland and the human rights struggle in Moore's, to which much of the world had turned a blind eye. The rule of law in Moore's homeland was apartheid—the systematic separation of races, categorized in descending order as whites, coloreds, and blacks, and the oppression of a black majority of twenty million persons by three million whites of Dutch descent called Afrikaners, who were convinced that God had mandated their right to rule.

"Arthur and I used to discuss interminably what to do about apartheid: what's meaningful and what's not," Moore said. "We were both vehemently opposed to apartheid, however we differed on how best to fight it."

Apartheid outraged Lt. Arthur Ashe, Jr., then a tennis-playing officer in the United States Army. Acceptance of injustice was never part of his persona. In 1967 he disturbed his superior officers with a public reference to South Africa's capital city: "Somebody should drop a hydrogen bomb on Johannesburg."

As Ashe and Moore continued to watch all hell break loose in Chicago, they talked about a quote they had seen in that day's newspaper from rock musician Frank Zappa, leader of a band called Mothers of Invention: "The way to stop all the violence in Chicago is for the hippies to cut their hair and infiltrate the police force."

The two discussed the concept of fighting against apartheid from the inside. Arthur then decided he needed to reach out to the South African government to receive permission to visit the country to compete in the South African Open tournament—not as an "honorary white" but as a black man—and build a platform in the United States to support such an unprecedented act. That, Arthur believed, would be the most effective way to show the apartheid regime in South Africa the error of its ways and begin to sway public opinion.

It would take years for Arthur to cut through the swath of political red tape and get a visa to visit South Africa. In 1969 and 1970 his applications were rejected by the South African government. In 1970 Arthur, then the No. 2 player in the world, and top-ranked Stan Smith visited four African nations (Kenya, Tanzania, Uganda, and Nigeria) for a series of tennis exhibitions and social events. Arthur would also visit Cameroon the following year. He spoke of his wish to be appointed U.S. ambassador to South Africa, but that notion sounded as fanciful at the time as his ever setting foot in that country. After all, why would a racially oppressive regime grant entry to someone who said its largest city should be bombed?

Arthur filed another visa application in 1973, and negotiations with South African officials continued. Among those advocating for Arthur were Robert Kelleher, a federal judge in Los Angeles who was Arthur's first Davis Cup captain; Donald Dell, a Washington, D.C., attorney and Arthur's agent; and Andrew Young, who in 1972 became Georgia's first black congressman since Reconstruction. The South African government did not want Arthur to visit, but it felt swayed somewhat by the argument that a trip by Arthur without incident could benefit the country's image enough to lift the international sports ban that kept South Africa out of the Olympics and other high-profile events. With both sides determined to get what they wanted from the deal, the visa application finally was accepted. In November 1973 Arthur visited South Africa.

"That trip was the start of change in South Africa—very small change," Moore said. "It was like Rosa Parks refusing to get up from her seat on the bus [in Montgomery, Alabama on December 1, 1955]. It was one small act that would have a much bigger impact."

Before the trip Arthur faced opposition from African-American activists. "People said, 'No, you shouldn't go. Why go all the way to South Africa for a cause when we've got problems right here?'" Moore remembered. "Uncle Tom" became one of the kinder criticisms leveled at Arthur. But Ashe argued that the situation for blacks in South Africa under the foot of apartheid was worse than the situation facing African Americans. As a black man he was not told by the U.S. government where to live. He could travel freely to any country on the globe, which would now include South Africa, whereas South African blacks were forced to live in government-created dwellings called homelands. South African blacks did not have the right to vote. South African blacks were forced to carry passes with their personal identification that were to be presented to white authorities on demand. South African blacks could be officially labeled "a banned person," or jailed by the government, as in the case of African National Congress leader Nelson Mandela, imprisoned since 1963 on Robben Island.

"I feel I have some credibility in talking about South Africa," Arthur wrote in his 1981 autobiography *Off the Court*. "I was brought up under a similar situation, having lived in the segregated South. I have more feeling being black, intuitively, than some northerner who may have a false feeling of integration." Arthur believed that in going to South Africa he "could play a significant role as far as raising the level of awareness within the white community both in South Africa and the United States."

Arthur set several conditions for his trip, all of which were approved by the South African government: (1) there would be no segregated audiences at the tournament in Johannesburg; (2) he would not have "honorary white" status, rather he would be recognized by white South Africa as a black man; (3) he would not have to stay in a segregated area; and (4) he could go anywhere he pleased and say anything he wanted. A few American sports journalists accompanied him on the trip, including Frank Deford of *Sports Illustrated*, with whom he wrote his first memoir, *Portrait in Motion*, in the 1970s, and Bud Collins of the *Boston Globe*.

Shortly after Arthur's arrival he had a chance meeting on the street with a colored South African poet and activist named Don Matera, regarded by his fans as "the poet of compassion." The apartheid regime had declared Matera a "banned person," meaning he could not work, could not appear at any public event, could not speak publicly, could not be quoted by any media, and could not be in the presence of anyone other than a family member. But when Matera heard that Arthur would be meeting that evening with a group of black South African journalists, he risked breaking an unjust law to try to talk with the American.

"When we were approaching the hall, there was a man standing by a telephone pole; it was Matera," Bud Collins recalled. "Arthur knew who he was. I didn't. He introduced himself, and there were guys across the street watching him. The police. He said, 'I can't talk to you long, but good luck.' The meeting with the black journalists was a real emotional setback for Arthur, because when he got up to speak—and we were told there were a lot of plants in the audience— a lot of people there were very critical of him. They were saying, 'Why did you come, Arthur? You're just making the government look good for letting you in. When you're gone, they'll still be kicking our black asses.' Things like that were said. I remember that very well. Arthur was very unsettled."

Had his critics in America been proven right? Was Arthur being used by a South African government intent on getting back into the Olympic Games with no real intention of granting basic human rights to an oppressed black majority? Had he done the wrong thing by setting foot in the land of apartheid? When Arthur left the hall Matera was still waiting outside. The words of an artist and activist whom Arthur respected, a man he did not expect to meet because of his "banned" status, fortified him and renewed his commitment to the cause.

"Obviously, Matera had known those sorts of statements would be made inside, and he could see Arthur was shaken," Collins said. "He said, 'Arthur, you have done the right thing to come here, because you have shown our black children that a black man can succeed in a white world.'"

Arthur also visited the South African homelands, white-created dwellings for blacks designed to disenfranchise them and dilute their political strength. He visited the impoverished township of Soweto, where in 1976 a violent uprising would take place resulting in the massacre of hundreds of blacks. On this day in 1973, a makeshift tennis court was fashioned under a bridge near a schoolhouse and hundreds watched, some hanging on to fences, as Arthur, the black tennis champion from America, and Moore, the white South African tennis star, shared their craft and instilled a sense of hope. A young black man named Mark Mathabane, then a tennis hopeful who idolized Arthur, wrote that he was inspired by the 1973 trip. Mathabane's life under apartheid and subsequent journey to America was chronicled in an autobiography, *Kaffir Boy*. ("Kaffir" is an Afrikaner slur equivalent to "nigger.")

The 1973 South African Open at Ellis Park was the first event under apartheid rule to have integrated seating. Moore, who did not compete in the event, made a point of sitting in a section previously reserved for blacks. There were black ball boys, and a few black South Africans competed in the tournament—dressing side by side with whites in an integrated locker room for the first time. The atmosphere in the locker room was said to be cold enough to store meat. Blacks, who had essentially been taught not to look a white person in the eye, did not initiate any locker-room chatter with their white counterparts. Whites, not used to being on equal footing with blacks, silently simmered rather than bring their resentment to a boil. For South Africa this constituted radical change.

Arthur partnered with Tom Okker, a Dutchman, to win the doubles championship, 6-2, 4-6, 6-4, but he lost to Jimmy Connors in the singles final, 6-4, 7-6, 6-3. He played quite well considering his full itinerary of meetings and fact-finding tours, and his startling encounters with the black journalists and with a distinguished professor from Stellenbosch University in Capetown who could not believe the intelligent and well-spoken Ashe was really black. "You are an exception," he told Arthur. "You are not completely black. You have some white blood in you."

Arthur hoped his trip would raise consciousness about South Africa among pro athletes, particularly tennis players, boxers, and golfers, who were accepting substantial appearance fees to compete in the country. "I asked Arthur what South Africa was like because I had considered going there for a tournament," said Kim Sands, the black pro from Miami. "He told me being in South Africa was like stuffing yourself with twenty pancakes and then having to eat twenty more. It just made you totally sick inside. After hearing that, I didn't go."

Arthur also hoped the international media would begin to hold accountable white South African athletes such as Gary Player, who routinely dismissed queries about apartheid with the line, "I'm a golfer, not a politician." But Arthur truly hoped that his first of several trips to South Africa would help bring an end to the apartheid regime. Change did not come as swiftly as he expected, but eventually it came. He had made a difference. In 1990 Nelson Mandela was released from prison. In 1992 South Africa returned to the Olympic Games for the first time in thirty-two years. In 1994 Mandela was elected president in South Africa's first all-races election.

Arthur remembered feeling "semi-satisfied" with his tennis performance on the 1973 trip to South Africa, because of the loss to Connors. Two years later he would have another shot at Connors and a chance to write history of a different sort.

In 1975 Jimmy Connors was invincible. Only twenty-two, the Belleville, Illinois, native played tennis with a youthful audacity. The left-hander was a boorish, bombastic, fiery, free-swinging force that no one could subdue. He brought to tennis the mentality of a prize-fighter, not one who dazzled judges with fancy footwork and rapid punches in combination, but one who knocked opponents out cold and sneered while admiring his handiwork. He swung from the heels, habitually treating a tennis ball like a glass jaw, and shot from the lip. Dictionaries of the day could have carried a headshot of Connors next to the word "brash."

A year earlier Connors had decisively won Wimbledon, the U.S. Open, and the Australian Open—three of the four Grand Slam events. The only logical reason he did not join Rod Laver and Don Budge as the only men in tennis history to win the Grand Slam was because the French Open banned him from its tournament for competing in Billie Jean King's World Team Tennis league. In the 1974 Wimbledon final, Connors could have been accused of elder abuse after a 6-1, 6-1, 6-4 thrashing of thirty-nine-year-old Aussie favorite Ken Rosewall.

Connors entered Wimbledon 1975 as prohibitive a favorite as anyone could remember. British bookmakers could get far more action on how many games he would lose in a given match, or in the entire tournament, instead of how many sets. Connors winning Wimbledon in a romp seemed the surest bet of all. In the Round of 16 he disposed of Aussie Phil Dent, 6-1, 6-1, 6-2. In the quarterfinals he defeated Raul Ramirez of Mexico, 6-4, 8-6, 6-2. And in the semifinals he dismantled Roscoe Tanner, a hard-hitting lefty from Lookout Mountain, Tennessee, 6-4, 6-1, 6-4. Six matches for Connors, six victories, all in straight sets. If Tanner could not withstand Connors's power and ferocity, went the conventional wisdom, what chance would his final-round opponent have? Why wait until after Saturday's match to engrave the men's trophy? Just do it now: James Scott Connors, 1975.

Arthur heard all the pro-Connors talk. He had played Connors three times before, including the 1973 final in Johannesburg, and had never beaten him. But at least Arthur was not in Connors's half of the draw. The only way they could meet at Wimbledon would be in the final, four days before Arthur's thirty-second birthday. And if an

Ashe-Connors match took place, it would make Arthur a Wimbledon finalist for the first time, his best result ever in a tournament he had not won in five previous tries.

Playing loose and relaxed tennis, Arthur moved quietly through his half of the draw. He ousted Graham Stilwell, 6-2, 5-7, 6-4, 6-2, in the Round of 16. In the quarterfinals he defeated a rising Swede named Bjorn Borg, 2-6, 6-4, 8-6, 6-1; it would be Borg's last defeat at Wimbledon before winning the next five titles in succession. In the semifinals Arthur outlasted Tony Roche, a tough Aussie, 5-7, 6-4, 7-5, 8-9, 6-4.

Not since Althea Gibson in 1958 had a black player qualified for a Wimbledon final. The British bookmakers made Connors a huge favorite and an even-money choice to win the match in straight sets.

"I remember being scared to death that Arthur was going to be terribly embarrassed," said Collins, who did the match commentary for NBC. "We almost didn't want the match to happen because Connors was going to beat him 1, 1, and Love [6-1, 6-1, 6-0]. We were glad for Arthur that he got to the final, but we didn't even want to watch. But we had to."

There was another reason for people to think that Connors would attempt to humiliate Arthur, and it had more to do with personal conflict than tennis: Connors was suing Arthur for $3 million, alleging slander and libel. Arthur, in his role as president of the Association of Tennis Professionals, had publicly criticized Connors for not joining the men's union.

Good thing Arthur did not solicit the opinions of the international sports media before the match. Otherwise he might not have arrived for the 2 p.m. first serve. Rather than buy into the gloom-and-doom about his chances, he approached a championship match against an unbeatable foe as though the grass court were a chess board. Strategy of the kind he had never before employed against Connors might just win the match, he thought. Brute force was not likely to work. You do not have to stand toe-to-toe with a slugger if you can outwit him.

In addition to the traditional white shirt and white shorts that players must wear at Wimbledon, Arthur strode onto Centre Court with a red, white, and blue sweatband on each wrist and in a blue Davis Cup jacket with USA in red letters on the back. Davis Cup, playing tennis for your country instead of yourself, was something Arthur loved and the iconoclastic Connors refused to do. So for one of the few times in the history of professional athletic competition between a black man and a white man, the black man represented the establishment.

Looking like a 6-foot 1-inch cigar with an Afro tip, Arthur revealed not a hint of nerves. Indeed, he looked positively serene. The book on Arthur's tennis game was that his backhand was the stronger shot, and he hit the ball hard and flat with virtually no topspin. But he liked what he had seen in the Connors vs. Ramirez quarterfinal, particularly the second set, which the challenger lost 8-6. Arthur had his game plan for the final: he would give Connors junk, more junk than Fred Sanford ever could.

Arthur hit forehand slices with underspin, mostly to Connors's two-fisted backhand, rather than take full healthy cuts. Making a player with a two-fisted backhand stretch for shots diminishes his power and control. Connors's backhand replies would float back, allowing Arthur time to rush the net and volley them away. He chipped and dinked the ball inside the baseline to lure Connors to the net, then lobbed the ball over him. He kept balls in the center of the court, forcing Connors to create his own angles. He seized the net at every opportunity. He served solidly without ever falling into a predictable pattern. And his forehand, his most inconsistent shot, held as firm as his resolve.

Connors held serve in the opening game, but Arthur took over from there. After two holds of serve and a pair of service breaks, the capacity crowd of nearly fourteen thousand at Centre Court was abuzz. The underdog had a 4-1 lead. During the changeover, when the players sit back to back and on opposite sides of the umpire's chair, Connors read a letter from his mother, Gloria, as he often did for inspiration during a match. Arthur closed his eyes and meditated, visualizing success. This he did during every changeover throughout the match, throughout the fortnight, through much of his career.

Arthur kept the momentum going and won the first set, 6-1, in twenty minutes, without ever facing a break point.

Could Arthur continue such tactically impeccable tennis and win two more sets? Press row was not yet convinced. "He wins the set, and we think, 'Well, that's great. He'll lose in four sets. He's not going to be embarrassed,'" Collins said with a laugh.

Arthur continued to dominate. Since Connors had a stronger backhand return, Arthur served mainly to his forehand. And Arthur's lobs were effective enough to keep Connors back. Two strong service games and a fourth consecutive break of serve gave Arthur a 3-0 lead in the second set.

"Come on, Connors!" a fan yelled.

"I'm trying, for Christ's sake," Connors replied.

Not even the rare occurrence of crowd laughter on Centre Court could delay Arthur's charge. On his fourth set point he unleashed a second serve that momentarily handcuffed Connors, causing a return into the net. Arthur had won another set, 6-1. He had a two-set lead before a crowd now solidly behind him, a crowd now wanting to see an upset, a crowd that undoubtedly wished it had stormed the betting parlors that morning and bet the underdog. Arthur was one set from becoming the first black man to win tennis's most coveted title.

But Connors was not about to roll over and die. Arthur had him down two sets but had not knocked the fist-pumping bravado out of him. After all, Connors was world No. 1 and Wimbledon's top seed for a reason. Arthur was up a break, 3-2 in the third set, but Connors broke right back. The two stayed on serve until the twelfth game when Connors rifled a crosscourt forehand winner for the service break that won the set, 7-5.

In the fourth set Connors raced to a 3-0 lead. Even if the defending champion thought he was capable of a remarkable comeback, Arthur stayed cool. During the changeover the handsome brown-skinned man seated with military-perfect posture, his eyes closed to the public, alone in his thoughts, was the coolest man on Centre Court. He would not employ a Plan B. He had come this far on a steady diet of junk, which still had not allowed Connors to find a comfortable rhythm. He had won the first two sets by showing enough poise and confidence to let Connors know he would not be intimidated. He stuck to Plan A. More junk.

Arthur held serve and trailed 1-3, then used a beautifully angled backhand winner, an overhead smash winner, and a beautiful lunging forehand winner to break Connors and get to 2-3. He held serve again to square the set and get an anxious crowd back on his side. With the set tied at 4-all and Connors serving, the defending champion made a major error. Thinking Arthur's return would sail long, Connors watched it clip the baseline. Point to Ashe: 15-all. Connors rushed the net, Arthur coolly whipped a backhand past him. 15-30. Arthur sliced a forehand return of a second serve low, forcing Connors to hit up at the ball. And into the net. 15-40, double break point. Arthur ripped a service return, Connors pushed a forehand wide. Game: Ashe. He led 5-4. The Wimbledon championship was now on his serve.

"Arthur was so cool; just the way he looked in the chair, you knew he was going to come out and finish it like a champion," said Bob Ryland, a two-time ATA champion who watched the match on television. Actually he watched taped highlights of the match. Ashe vs. Connors was not televised live or in its entirety in the United States. The 1975 Wimbledon gentlemen's final was presented to America as part of a ninety-minute telecast after the Major League Baseball Game of the Week. And if the baseball game ran long in your area, the tennis highlights were cut even further.

But if you managed to get through the morning and afternoon of July 6 without knowing the outcome of the match, you could have watched NBC's taped coverage and seen Arthur open his eyes after the fifth changeover in the fourth set, walk briskly to the service line to a hearty round of applause, and been surprised.

Point one—Arthur scores on a service winner. Three points from the championship.

Point two—Connors responds with a forehand crosscourt winner. Still three points from a championship.

Point three—the players rally for one of the few times in a crisply played match. Connors, forced again to hit up, dumps a forehand into the net. Two points from the championship.

Point four—Arthur smacks another service winner. Championship point.

Point five—Arthur does not change a thing: he slices a serve deep to Connors's backhand, pulling him off the court. The weak return floats toward the net. Fittingly, Arthur concludes a superior strategic match with the easiest of smash volleys into a wide open court. Game. Set. Championship.

Arthur turned to Dell, his agent and former Davis Cup captain, in the friends' box and displayed the second most famous clenched fist ever by a black athlete, the most famous being the black-glove salute of Tommie Smith and John Carlos, gold and bronze medalists respectively, in the 400-meter dash at the 1968 Olympics in Mexico City. The gesture by Smith and Carlos, an expression of Black Power at an Olympiad boycotted by many black athletes, had turned the sprinters into pariahs in the eyes of the establishment. A clenched fist seven years later by Ashe, on the day he represented the establishment against the tennis outlaw Connors, raised nary an eyebrow.

For British fans that had not seen one of their own win the Wimbledon gentlemen's singles title since Fred Perry in 1936, the almost lustful applause on Centre Court made it sound as if it they had temporarily adopted the lean, graceful black man from Richmond, Virginia. They had come expecting to see yet another unpopular thrashing by Connors. Instead they were witnesses to history: a black man had won Wimbledon.

"I walked into the locker room," Arthur wrote, "and the first person I saw was Neale Fraser of Australia, who beat Rod Laver for the 1960 Wimbledon title. Neale stuck out his hand and said, 'Welcome to the club.'"

And perhaps out of newfound respect for Arthur, Connors dropped the lawsuit. Eventually he joined the ATP and played Davis Cup for the USA.

As the gentlemen's singles champion of Wimbledon, Arthur received three trophies. The one presented on Centre Court by the Duke of Kent was the All-England Tennis Club Trophy, which reads, "Single-handed Championship of the World." The others were the Renshaw Cup, named for William and Ernest Renshaw, British brothers who combined to win eight Wimbledon titles in the late nineteenth century, and the President's Cup. "My first thought and only sad moment was that Dr. Johnson had not lived to see my greatest victory," Arthur wrote in reference to the man who molded him into the champion he became.

As a boy, Arthur had tennis right outside his door. His family lived in a city-owned house inside Brook Field Park, the park for blacks in segregated Richmond. His dad, Arthur Sr., was a police officer in charge of the park, which had four tennis courts. As befitting his position, Arthur Sr. was a stern, no-nonsense man who tolerated no backtalk from his namesake. When Arthur was six, his mother, Mattie, died of a toxemic pregnancy caused by hypertension and cardiovascular disease. Asked by his dad if he wanted to attend the funeral, Arthur said no. Evidently the sight of adults wailing and losing control traumatized him. No one attempted to change his mind.

The all-black Richmond Racquet Club used Brook Field Park as its home base, and students from nearby Virginia Union University, a historically black school, also practiced there. At age seven Arthur watched Ronald Charity, a nineteen-year-old VU student, practicing serves, forehands, and backhands, and became captivated. Charity, who also played in the American Tennis Association, offered to teach Arthur a game for which his dad did not have much use. Unusually thin for his age, Arthur nonetheless showed decent athletic skills and, most important, an eagerness to learn and work hard. He was a quick study. Charity entered him in ATA events, the only tennis competition open to blacks in Richmond, and by age ten Arthur had won ATA twelve-and-under tournaments in Washington, D.C., and Durham, North Carolina.

There was something different about Arthur. Not only his crispness in striking the ball and his ease in moving about the court, but also the self-assuredness he showed even against older, more experienced players. Charity knew that Dr. R. Walter Johnson, a Lynchburg, Virginia, physician and the architect of the ATA's junior development program, had been trying to convince the USLTA to integrate its youth tournaments in the region. Charity brought Arthur to Lynchburg to see the man known as "Dr. J."

If anything, Dr. J was even more enthusiastic about Arthur's talent, poise, and potential. This could be the player, he decided, to literally change the complexion of junior tennis in the region. To spur the development of Arthur's game, Dr. J convinced Arthur's father to let the boy join his brood of talented boys and girls during the summer in Lynchburg. There Arthur refined his strokes, learned court etiquette, practiced with older boys, and, once Dr. J's pushing and prodding of the region's USLTA officials effected change, entered tournaments against the best white players in the area.

It was not unusual for Arthur to have to serve five hundred balls before breakfast and another five hundred afterward. And he had chores, as did all of Dr. Johnson's pupils. Chores included smoothing the clay court in Dr. J's backyard and picking up trash. The idea was to build in Arthur mental toughness and endurance. "Don't be as strong or as tough as those white boys," Dr. J said. "Be stronger. Be tougher." Among the rules of etiquette he taught Arthur was always to give the point to an opponent on a close call. He drummed this rule into all his charges, so they would do it instinctively in a match against white players—to better ensure that the well-mannered blacks would be allowed to compete again in those same tournaments.

Under the tutelage of Dr. J and his son, Bobby Johnson, Arthur became the predominant junior player in ATA competition. He won the boys' twelve-and-under title in 1955, and the boys' sixteen-and-under title in 1957 (when he was fourteen) and again in 1958. By this time Dr. J had wedged open the doors of certain white-run tournaments in the state—though not in Arthur's hometown of Richmond—

and Arthur excelled in them as well. As the lone black in a tournament he won in Charlottesville, Virginia, he suffered an indignity he would never forget. When the boys decided to attend a movie after the matches, Arthur was stopped at the box office and denied admission. How far had he come, really, if he was still treated like a second-class citizen in his home state?

Dr. Johnson decided that Arthur's game could only stagnate under the weight of entrenched racism in the South. He arranged for Arthur to move to less oppressive St. Louis and finish high school while living with the family of a friend, Richard Hudlin. Hudlin was a college professor who had been captain of the University of Chicago tennis team in 1924.

In St. Louis, Arthur played indoor tennis on linoleum floors for the first time, which forced him to develop a serve-and-volley game, something he never learned under Dr. J. Although a tennis enthusiast and a tireless advocate for black achievement in the sport, Dr. Johnson's major sports interest was football, which he played in college and later coached. Arthur said in later years that his late start as a serve-and-volley player contributed to his being often erratic in that critical phase of the game.

In 1960 Arthur achieved major firsts for an African American in a white-run tournament, winning the U.S. Nationals Interscholastic title and the U.S. Nationals Indoor title. He repeated as U.S. Indoors champ the following year amidst the stifling atmosphere that came with being a promising black star in a country-club sport. "I played in clubs where the only blacks were waiters, gardeners, and busboys," he said. "The game had a history and tradition I was expected to assimilate, but much of that history and many of those traditions were hostile to me."

Ashe became an All-American at UCLA playing under famed coach J. D. Morgan. Being a black tennis player made Arthur stand out. Being smart while projecting an air of nonthreatening self-assuredness made fair-minded whites feel comfortable around him. He would have missed out on playing in major tournaments abroad during the summer of 1963, but a white woman named Joan Ogner, the wife of a Beverly Hills auto dealer, approached him after an exhibition match at the California Club and gave him the eight hundred dollars for the trip. According to someone who was there, the budding African-American star was never ostracized on the tennis circuit.

"Arthur was always accepted in the locker room," Drysdale said. "There were no racial overtones. I think everyone respected him. The locker room was, as it is now, very international, and my sense was that anyone who got into that locker room, particularly having qualified for the majors—Wimbledon, the U.S. Open, the French Open, the Australian Open—was seen as an equal."

An equal on the court, Arthur was nonetheless a curiosity to his peers. The coach of 1970s Russian player Alex Metreveli threatened to stare a hole through Arthur while watching the black man groom his hair in the locker room one day. Never before had the Russian been close enough to a black man to compare hair textures. Arthur allowed the coach to have a feel. As the locker room erupted in good-natured laughter, the Russian marveled at the softness of Arthur's hair, apparently expecting it to feel like a Brillo pad.

While at UCLA, Arthur took ROTC training, as was required of every male student. After graduating in 1965 with a degree in business administration, he joined the army and reported to Fort Lewis, Washington. (His brother, John, became a decorated career Marine who served two tours of duty in Vietnam.) Tennis was still an amateur sport, so Arthur wasn't missing out on any big purses while serving in the military. He became a lieutenant and played in tournaments as often as he could. This he managed to do because he had been named to his first U.S. Davis Cup team. That allowed him to go on temporary duty to represent the United States in international competition. By the end of 1967 he was the No. 2–ranked player in the country behind former UCLA teammate Charles Pasarell.

A year later Arthur debuted in the Davis Cup, combining with Pasarell, Captain Donald Dell, Dennis Ralston, Stan Smith, Clark Graebner, and Bob Lutz to trounce Australia 4-1 in the final. The triumph began a string of five consecutive Davis Cup titles for America. But during that run Arthur endured an appalling racial incident in his own country. The U.S. vs. Mexico matches scheduled for the Dallas Country Club had to be moved because club members objected to having a black man on the team. The matches were played in Samuel Grand Park, a public facility.

The 1968 Davis Cup title was the first in a triple crown of success for Arthur that year. The second was his winning the penultimate U.S. Nationals title in Boston, defeating Lutz in a five-set final. The third came at Forest Hills, where the rules of tennis had changed forever because of the first-ever U.S. Open tournament for prize money.

The only way Arthur could compete in the 1968 Open was as an amateur since he was stationed at West Point at the time. He was seeded sixth and caught a huge break when Drysdale upset Laver, whom Arthur had never beaten, in the Round of 16. Arthur then beat Drysdale in four sets in the quarterfinals and ousted Graebner in four sets in the semifinals. He caught another break when Okker upset Rosewall (the winner of 70 percent of his career matches against Arthur) in the other semifinal. In a two-hour and forty-minute final, Arthur wore down Okker with superior power and court coverage, 14-12, 5-7, 6-3, 3-6, 6-3.

"The award ceremony that day will always hold a special place in my heart," Arthur wrote. "My father came onto the court with me, and it felt wonderful to share that moment with him. Dr. J was in the stands." As an amateur, Arthur could not accept the $14,000 first prize, but he did achieve the world No. 1 ranking among amateur players. His only monetary payment from the U.S. Open was $28 a day in expense money, to which he was entitled as a U.S. Davis Cup player. But from an anonymous donor Arthur received 100 shares of General Motors stock, which in September 1968 sold for $84 a share.

Winning the inaugural U.S. Open made Arthur a name that even those unfamiliar with tennis recognized, a name with which the black community, in the heat of an all-consuming struggle for self-determination in their own country, wanted to associate. Unlike Althea Gibson a decade earlier, Arthur did not try to distance himself from the civil rights struggle. Unlike Althea, he did not tell reporters he was concerned about himself and no one else. Regardless, Arthur faced heat from those in black America who believed he was not giving enough of his time to black causes. His reply was essentially that it was impossible for any black person's efforts to be considered sufficient. "You can do clinics—and I've done my share—but you can never do enough," he wrote. "They want you to be great as well as spend all your free time in the black community, and you can't do both. You can't be No. 1 on a tennis court and spend all your time in the black community. Muhammad Ali didn't do it, Martin Luther King didn't do it, no one's done it. It can't be done."

A black cause Arthur enthusiastically endorsed was the United Negro College Fund, the largest tax-exempt charitable organization in the African-American community. "I support the UNCF because of the high value I place on [black] colleges and because the fund is non-political and highly efficient," he wrote in his 1993 memoir. Ashe may never have addressed a group of black children without expressing something akin to the UNCF's slogan, "A mind is a terrible thing to waste."

It was at a UNCF benefit at Madison Square Garden on October 14, 1976, that Arthur first met the love of his life. An NBC staff photographer was among those who jockeyed for position to shoot him that night. Her name was Jeanne Moutoussamy, a café au lait–skinned beauty of black and East Indian origin. "Jeanne captivated me," wrote Arthur, who had for years declared himself a confirmed bachelor. "In looks, she was easily a '10,' but she did something else to me. She was a photographer and graphic artist who was bright, articulate, sensitive. Even with all my traveling in late 1976, to Europe and Australia, I knew I wanted to marry Jeanne. It was intuition mingled with being able to recognize genuine feelings for someone."

There was no marriage proposal. Arthur hid an engagement ring in an envelope in Jeanne's medicine cabinet. She found it three days later. With Arthur on crutches from having had bone spurs removed, he married Jeanne on February 20, 1977, with Andrew Young, then the U.S. ambassador to the United Nations, performing the ceremony.

The Ashes resided in Mount Kisco, New York, a suburb forty minutes north of New York City. One of their neighbors was Ilie Nastase, the irrepressible Romanian who won two Grand Slam singles titles and threw countless tantrums in a twenty-year pro career. Arthur and Ilie were friends despite two incidents that highlighted the volatility of a player nicknamed "Nasty."

In 1976 Arthur played against Nastase in the final of a nationally televised tournament called the Avis Cup, sponsored by the rental car company. "At one point Nastase was losing and he said, 'That goddamn nigger,'" said Collins, the NBC broadcaster that day. "Everyone on television heard it because we had microphones around. But no one in the stadium heard it. He said it pretty softly. Ashe was shocked, but he didn't get angry. He said later, 'That's Ilie. You never know what he's going to say.'"

Or what he's going to wear. Arthur and Nastase played doubles together in a tournament sanctioned by World Championship Tennis (now defunct). A WCT rule mandated that doubles teams had to be similarly attired. So after Arthur came out first, Nastase took the court . . . in blackface. Arthur made "Nasty" go back to the locker room to wipe his face before play began.

With Jeanne at home and Nastase in the neighborhood, Arthur might have felt like the star in his own version of *Beauty and the Beast*. At age thirty-three he found his life partner after years of bachelorhood and as ascetic a lifestyle as a world-recognized professional athlete could have. Before his marriage, a newspaper reporter wrote, "Ashe travels to 20 countries yearly and owns no homes, cars, furniture or other trappings." Evidently Arthur believed in saving for rainy days. As greater prize money came into pro tennis in the early 1970s and his performance improved, his earnings from the court skyrocketed:

    1970 $140,000
    1971 $350,000
    1972 $500,000 plus

He had endorsement deals with AMF Head racquets, Bufferin, Benefit cereal, and Volvo. And he held the job of head teaching pro at the Doral Resort and Country Club in Miami.

Marrying Jeanne in 1977 undoubtedly made it easier for Arthur to endure a year in which nothing went right on the court. Still a young man in the real world, he was in the twilight of his tennis career, a time when injuries exact a heavy toll. His world ranking, No. 2 in 1976, plunged to No. 257 because of heel surgery and eye problems. Injuries caused him to miss three of the four Grand Slam events that year; in the only one he played, he lost in the Australian Open quarterfinals.

But in 1978 Arthur battled back and appeared in every Grand Slam event. Despite a first-round upset loss at Wimbledon, he reached the semifinals of the Australian Open and the fourth round at the U.S. Open and French Open, and finished the season ranked No. 7 in the world and as the ATP Comeback Player of the Year.

On July 31, 1979, less than a month after another first-round upset loss at Wimbledon, Arthur suffered a heart attack minutes after conducting a clinic at the East River Tennis Club in Long Island City, New York. Thinking the attack to be an aberration, he attempted a comeback several months later. But after a second heart attack he retired from the game. He underwent quadruple bypass surgery on December 13, 1979, at age thirty-six, and would undergo a second heart operation in 1983. One of the more remarkable careers in sport had come to an abrupt end.

Arthur fit comfortably into the role of a tennis elder statesman. In addition to his charitable works and corporate affiliations, he became a tennis commentator, covering Wimbledon for HBO and regular tour events for ABC and PBS. He captained the Davis Cup team. He wrote a weekly tennis column for the *Washington Post*. He enjoyed spending more time with Jeanne. And he became a doting father to their only child, a daughter Camera, born December 21, 1986.

In July 1985 the International Tennis Hall of Fame in Newport, Rhode Island, inducted Arthur in his first year of eligibility. During the outdoor ceremony he referred to his status as tennis's first black male professional champion, saying, "It was always interesting being in my position. I never wanted to be in another sport or not to be in the minority. I always thought the system was wrong, not that it was me that was wrong." In referring to Arthur Ashe, Sr., he said, "My father always told me that you should leave something better off than when you found it. That's what I've always tried to do." And of his staunchest tennis benefactor, he said, "If there is one person I wish could be here, it would be Dr. Johnson. He is not alive now, but he would be very pleased about [my induction]."

The Johnson family, however, was not pleased with Arthur after he chose not to attend his benefactor's funeral. Dr. J died on June 28, 1971, of a malignant tumor at age seventy-two. Althea Gibson, Johnson's other famous tennis protégé, at the time a struggling competitor on the women's pro golf tour, attended the memorial. Arthur chose to remain at Wimbledon, where he had already lost in singles to Marty Riessen but remained in contention in doubles with partner Dennis Ralston. Arthur's explanation that he felt uncomfortable at funerals—remember, at age six he had chosen not to attend his own mother's funeral—did not sit well with the Johnsons.

In later years Arthur weathered criticism from young African-American tennis pros such as Juan Farrow, Luis Glass, Horace Reid, and Arthur Carrington, all of whom argued that Ashe had not done enough to advance their careers. Sydney Llewellyn, who coached Althea in the 1950s and coached Carrington in the 1970s, said about Arthur, "He only gave a handout here and there. Ashe never sincerely helped any of those kids." Farrow, the last promising ATA junior to be trained by Dr. Johnson, criticized Arthur for not playing doubles with him in pro events. "Arthur wanted to make sure that he was the only one [to succeed]," said Farrow, a tennis coach in Macon, Georgia. Farrow seemed to suggest that a doubles pairing with Arthur would have increased his exposure and allowed him to attract sponsors. But Farrow was a teenager in junior tournaments in 1977, the year Ashe had injuries and rarely played. By the time Arthur retired in 1979, Farrow had done nothing on the pro circuit. The highest pro ranking he achieved was No. 227 in 1985.

Other African Americans in tennis tell a different story about Arthur. Kim Sands, who became the head women's coach at the University of Miami after her playing career, worked with Arthur when he taught tennis at the Doral Country Club. "Arthur was a great coach and always supportive," she said. "I came to tennis late, while I was playing basketball in high school. Arthur taught me how to play. He taught me how to serve. Today I teach the serve exactly the way he taught me: point your arm toward the net post on your toss; don't vary the direction of your toss so your opponent won't know where you're going to hit it. He taught me so many technical things about the game, and he was always so positive." Rodney Harmon, a former pro from Ashe's hometown of Richmond, said, "Arthur was not the kind of person who would publicize what he was doing to help other black players. That was not his way. He did what he thought was right in a quiet, thoughtful way. Some black players he helped financially, but he did it without wanting any publicity. You know the saying, 'Where good news travels, bad news travels faster'? It's so easy for people who didn't go as far in tennis as they think they should have to say that Arthur didn't help other blacks. But I can tell you as a black man myself and as a former player that Arthur was very helpful to me."

Arthur also helped Yannick Noah, whom he spotted as a boy in 1971 during a trip to Cameroon. He contacted the French Tennis Federation, which guided Noah to a career that included a French Open title in 1983, a Davis Cup title in 1991, and induction into the Hall of Fame in 2005. In response to the African-American players who argued he should have done as much for them as he did for Noah, Arthur said, "What they didn't realize was that I wasn't helping Yannick that much. Yannick Noah is not my protégé. I didn't teach him a single stroke."

"With Arthur, I would say that if he saw you helping yourself along, he would help you," said Harmon, the USTA director of men's tennis. "If he thought you were not helping yourself, he would not help you. That's what I saw."

Arthur criticized the USTA when he believed America's largest tennis organization was not doing the right thing. On the USTA's unwillingness to keep Althea Gibson in the sport by giving her a job, he said, "As good as she was, she was the only great U.S. champion I

R FIVE

ly show in town"

• • • • • • •

a did not always have world rank-
 on racial prejudice, they were kept
ajor national and international tour-
r stopped blacks from playing. For
players had tennis rankings and won
rganization of their own, an organi-
terests of the white-owned print and
n where all the top players knew one
ne another, through the black news-
ion that, quite intentionally, did not
 name, because the American Tennis
ig more inclusive than the rest of the
 of Famers Althea Gibson and Arthur
ire pro stars Zina Garrison and Lori
iship trophies. The ATA is where John
Thomas, Jr., and Nehemiah Atkinson,
pions, started. The ATA was founded
layed tennis even earlier than that.
is credited with introducing the game
in 1874. Blacks in the Northern and

know who had financial problems. If she were white, there's no question she would have been helped." He also rebuked the organization
for not offering a coaching position to John Wilkerson, a black coach
from Houston who developed future champions Zina Garrison and
Lori McNeil from his public park program.

Speaking truth to power—not in a loud and abrasive voice, but
in a mannered and well-reasoned tone—was Arthur's way. His important voice would be stilled under the most tragic of circumstances. During either of two blood transfusions, in December 1979
or June 1983, he contracted the virus that causes Acquired Immune
Deficiency Syndrome (AIDS). He tested positive for the virus in September 1988 after undergoing brain surgery. At the time only family
and a few close friends knew that he had AIDS. "We were at a tournament together," Cliff Drysdale said, "preparing to broadcast a
match for ABC. Arthur said, 'There's something I've got to tell you.'
I said, 'Oh, geez, Arthur, don't tell me you're having heart problems
again.' Then he told me about his condition. I was mortified. It was
just awful."

The public found out on April 8, 1992, at a news conference
hastily arranged so that Arthur could break the news himself before
the newspaper USA Today could. Two days earlier USA Today tennis writer Doug Smith, a respected journalist and author, came to
New York seeking confirmation from Arthur of a telephoned tip that
he had AIDS. Both Smith and Arthur had grown up in Virginia, competed against each other on the ATA circuit, and were friends for
decades. Arthur confirmed to Smith that he indeed had AIDS, but
asked Smith not to print the story until he could speak to USA Today
sports editor Gene Policinski. He hoped Policinski would respect his
privacy and not run the story. He did not want the public to see him
differently, treat him differently, pity him because he had AIDS.
Arthur's intention had been to reveal the news only if he was close to
death. The editor informed Arthur that the newspaper would not sit
on the story. Although the news did not appear in the April 7, 1992,
edition, Arthur knew it soon would. He canceled an appearance that
day for his Safe Passage Foundation in Newark, New Jersey, and

another in Washington, D.C., with Donald Dell and Stan Smith. With Jeanne at his side at the offices of HBO on Avenue of the Americas and Forty-second Street in Manhattan, Arthur spoke into a cluster of microphones and revealed he had AIDS. He answered a few questions afterward, including these:

"*Do you plan to sue the hospital where you received the tainted blood?*"

"*No.*"

"*Do you feel forced out?*"

"*Absolutely. If the person hadn't called the newspaper, I'd still be leading a normal life.*"

"*Do you have any advice for AIDS sufferers?*"

"*Yes. Take care, because you never know what breakthrough lies around the corner.*"

In his final year he founded the Arthur Ashe Foundation for the Defeat of AIDS. The foundation raised more than five million dollars by the end of 1993 to educate the public about AIDS, and distributed funds to organizations devoted to AIDS research, clinical trials, and patient support. In August 1992 Arthur played host to tennis greats at a fund-raiser at the National Tennis Center the day before the U.S. Open. Today the annual event is known as Arthur Ashe Kids' Day, and it occurs at the same site two days before the U.S. Open. Requests to interview Jeanne Moutoussamy Ashe and Camera Ashe at the 2006 U.S. Open were denied. Both are extremely private women. Both shared a life with a man who touched his many friends and countless others he never met with uncommon grace and dignity.

Unlike Earvin "Magic" Johnson, the basketball Hall of Famer who announced in 1991 that he had the AIDS virus yet has survived and flourished since, Arthur lost his private battle. He died February 6, 1993. The official cause of death was pneumonia. In his forty-nine years he showed us how a life combining academic and athletic excellence, intellectual curiosity, and social activism can be an inspiration to others—and the clearest expression of humanity. On the fourteenth anniversary of his death, the Web site www.arthurashe.org was launched, allowing everyone to learn more about a remarkable man.

CHA

"We were the

· · · ·

Black tennis players in Am
ings. For reasons based so
out of Grand Slam events and
naments. But those barriers n
decades, generations really, bla
championships in an American
zation that existed outside the
broadcast media. An organizat
another, or soon learned abou
papers of the day. An organiz
put "Colored" or "Negro" in
Association prided itself on be
country. The ATA is where Ha
Ashe were nurtured, where fu
McNeil held their first champi
Wilkerson, Benny Sims, Willis
all of whom coached pro cha
in 1916. Yet black Americans

Walter Wingfield of Britai
of tennis as we know it today

For many, Arthur was the first prominent black tennis player they had seen. But were it not for a tennis association created by African Americans nearly a hundred years ago, in an era of virulent racial segregation, it is unlikely that Arthur would have taken up the game at all. This league showed Arthur as well as those who came before and after him that black tennis players are not oxymorons. Instead they could be champions—in a league of their own and in the world.

CHAPTER FIVE

"We were the only show in town"

● ● ● ● ● ● ● ● ● ● ●

Black tennis players in America did not always have world rankings. For reasons based solely on racial prejudice, they were kept out of Grand Slam events and major national and international tournaments. But those barriers never stopped blacks from playing. For decades, generations really, black players had tennis rankings and won championships in an American organization of their own, an organization that existed outside the interests of the white-owned print and broadcast media. An organization where all the top players knew one another, or soon learned about one another, through the black newspapers of the day. An organization that, quite intentionally, did not put "Colored" or "Negro" in its name, because the American Tennis Association prided itself on being more inclusive than the rest of the country. The ATA is where Hall of Famers Althea Gibson and Arthur Ashe were nurtured, where future pro stars Zina Garrison and Lori McNeil held their first championship trophies. The ATA is where John Wilkerson, Benny Sims, Willis Thomas, Jr., and Nehemiah Atkinson, all of whom coached pro champions, started. The ATA was founded in 1916. Yet black Americans played tennis even earlier than that.

Walter Wingfield of Britain is credited with introducing the game of tennis as we know it today, in 1874. Blacks in the Northern and

Eastern states played tennis before the turn of the nineteenth century. Professors at Tuskegee Institute, the historically black college in Alabama, noticed this and soon the game spread to the South. In 1898 a Philadelphia minister named W. W. Walker sponsored the first interstate tournament for blacks. Edgar Brown, a black pioneer in the game, is credited by some with introducing topspin—hitting the top of the ball to produce a higher and trickier bounce—around 1900. Tennis caught on quickly among the black elite—doctors, lawyers, college professors, businessmen, and other professionals. Blacks skilled enough to coach the sport began to emerge. Soon it hardly mattered that white tennis clubs were closed to blacks because blacks began forming their own clubs.

Representatives from more than a dozen of these clubs met on November 30, 1916, in Washington, D.C., and created the ATA. Its mission included:

• giving black tennis enthusiasts a place to play the game and socialize;
• holding an annual tournament; and
• promoting the game among other blacks.

The ATA founders included Ralph Cook, Henry Freeman, Tally Holmes, Dr. Harry S. McCard, Dr. B. M. Rhetta, and Dr. William H. Wright. Holmes, of Washington, D.C., became one of the ATA's dominant players. The first ATA tournament was staged in Druid Hill Park in Baltimore in August 1917 with thirty-nine competitors representing thirty-three clubs. Holmes won the men's singles, Lucy Slowe the women's singles, and Holmes and Sylvester Smith the men's doubles. Women's doubles, mixed doubles, and boys' singles were added in 1924.

The ATA, a not-for-profit organization since its inception, has been open to all, regardless of race. Indeed, Althea Gibson's first championship, as a fifteen-year-old, came against a white Jewish girl named Nina Irwin at the Cosmopolitan Tennis Club, an ATA member club. Historically black colleges and universities (HBCUs) were the venues for most of the early ATA tournaments, schools such as Wilberforce University, the oldest private African-American university in the country, in Wilberforce, Ohio, which had been a stop on Harriet Tubman's underground railroad; Central State University, also in Wilberforce; Hampton Institute in Hampton, Virginia; Tuskegee Institute; Lincoln University in Lincoln, Pennsylvania; and South Carolina State University in Orangeburg.

Staging the tournament at HBCUs accomplished two objectives. Since ATA competitors often brought their families, children were made aware of black college campuses at an early age, and the schools provided lodging and meals for blacks in an era when public accommodations, particularly in the South, were segregated. The HBCUs also benefited from having potential donors from the black elite visit their campuses.

"Most people used to play and have their vacation at the ATA championships," said Wilbert Davis, a former ATA president. Indeed, ATA tournaments were festive weeklong affairs, combining serious competition with fashion shows, dinners, and formal dances. Through the ATA came the affirmation that as a black tennis player in America there were many other people like you. A quarter-century after the first ATA tournament there were 145 black tennis clubs in America with more than 1,000 members.

The tournaments were covered each year by the leading black newspapers. Through publicity in such publications as the *Chicago Defender*, the *Philadelphia Tribune*, the *New York Amsterdam News*, and the *Afro-American* chain that served several cities, ATA champions became known in the black communities. Most of the images of these stars in action have been lost over time. Their names, however, should not be forgotten:

Tally Holmes, who won singles titles in 1917, 1918, 1921, and 1924, was said to have smooth strokes and a great backhand.

Edgar Brown, the champion in 1922, 1923, 1928, and 1929, was a master of topspin and a versatile shot-maker.

Ted Thompson, champion in 1925 and 1927, was thought to have one of the best forehand slices in the game.

Dr. Reginald Weir starred at City College of New York and won the ATA men's title in 1931, 1932, 1933, 1937, and 1942. In 1948 the graceful Weir was the first African American to play in the USLTA National Indoor Championships. He lost in the second round to top-seeded Tony Trabert, the eventual champion and a future Hall of Famer.

Ora Washington of Philadelphia, nearly six feet tall, was the first dominant woman in ATA tournaments. She won seven straight singles titles from 1929 to 1935, and another in 1937. Between 1925 and 1936 she teamed with three different partners to win twelve doubles crowns. She also was the star center on a women's basketball team sponsored by the *Philadelphia Tribune*.

Washington had an unusual way with a racquet. She left space between her right hand and the end of the racquet, not unlike a baseball player "choking up" on the bat. And she rarely took a full swing, preferring to slice the ball. The strategy worked—her record for consecutive ATA singles titles stood for more than thirty years until broken by Althea. "Ora was really angry about never getting a chance to play against the best white women," said Bob Ryland, a former ATA champion. "She'd hear about the white women winning at Wimbledon and the U.S. Nationals, and those other [Grand Slam] tournaments, and she'd be saying, 'I could beat them.' She had to work as a domestic, and she was really angry that she couldn't play in the big leagues."

Isadore Channels, Lulu Ballard, and Flora Lomax, each of whom won four ATA singles titles in the first half of the twentieth century, also did not get their chance either against the top white female stars—Suzanne Lenglen, Helen Wills Moody, Helen Jacobs, Alice Marble, et al. And the most prodigious doubles team in ATA history, Margaret and Roumania Peters—tennis's original Sister Act—was denied a chance to be considered the world's finest doubles team. The WTA honored the Peters sisters during the 2003 Federation Cup matches in their hometown of Washington, D.C. Roumania Peters died that year of pneumonia at the age of eighty-five. Margaret Peters died the following year; she was eighty-nine.

Margaret and Roumania were known as "Pete" and "Re-pete" because they won four consecutive ATA titles from 1938 to 1941 and a remarkable ten in a row between 1944 and 1953. Crowds clamored to see them whenever they played at the Twentieth Street court in the Georgetown section of Washington, D.C. Gene Kelly, the famed actor-dancer and an avid tennis fan, was stationed at a nearby naval base during World War II and stopped by the court one day in 1944 to watch the Peters sisters. Everyone learned how close the sisters were when Margaret waited for Roumania to finish high school so they could attend Tuskegee Institute together from 1937 to 1941. Both graduated with degrees in physical education.

As a single act, Roumania Peters won the ATA title in 1944 and 1946. In the 1946 final she defeated Althea Gibson in three sets—the only match Althea ever lost to a black woman.

George Stewart, a left-hander, emerged as the most prolific men's singles champion in ATA history, capturing the title seven times and winning the last one seventeen years after the first (1947, 1948, 1951, 1952, 1953, 1957, and 1964). A student at South Carolina State, Stewart was the first African American to compete in the NCAA championships, with Ryland of Wayne State University in Detroit the second. In 1945 Ryland advanced to the NCAA quarterfinals. The following year he lost in the third round to the eventual champion, Bob Falkenburg of the University of Florida. Two years later Falkenburg won the title at Wimbledon, a major event still closed to the ATA stars.

All the big-league tournaments were closed to Oscar Johnson, the 1950 ATA champion. In 1948 Johnson became the first African American to win a national championship, the National Public Parks tournament at Griffith Park in Los Angeles. They were closed to Eyre Saitch, who captured the 1926 ATA title before he won basketball championships as a member of the Harlem Rens in the 1930s. They were closed to Jimmie McDaniel, who won four ATA championships between 1939 and 1946. And they were closed to Ryland during his prime tennis years—he won ATA titles in 1955 and 1956.

"When I won the ATA, I thought I was as great as the Wimbledon champion," Ryland said. "They wouldn't let me play there, but I could play here. All of us should have made it to the big leagues. All of us were good enough. We all thought that things would change, even before Jackie Robinson got into Major League Baseball [in 1947], and we'd get to play in the big leagues. When we got to compete against the white players back then, they were exhibitions."

One such exhibition drew more than two thousand fans to Harlem's Cosmopolitan Tennis Club at 149th Street and Convent Avenue. Hundreds more without seats in the bleachers watched the outdoor match from apartment windows and trees on July 29, 1940, the day a Grand Slam champion came uptown. Don Budge, who in 1938 became the first player to win the Grand Slam, played a best-of-three-set match against McDaniel, the reigning ATA champion and a student at Xavier University in New Orleans. Between 1939 and 1943 McDaniel won thirty-eight of forty-three tournaments.

The Budge vs. McDaniel exhibition was sponsored by Wilson Sporting Goods, for whom Budge did promotional work. Unfortunately for McDaniel, the match was played on clay, and he was a hard-court player from California unaccustomed to the slower surface. He lost, 6-1, 6-2. His jitters combined with Budge's experience and mastery of all playing surfaces produced a one-sided affair. A reporter covering the match for the *New York Herald Tribune* wrote, "It is not quite fair to McDaniel or to Negro tennis in general to judge by this one match."

On August 19, 1944, the Cosmopolitan Club staged an exhibition match involving two black ATA stars and two white women from the big leagues. Private First Class Ryland of the Walterboro (South Carolina) Air Base teamed with Alice Marble, the top-ranked player in the world, against Dr. Weir and Mary Hardwick of England. "I was the No. 1 seed in the ATA then, and the army thought it would be good publicity to send me to New York for the match," Ryland said. "It was two black men and two white women, but we were in Harlem, so the army didn't worry about anyone getting upset. We couldn't have done that in the South, though." Marble's participation in the match and subsequent conversation with Ryland about Althea Gibson, an ATA rising star, prompted her to advocate that Gibson in particular and blacks in general be allowed to compete in the U.S. Nationals.

While Marble pushed for change from one end, the ATA leadership pushed even harder from the other end. An ATA vice president, Dr. Robert Walter Johnson, made the strongest push of all. Johnson came to tennis after starring as a running back in the 1920s at Lincoln University, where he acquired the nickname "Whirlwind" for his ability to use speed and spinning moves to elude would-be tacklers. He coached football, baseball, and basketball at various HBCUs while putting himself through medical school. While at Meharry Medical School in Nashville he got hooked on tennis. After graduation, he established his own clinic in Lynchburg, Virginia, because blacks there were not permitted to practice in white hospitals.

Dr. Johnson used his own money and resources to begin a program to train talented black youngsters to play tennis. Dr. J, as he was known, ran the Junior Development Program for twenty years, until his death in 1972. The success of his program earned him another nickname, the Godfather of Black Tennis. An intense, bespectacled man, Dr. Johnson invited ten to twelve teenagers and preteens into his home each summer for tennis instruction on his backyard clay court and military-style discipline. He reasoned that tournaments run by the USLTA eventually would be opened to blacks, and when the racial barriers came down he wanted players ready to make an impact.

"It was a strict regimen," said Juan Farrow, the last junior coached by Dr. Johnson to compete on the pro tour. "We were up at six in the morning. We hit about a thousand balls a day from a ball machine. He would come out and sit and yell and scream."

Dr. Johnson insisted his young charges do things his way. In exchange for a tennis-intensive summer with room and board, he made the youngsters do chores—clean the house, roll the clay court, sweep the court, take out the trash. "You had to do what Dr. Johnson told you to do," said Willis S. Thomas, Sr., a former ATA treasurer. "He'd send you home in a minute if you didn't measure up to what he wanted."

The youngsters got three meals a day, but not exactly gourmet meals. Ryland remembers buying a steak for John Lucas, a pupil who became a star in the National Basketball Association. "Dr. Johnson yelled at me, 'Don't you give him a steak. I'll send you home if you do that again. Give the boy neck bones. You gotta keep him hungry.'"

Blacks motivated and hungry to prove themselves made for the best pupils for Dr. Johnson's lessons in tennis and in life. More than one hundred of his juniors earned college scholarships. And if big-league tennis potential was there, he did everything to bring it out.

In a 2004 biography of Johnson, former tour pro Leslie Allen said, "When my mother sent me to Dr. J's, I knew I was going to a place of tradition, and when Dr. J spoke, we listened to him like he was the king. . . . You knew that everyone had your best interests at heart, and you never felt threatened because someone was better than you. What I liked most about his approach is that he made it simple for you to understand what you had to do to get better. And a lot of it wasn't about stroke production."

Dr. Johnson, who won seven ATA mixed doubles titles with Gibson, saw his junior development program as a finishing school for promising black youth. "When we trained them, we were not interested in just changing their grips. We intended to improve their game from a minor-league status to a big-league status. In the minors a pitcher tries to throw a strike over the plate to reach the big leagues. A pitcher in the big leagues must throw for the corners. So our job was to teach the players how to serve for the corners and the lines instead of down the middle of the court."

Althea Gibson and Arthur Ashe, the stars of Dr. Johnson's program, carried the banner of the ATA into the big leagues and onto the victory stand at Grand Slam tournaments in the fifties, sixties, and seventies. Largely through the efforts of this trio, the tallest barriers to black progress in tennis had been toppled. But other barriers remained to upset another of Dr. J's pupils.

Arthur Carrington of Elizabeth, New Jersey, was twenty-six when he won the 1973 ATA singles title in Boston. ATA officials told him the winner of the event would be assured a spot in the U.S. Open at Forest Hills. But Carrington's name was not called when the singles draw was announced. Dr. Clyde Freeman, ATA president, said he received an assurance from a member of the U.S. Lawn Tennis

Association that the ATA champion would get a wild card into the main draw. The USLTA said there had been a misunderstanding: no such agreement existed in 1973, though it had in earlier years. Indeed, during the 1950s and 1960s an agreement between the two organizations allowed four ATA players to compete in the U.S. Nationals every year. But USLTA president Walter Elcock claimed that the advent of the U.S. Open in 1968 necessitated a policy change. The USLTA wanted only the ATA champion to be considered for a wild card only into the qualifying rounds, not the main draw. The USLTA ruled Carrington could not compete in the Open unless someone withdrew from the main draw.

Carrington, tall and brown-skinned with a short-cropped Afro hairstyle and a mustache, accused the USLTA of racism "just because I wear alligator shoes and drive an Eldorado and look like a pimp." He had been on the pro circuit for only a few years, and his largest paycheck from an ATP event was $500.

"There's a reason why there's not many blacks in tennis," he told reporters on the eve of the Open. "It's rough. It's like pioneering. We can't say Althea Gibson and Arthur Ashe have opened the doors because no one has followed them up. We have to do it all over again."

Instead of being able to concentrate on preparing for a first-round match at the Open, Carrington spent an anxious day hoping to get into the tournament at all. At the eleventh hour he was allowed to compete after John Paish of Britain withdrew. Facing Ove Bengston of Sweden, Carrington lost, 6-3, 6-4, 6-3. "I'm satisfied now," Carrington said afterward. "I believe I can play with those guys if I'm given a chance. This was my first experience on grass, and I couldn't get used to the heavy ball and the lack of bounce. If this just opens some doors so I can play in more tournaments, I'll be happy."

Carrington's stay on the pro tour was brief. His highest ranking was No. 241 in June 1974. He was another player to whom the burdensome label "the next Arthur Ashe" had been affixed. He and Ashe had ethnicity in common but not much else. "Arthur presented one kind of image and I presented another one," he said. "A kind of urban thang." Carrington said he was raised "in a militant atmosphere." He used to listen to speeches by Malcolm X and other fiery speakers, the polar opposite of the world he encountered in pro tennis. "I had an identity crisis on the pro tour," he said. "I couldn't relate to white people." Relating to the tennis etiquette lessons given in Dr. J's summer program also proved difficult for Carrington. He had been reared not to believe in giving away a point on a close call, or to turning the other cheek if provoked. He said Dr. J sent him to black-run junior tournaments in the 1960s instead of the white-run tournaments because the doctor thought he had "a bad attitude."

Bad experiences as a pro did not diminish Carrington's love of tennis. He and his son, Lex, run a tennis academy at Hampshire College in Amherst, Massachusetts, where he coaches people of all backgrounds. "You can always make good money with the rich white folks," he said. Lex Carrington played briefly on the pro tour, coached Vera Zvonareva of Russia, a former Top 10 player, and became a hitting partner for Andre Agassi, Pete Sampras, and Jim Courier. "We're a third-generation tennis family," Arthur Carrington said. "My mother and grandmother played tennis in the 1930s, and my brother runs a tennis academy in Florida."

"An awful lot of people were given the opportunity to learn the sport through the scholarships the ATA provided to member clubs," said Bob Davis, a former ATA champion and board member. "The Modern Tennis Club of New York City sponsored all my tennis lessons. My parents didn't have the financial wherewithal to provide those lessons for me."

In the decades before the U.S. Tennis Association sought to develop players in the African-American and other nonwhite communities, the ATA filled the breach. Some of the African Americans who won pro tournaments or achieved world rankings were Zina Garrison, Lori McNeil, Juan Farrow, Leslie Allen, Arthur and Lex Carrington, Rodney Harmon, MaliVai Washington, Mashona Washington, Michaela Washington, Katrina Adams, Camille Benjamin, Chip Hooper, Renee Blount, Marcel Freeman, Bruce Foxworth, and Kim Sands. Players in the ATA knew they were accepted and respected. The insidious practices that commonly befell black players in USTA events, such as being defaulted from a tournament because of being purposely given an incorrect starting time, did not happen in the ATA.

"The ATA was amazing," said Kim Sands, the 1976 singles champion. "Before I went to the tournament I didn't realize how many people of color there were playing tennis. Just to be in that environment really emphasized to you that you were not alone. I never saw so many beautiful shades of black—black people, brown people, yellow people, red people like me. And it was all very traditional; most of the people wore tennis whites. When I won the ATA title that let me know I was ready for Chrissie and Billie Jean on the next level."

Leslie Allen, who in 1981 became the first black woman to win a professional tournament in the open era (Althea won hers before 1968), followed her parents into the ATA. "Through the ATA network, we'd know the up-and-coming black players before the general public ever saw them," the 1977 champion said. "I met Venus and Serena when they were kids. Same with Zina and Lori. Same with Chanda Rubin."

Rubin caught the tennis bug when she was five. She tagged along with her parents when they brought older sister La Shon from their home in Lafayette, Louisiana, to Houston to meet renowned tennis coach John Wilkerson. "Her parents thought the older sister would be the star," Wilkerson said, but it was like Chanda said to herself, 'Y'all don't know. I'm going to be the one.'" La Shon became a schoolteacher. Chanda became one of world's Top 10 players in the mid-1990s, reaching a career best No. 6 in April 1996. That same month she achieved her best-ever doubles ranking of No. 8.

A player with a steady but unspectacular game, Rubin has shown an ability to beat any player on a given day. While Serena was in the process of winning four consecutive Grand Slam titles between June 2002 and January 2003, Rubin defeated her in August 2002 in the quarterfinals of the Chase Open in Los Angeles after trailing 1-4 in the third set. Rubin went on to defeat Jelena Dokic and Lindsay Davenport to win the tournament. But it's another match against a Williams sister for which Rubin is best known.

Amanda Falker, third from left, was one of the first women tennis players. She is pictured here with, from left, Margaret Wylie, Florence Hass, and Florence Felton in Chicago in 1910. [Chicago Historical Society]

Bob Ryland, now a coach in his eighties, was one of the first blacks to compete in a major college tournament. [Private collection of Zack Davis and Robert Ryland]

Margaret and Roumania Peters, at left, prepare to face Ora Washington and Doris Miller in a doubles match at the 1947 ATA Championships in Baltimore. [Private collection of the heirs of Matilda Roumania Peters Walker and Margaret Peters]

Seven-time ATA mixed doubles champions Whirlwind Johnson and Althea
Gibson, at right, after defeating George Stewart and Ora Washington in
the 1948 final. [From Doug Smith, *Whirlwind: The Godfather of Black
Tennis,* Blue Eagle Publisher]

In 1957 Althea Gibson
became the first black
woman to win the
Wimbledon title.
[AP Images]

Arthur Ashe defeated
Jimmy Connors in the
1975 final to become
the first black man to
win Wimbledon. [Tony
Triolo / *Sports
Illustrated*]

Arthur Ashe and Althea Gibson at their induction into
the USTA Eastern Division Hall of Fame in 1988.
[*Black Tennis Magazine*]

Renee Blount, former
University of Virginia
assistant women's coach,
excelled in junior tennis and
played eleven years on the
pro circuit. [*Cavalier Daily*]

Evonne Goolagong Cawley
defeating Betty Stöve en
route to her second
Wimbledon title in 1980.
[George Herringshaw and
sporting-heroes.net]

Rodney Harmon, now the USTA's director of men's tennis,
reached the 1982 U.S. Open quarterfinals. [*American Tennis
Association Magazine*]

France's Yannick Noah, a 2005 Hall of Fame inductee, won the French Open in 1983. [George Herringshaw and sporting-heroes.net]

MaliVai Washington reached the 1996 Wimbledon final. [Ron Waite / Photosportacular]

Zina Garrison won the 1988 Olympic doubles gold medal with Pam Shriver. Garrison now coaches the U.S. Olympic and Federation Cup women's teams. [Michael Cole]

Sande French was the chair umpire for the 1993 U.S. Open women's final. No African American has chaired a Grand Slam final since. [Sande French]

Venus, left, and Serena Williams made tennis history in 2002 as the only sisters ever to be ranked world No. 1 and No. 2 simultaneously. The sisters display their wares after Serena defeated Venus 7-6, 6-3 in the Wimbledon final on July 6, 2002. [© Fred Mullane / cameraworkusa.com]

James Blake ended 2006 ranked No. 4 in the world, the highest ranking by a black man since Arthur Ashe in 1976. [© 2002 M. McCarron]

Shenay Perry, an up-and-coming star, was the only American to reach the fourth round at Wimbledon in 2006. [© 2004 M. McCarron]

Scoville Jenkins became the first black to win the USTA National Hardcourt title in 2004. [Scoville Jenkins]

Donald Young, two-time USTA National Hardcourt champion, competing in the 2006 U.S. Open. [Benjamin Woods]

Coming off her second left knee operation in two years, Rubin was two games from ousting Venus in the third round at the 2002 U.S. Open. She used a potent forehand and a net-rushing strategy to take a 4-1 lead in the third set. As the Ashe Stadium crowd anticipated a major upset, the second-seeded Venus raised the level of her service and baseline play to escape with a 6-2, 4-6, 7-5 win. "People tend to single that match out," Rubin said with a grin. "I wouldn't always single it out because of how it ended. But I learned a lot in that match about being competitive, point in and point out, and performing well on a big stage."

Rubin and Venus teamed to represent the United States in doubles at the 2004 Olympics in Athens. The first-time pairing was short-lived. An unheralded Chinese duo of Tian Tian Sun and Ting Li upset them in the first round, 7-5, 1-6, 6-3. No one then could have known Sun and Li would win the gold medal, a first for China in tennis. Hence the media asked Venus if she missed Serena, with whom she had won a doubles gold medal at the 2000 Olympics in Sydney. "Is that why the press conference was called, so you could ask me that?" Venus bristled. "I'm here playing for the USA. I love playing with Chanda Rubin. That's not even part of the equation."

Chanda, whose name means "bright or fierce" in Sanskrit, won the 1992 Wimbledon juniors title and was ranked second in the world. The informal ATA network began touting her after victories in the Orange Bowl event in Miami for girls twelve and under and the National Championships in the girls twelve-and-under and fourteen-and-under divisions. She seized the spotlight as a sixteen-year-old with a first-round upset of veteran Katerina Maleeva of Bulgaria at the 1992 U.S. Open. Had she been in Lafayette that day, she would have been taking classes in the twelfth grade at the Episcopal School of Acadiana. After graduating from high school, she joined the pro circuit full time. She has won seven WTA titles and been a finalist twelve times in singles; in doubles, she has ten tournament wins and seven second-place finishes.

The caramel-skinned Rubin has a Jewish surname. She said her family is not Jewish, but she has not traced her genealogy to find out how her father, Edward, a judge, got the surname. Her mother, Bernadette, is a retired schoolteacher. Both parents instilled in Rubin the importance of giving back to society, and she is perhaps the most philanthropic player in tennis. From 2001 to 2006 the Chanda Rubin Foundation sponsored eight satellite tour events across America for female juniors. "I did everything with the goal of giving kids more opportunities to play," she said. "As a professional athlete, you should be willing to give back and set a positive example for the next generation of players. So many people made it possible for me to play tennis. It's only right that I help other people."

Rubin, who has more than $4.5 million in tennis earnings, has contributed to numerous groups and causes, including the Hurricane Katrina Disaster Relief Fund; Athletes Against Drugs; the American Heart Association; Special Olympics; the Bishop Charity Fund, which helps the needy in her hometown; the Women's Sports Foundation; the United Negro College Fund; a grassroots tennis program she started at several Louisiana schools; and the ATA. In 1995 she became the first tennis player to be named U.S. Olympic Committee Athlete of the Year. *USA Weekend* magazine named her one of the "Most Caring Athletes" in 1997, the same year she received the Arthur Ashe Leadership Award. "My parents always encouraged me early on," she said, "and certain causes that I really feel are worthwhile I just want to give some time to."

After sixteen seasons on the pro circuit, Rubin remains passionate about tennis. But injuries have taken a toll on her thirty-one-year-old body. Her last tournament win came in 2003 in Luxembourg. She played in only three events in 2005 after a third left-knee operation. In 2006 she competed in seven events and withdrew from six others because of knee and ankle problems. She made a cameo appearance at the U.S. Open, losing to No. 9 seed Nicole Vaidisova of the Czech Republic in the first round. "I'm just trying to stay positive," said Rubin, who ended the year ranked No. 481. "This being the U.S. Open, there was incentive for me to try to compete at a high level. Unfortunately I wasn't able to do that."

"I hope I'm wrong," said Wilkerson, the coach who first saw her twenty-six years ago, "but I don't believe she can get back to where she was. She's at that age when women want to move on and do other things—get married, have children. She's had a lot of injuries. We'll see."

Even if Rubin does not recapture past glory, she made her mark as the fifth African-American woman in the open era to reach the world Top 10, joining Venus, Serena, Garrison, and McNeil. And her 1995 ATA Athlete of the Year award is indicative of her role in continuing a tradition of black junior champions who have excelled in the pros.

As Rubin attempts to prove in 2007 that her best days in tennis are not behind her, the ATA faces a similar challenge. The tennis world in which the ATA operates today is far different from the era of Dr. Johnson's junior development program. "There is no absolute necessity for the ATA," said Bob Davis, the former ATA board member. "Once we were the only show in town. But our lives are very different today. You have to want to be a member. You have to want to be part of that black experience."

Because of racial integration and the USTA's multi-cultural player development program, which had grown in the past decade, the ATA must reinvent itself. The organization has five thousand members, of whom one thousand are life members. The group is lobbying the International Tennis Hall of Fame for the enshrinement of Dr. Johnson, a worthy endeavor. But the ATA has yet to initiate a program in the twenty-first century that can increase its influence.

"The current direction of the ATA," president Willis Thomas, Jr., said, "is not to get involved in things we know we cannot do at this time, such as a junior development program, which implies sustainability and longevity." Thomas, elected in 2004 and reelected to his final term in 2006, said even the USTA, with all its resources, does not run an effective junior program. "If they did," he said, "the U.S. wouldn't be so far down in the world of tennis."

Considering that no American player won a Grand Slam event in men's or women's singles in 2006—something that had not occurred in sixty-nine years—Thomas's jab at the USTA was warranted. He brings solid tennis credentials to his job. A successful player in the ATA and at Texas Southern University, he coached tour pros Garrison, Harmon, and Adams. He and his father, Willis Thomas, Sr., a former ATA treasurer, are inductees in the Mid-Atlantic Tennis Hall of Fame. Thomas Jr. is also the director of tennis at the Washington, D.C., Tennis and Education Foundation, which seeks to build self-esteem in inner-city youth through education and life-skills training while also helping teens to develop their tennis skills to earn college scholarships.

Under his direction the ATA provides grants for young players to join tennis programs or attend academies, such as the Bolletieri Academy in Bradenton, Florida. Current pros Shenay Perry, Jamea Jackson, and Ahsha Rolle have received ATA grants. The ATA also provided grants to allow ten junior players to come to the 2006 ATA tournament in San Diego. "Allowing kids to compete in our championships allows them to play at a national level," he said. "That's a chance they would not get in the USTA."

In December 2006 the ATA held a weekend workshop for young players in Coral Springs, Florida. A seasonal tennis workshop is a far cry from the days when the ATA developed champions. Although Thomas argues that that is an unrealistic goal today, others with roots in the organization believe it can be accomplished if the ATA were to alter its vision.

"The governing board has to make the ATA more than a national tournament. That is essentially what the ATA has become," Bob Davis said. "The ATA must get blacks more involved in tennis, and to do that the sport needs to be in black neighborhoods. The ATA website still touts its annual tournament and Arthur and Althea. As great as Arthur Ashe was, he's been dead for fourteen years. To a lot of our youth, he's an historical figure. Althea hasn't been on television for twenty years. A lot of our people have never seen her."

Black amateur players no longer must compete in ATA events to get noticed or to cultivate their skills. The USTA multi-cultural player development program has many black former players, including Mc-

Neil, Garrison, Martin Blackman, and Roger Smith, serving as coaches or board members. Further, an amateur player today with an ATA ranking does not impress colleges offering tennis scholarships. But scholarships *are* awarded to players with a high ranking in USTA events. Hence black tennis players can earn college scholarships today without joining the ATA.

"I've always considered the ATA as a feeder into the higher levels of tennis," said Wilbert Davis, a former ATA president and an eleven-time ATA champion. "I really don't see us competing with the USTA. If we could prepare our players to compete in their environment, that would be fine with me."

But for the ATA to become a feeder system many believe the organization needs a facility of its own where youngsters can be trained by expert coaches in tennis, fitness, and the mental side of the sport without feeling like a distinct minority at a predominantly white academy. Many black-owned venues that used to present ATA tournaments in generations past no longer exist. Harlem's Cosmopolitan Tennis Club, for example, was replaced decades ago by a church and apartment buildings. Bob Davis tried to establish such a tennis facility in 1982 in Plattekill, New York, some sixty miles north of New York City. He called the facility Taromar, taking the first letters from the names of his daughters Tanya and Robin and his then-wife Mary. Taromar had dormitory space to accommodate forty people, a dining room, a swimming pool, two tennis courts on site, and an agreement to lease an additional fourteen courts from the nearby State University of New York at New Paltz. Today Taromar no longer exists.

"My dream was to give black children a chance to learn tennis as I did," said Bob Davis, the younger brother of Wilbert Davis. "The reality was, I had to pay the bills. To keep the doors open I had to bring in more children whose families could pay. I asked the ATA to endorse Taromar as its national training center. The ATA declined. For the life of me, I can't tell you why. It was the only black owned-and-operated tennis facility in the world."

"The ATA is run by its board," said Sallie Elam, who as the executive secretary handles the day-to-day business. "If the board does not vote for something, it doesn't happen." That alone does not explain why Taromar was rejected, or why an attempt to create an ATA training facility at Texas Southern University in Houston failed, or why a proposed training complex scheduled to open in Florida in 1997 did not.

"The ATA does not have a business plan to get funding for a facility that could be used to house an ATA program," said Albert Tucker, who in 1996 served as executive secretary. The ATA had a verbal agreement with officials in Fort Lauderdale to build a twenty-two-court facility that would have become the permanent home of the annual ATA tournament. The Convention and Visitors Bureau said it expected the facility to attract visitors who would add up to fifteen million dollars to the city's economy each year. Nothing happened. Not one shovel hit the ground.

According to Elam, the 1996 election of Bernard Chavis as president sent the ATA into a turmoil from which it is still trying to recover. Chavis sued the organization over philosophical and financial differences, which led to years of costly litigation, she said. That's the ATA response to why the Fort Lauderdale deal fell apart.

According to Tucker, who lives in Fort Lauderdale and has left the ATA, older board members charged that as executive secretary he made too much money from the annual tournament—an event that adds up to $2.5 million a year to the host city's economy—and that he, not necessarily the ATA, would benefit from having a training facility in his city. "The focus of the ATA should be on youth development," Tucker insisted. "There needs to be a program similar to what Dr. Johnson ran, with no adult component. I don't believe the ATA should be about adult tennis anymore."

Yet it is. And always will be, Elam said. She began playing in ATA events as a ten-year-old. She will compete in doubles at the 2007 ATA tournament in July in New York City (at the Billie Jean King National Tennis Center and eight other venues). Fifteen hundred players will compete in a tournament that long ago outgrew the historically black colleges that used to play host to it. Elam will compete in the sixty-and-over division. People into their eighties will compete as well. People who remember Althea Gibson and Arthur Ashe as teenagers. People who remember Dr. J and the fresh faces he brought to his backyard clay court in Lynchburg every summer. People who remember when the ATA was the only game in town. And for them, it still is.

The existence of a tennis organization that is ninety-one years old and led by African Americans is laudable. The reality of that organization being of such diminishing influence that African-American youth in a sports-mad nation barely know it exists is unfortunate. Those same young people can readily name two African-American tennis players, Venus and Serena. Now they are becoming familiar with another, a young man whose talent, demeanor, and ability to inspire others has invited comparisons to tennis's first African-American male superstar.

CHAPTER SIX

"You tell me what the similarity is"

• • • • • • • • • • •

J ames Blake found the question amusing: "Who would you want to play you in the film version of your life?" Not just any tennis player would merit such a question. That he essentially learned to play tennis in the African-American mecca of Harlem, in New York City, and attended college at the Harvard of the East, Harvard University itself, is intriguing enough. But that is just part of what gives his story appeal. Not just any tennis player could overcome a spinal abnormality as a boy, and then as a professional go in two years' time from being bedridden with a career-threatening injury to losing his father to cancer to being stricken with a shingles-like condition that deprived him of hearing, vision, and feeling on one side of his face to a return to world-class tennis and a string of major victories that carried him to No. 1 status in America and the No. 4 ranking in the world.

Had a Hollywood screenwriter created such a storyline, it surely would have been rejected as implausible. But in Blake's case the truth of his tennis career has been stranger, and more gratifying, than fiction.

So Blake again considered the question. He decided on Boris Kodjoe, a dashing model-turned-actor born in Vienna, Austria, thirty-three years ago to a German father and a Ghanaian mother. Kodjoe, who appeared in the film *Brown Sugar* and the television series *Soul Food*, played junior tennis in Europe before a back injury convinced him to fashion a career out of being tall, dark, bald, and handsome. But Blake added one caveat to his casting choice: "Only if he can still play tennis."

Blake might have to help out on the action scenes, for no one in the game hits an atomic forehand quite like his. And perhaps no other player is as quick around the court. These are assets you cannot leave to a mere actor. But Kodjoe fits two important criteria in a Blake story: ethnicity and appearance. Blake, too, is the product of interracial parents. He was born twenty-seven years ago to an African-American father and a white British mother who met in a New York City suburb while indulging in their favorite pastime: tennis.

While not possessing acting chops, Blake himself has the look of a matinee idol: 6-1 with an athletic physique that he accentuates on the court with sleeveless, skin-hugging shirts, sharp facial features blending Africa with Europe, a bald dome, light caramel skin, and an endearingly crooked but straight-toothed smile. In 2002 he signed with the modeling division of his sports management agency before even winning a professional tournament. A year later he had a ten-page pictorial in *Gentleman's Quarterly*. Before the 2006 U.S. Open he appeared in the pages of *Men's Vogue*.

Blake devoted his time in 2006 to a dedicated climb up the world rankings—to Top 10 status for the first time in March, to a career-high five tournament titles and seven ATP Tour finals, to establishing his status as the foremost African-American player in tennis and, arguably, the sport's most gentlemanly player, to the first victories of his career against countryman Andy Roddick and an Australian nemesis named Lleyton Hewitt.

No black man has been ranked as high as Blake since Yannick Noah reached world No. 3 in 1986. Blake is one of only four African Americans to win an ATP Tour title in the open era, joining Bryan Shelton, MaliVai Washington, and Arthur Ashe. And no other American male outperformed Blake in 2006. "To finish the year as the No.

1 American, I hadn't even thought about it coming into the year," he said. "To have that as a reality is an honor."

Blake completed his coming-out party as a finalist in the 2006 Tennis Masters Cup in Shanghai, China, an elite tournament open only to the top eight players in the world. In Shanghai he finished first in a group that included Rafael Nadal of Spain, a two-time French Open champion; Nikolai Davydenko of Russia, a 2005 French Open semifinalist; and Tommy Robredo of Spain, a two-time French quarterfinalist. Because the Masters Cup format required Blake to play the second-place finisher in the other group in the semifinal round, he met for the first time David Nalbandian, a stylish Argentine who was the 2002 Wimbledon runner-up. In a thrilling display of power-hitting, Blake dismissed Nalbandian, 6-4, 6-1.

Before that match, Roger Federer of Switzerland, the world's No. 1 player, defeated Nadal in the other semifinal. Reporters asked Federer, "Who would you like to play in the final?" a standard query that tennis players usually handle diplomatically rather than risk offending another player. But without hesitation Federer said, "I would like to play James, to be honest. He's one of the fantastic stories in our game."

Perhaps Federer had an ulterior motive for wanting to play Blake. Nalbandian had defeated him in the Masters Cup final the year before while Federer had never lost to Blake. And he still had not through the year 2006 after defeating Blake, 6-0, 6-3, 6-4, in a best-of-five-sets final in Shanghai.

Yet Federer is correct in his assessment of Blake's story and the potential it has to raise the national and global popularity of tennis. Blake's tennis resumé, notable as it is, does not reveal the full measure of why his story holds such resonance. Neither does his battle to overcome adversity and familial misfortune. There is a likability quotient that propels him, something that advertisers and media professionals refer to as a Q rating.

People love a good comeback story. Blake's began on May 6, 2004, at the AMS Roma tournament in Italy. That morning Blake practiced for the event on a clay court with fellow American Robby Ginepri.

They pushed each other hard. The rallies were spirited and intense, close to tournament competition without being so. With Blake on the baseline, Ginepri sliced under the ball, producing an angled drop shot. As Blake raced in, his right foot stuck in the red clay, throwing him off balance and sending him careening forward. His head hit one of the posts holding up the net, a post driven into the ground that did not give upon impact. He fractured vertebrae in his neck. He had to be helped onto a plane back to America. He felt fortunate when told he would be sidelined for only two months. At the time he knew his father, Thomas Blake, Sr., was battling cancer in a hospital in Fairfield, Connecticut. While James Blake struggled to regain his health, the father's condition worsened. The father told James and his other tennis-playing son, Thomas Jr., "You guys cannot change your lives one bit because of my health. You have to live your lives."

In July the Blake boys entered a grass-court tournament in Newport, Rhode Island, on the grounds of the International Tennis Hall of Fame. James competed in the main draw. Thomas played in the Challengers event. In tennis the Challengers circuit is one level below the ATP Tour. On a Friday afternoon, with their father's health fading, James watched Thomas win a match in a third-set tiebreak. The next day James won his opening-round match. Afterward James told his agent, "If I win the next match, I'm going to need you to talk to the tournament director. I need to get a day off. I need to go to a funeral." That is how he conveyed the news that Thomas Blake, Sr., had died. He honored his father's final wish and did not withdraw from the tournament. He lost his next match, as did Thomas.

For James, the stress of losing his father literally paralyzed the left side of his face. The condition is called Zoster. He could not close his left eye or hear from his left ear. He would often lose his equilibrium when attempting to walk. "I just tried to keep my spirits up," he said. "My brother and my friends would come visit me and crack jokes about how bad I looked. They did anything to try to lighten the mood."

Thomas Jr. said, "We never put tennis on TV, never talked about tennis. While James kept his doctor's appointments, we didn't try to keep up with what was going on in the sport. We didn't want him to get depressed."

James made just one public appearance with his face half-paralyzed: he attended Arthur Ashe Kids' Day in New York two days before the 2004 U.S. Open, because he always did, out of respect for his role model. Had he stayed off the pro tour for at least six consecutive months, he would have protected his world ranking, then No. 23, when he returned. A rule allows players to protect their ranking if they miss six successive months because of an injury. But Blake decided to honor a previous commitment and play a tournament in Delray Beach, Florida, in mid-September. He lost in the second round and did not play again that year. His ranking plummeted.

The way the ranking system works in tennis, a player who earns points in a tournament in a given year must compete in that same tournament the next year and perform as well to protect his ranking points. Missing the tournament altogether means losing all the points. When Blake finally returned to the circuit in 2005, his ranking was No. 210. By that time he had one ATP Tour championship on his resumé, the 2002 Legg Mason Classic in Washington, D.C.

This is where Blake's Q rating helped him enormously. Tournament directors gave him wild cards into the main draws of their events. He received eleven wild cards in 2005 alone, more than any black tennis player has ever been given in one year. Hence he did not have to play in nearly as many Challengers events to try to boost his ranking as a typical player outside the world's Top 200 would have. "Blake got all those wild cards because he's biracial," said William Washington, the coach and father of Mashiska Washington, a black player on the Challengers circuit. "I've been in tennis forty years and I've never seen any person of color get so many wild cards."

Blake is likable. He plays an exciting style: fast, athletic, and hard-hitting. He is good copy. He has a following. Women have been known to consider him a pleasant sight. He has his own booster club, called the J-Block, composed mainly of people he knows from Fairfield, Connecticut, where he once lived, and from the Tampa, Florida, area, where he now resides. The J-Block cheers and chants for Blake at every American tournament he plays. Actually the J-Block more closely resembles a cement block: solid and all-white. But Blake has many black fans as well. He won more of them in August 2006 when he paid to have busloads of black children from New York–area tennis programs brought to the Pilot Pen tournament at Yale University. Most had never been to a professional tournament before.

A less agreeable player would not have received the wild cards into the main draw of tournaments that Blake received in 2005. Without question, the assist aided his comeback effort. There are more points to be earned and more money to be made when competing at the highest level of tennis. But Blake still had to do something with those wild cards. He won ATP events in New Haven and Stockholm, and reached the finals in Washington, D.C., and the quarterfinals at the U.S. Open. He finished 35-21 for the year, improving his ranking to No. 24. He was back. He had overcome adversity. And he became a hot property, telling his story to Oprah Winfrey, David Letterman, *60 Minutes*, and *Nightline*, and in *Oprah*, *People*, and *Esquire* magazines. In nearly every media appearance, and in most of his appearances since then, he has been likened in some regard to his role model.

"It's an honor any time I hear my name linked to Arthur Ashe," he said. "It takes me back a second to think about how incredible he was, and also to think about what he did with his fame and with his influence. It overshadows what he did on the tennis court. When I'm linked to him, I know it's just in tennis terms, and I've got a very, very long way to go to be linked to him in terms of what he did off the court. That's something I'll attempt to do, but I know it's going to take a lot more work."

What Blake has going for him now is an Obama Factor. As in Barack Obama, the U.S. senator from Illinois, born in Hawaii to a Kenyan father and a white American mother who had been raised in the center of the American map in Kansas. Like Obama, a multi-ethnic African American who appears completely at ease in any group of people, Blake handles himself in a way that makes him popular without looking rehearsed, classy without seeming contrived, sportsmanlike without appearing anachronistic. Were pro tennis's first African-American male champion alive today, he would undoubtedly give Blake his stamp of approval.

"I don't think anyone could make Arthur Ashe more proud than James Blake," said Bob Davis, who played doubles with Arthur in the American Tennis Association in the 1960s and ran a tennis camp Blake attended in the 1980s. "James went to Harvard. He is articulate. He is not an angry young brother. He is a well-educated, family-oriented tennis player. Arthur would be thrilled to see James Blake today."

Arthur did see Blake once, among a sea of young brown faces during a visit to the Harlem Junior Tennis Program when James was only three. Years later Blake absorbed Arthur's pronouncements about the importance of education, sportsmanship, and good character. "He's a man I never heard one person say a negative thing about," Blake said. "He's someone who could take even a terminal disease like AIDS and use that for good. He could take a negative and find a way to make it into something positive. I think he saw the inherent good in people, and I try to live my life the same way."

When Ilie Nastase grunted "That goddamn nigger!" on national television, Arthur defused a racial powder keg by chalking up the outburst to Nastase's fiery temper and forgiving him. On the afternoon of August 31, 2001, James Blake played in a nationally televised second-round match at the U.S. Open—a time in his career when he generated more interest for his looks than his game, when his face appeared on a giant American Express billboard outside the National Tennis Center. On that day his opponent, Lleyton Hewitt, an Aussie antagonist direct from central casting, was falling behind two sets to one when he played the race card.

A close call in the third set by Marion Johnson, a black linesman, went against Hewitt, giving a point to Blake as the New York crowd, sensing a major upset, cheered wildly. Hewitt stormed toward the chair umpire, then pointed to Johnson and shouted, "Look at him!" Then he pointed to Blake and bellowed to the umpire, "Look at him! You tell me what the similarity is!" Hewitt insidiously suggested that a black linesman had made a call in favor of Blake because of race. Blake acted on court as if he had not heard Hewitt. But everyone else, those in Arthur Ashe Stadium and those watching on television, knew Hewitt had injected race into the match because there was a boom microphone below the umpire's chair at courtside. The stadium crowd gave infinitely more abuse to Hewitt, who would win the match 6-4, 3-6, 2-6, 6-3, 6-0, and eventually win the tournament, than had Blake. Indeed, Blake suffered more from dehydration and stomach cramps—which caused him to vomit on court during the match and receive three bags of intravenous fluid afterward—than from Hewitt's race-baiting.

Blake had in fact heard Hewitt and immediately understood the racial insinuation behind the remark. He simply chose not to make it an issue on the court. "We talked about it in the locker room, and he did apologize," Blake said in a tone indicating he considers the matter closed. "What he said was wrong. And he said he didn't mean for it to come out the way it did. I didn't know him well at all at the time. But I knew we would both be on the tour for a long time, and I told him that if he said anything like that again, I wouldn't be so kind. I'm not a pushover. I just made the decision that I was going to give him the benefit of the doubt that time."

Just as with Ashe's handling of the Nastase incident a quarter-century earlier, this is not to suggest that Blake's decision to defuse the issue—effectively to give Hewitt a public pass when he could have skewered the Aussie with his own words—was the only way to handle it, or the right way. It was simply Blake's way.

In response to a reporter's suggestion that having parents of different races somehow insulated him from racial matters, Blake said, "I wouldn't say I completely ignore racial issues. It's tough to concentrate on racial issues at the same time as concentrating on my tennis. I feel I will definitely be active in [African-American causes] when my career's over or my career's coming to an end."

Despite having a mother born and reared in Coventry, England, Blake has always referred to himself as an African American. Because he is. His father is of African ancestry and was born in America.

Blake is black according to the "one drop of black blood" principle that has identified Americans of mixed race as "black" or "African American" for as long as they have lived in America. Blake's on-court appearance in 2001 was unmistakably black: He wore his hair in long, free-flowing brown dreadlocks reminiscent of 1980s star Yannick Noah, or a follower of Rastafarianism. It is a look he has since abandoned in favor of a shaved head because the Blake boys were constantly being mistaken for each other. (Thomas still wears dreadlocks.) But James Blake's speech is not stereotypically black. Close your eyes when listening to him and you hear a well-spoken young man, clearly American, clearly educated. He does not speak in a way that those with only limited exposure to black Americans would immediately identify as black. Yet there is no internal struggle for self-identification within Blake's mind. He is an African American.

Blake's parents, Thomas Sr. and Betty, attended the Hewitt match. They told a courtside reporter for the USA Network that their son tries to ignore issues of race. James Blake clarified the statement after the match, telling reporters that he does not ignore race matters but instead tries not to focus on them during a match, because the task of playing winning tennis against world-class competition is hard enough. Blake's view is seconded by Roger Smith, a former tour player from the Bahamas, who said, "If you're black and you're on the court thinking about some racial thing that happened to you and your opponent is white and he's just thinking about beating you, he has the advantage. He's more focused on the task at hand than you are."

When James was born, the Blakes lived in Yonkers, New York, a suburb north of New York City, where whites generally live on the East Side and African Americans and Latinos on the West Side. The Blakes were East Siders. Betty was an editor at Fairfield University, Thomas Sr. a salesman for the 3M Company.

"My dad learned tennis from an Army buddy," said Thomas Blake, Jr., who retired from tennis in January 2006. "My parents were tennis players before they met. They met at a local park in Yonkers and hit it off. When we were kids, it seemed like every day we were watching them play tennis."

Since the age of twelve Blake has been coached by Brian Barker—
an unusual display of loyalty in a sport where top players routinely
replace coaches as if they were worn-out shoes. Before Blake's climb
from No. 210 to elite status, he resisted the advice of observers who
thought he should change coaches for the sake of change. "Brian and
I joke about that all the time," he said. "So often guys refuse to take
the blame themselves when they lose, and put it on the coach. The
coach isn't out there hitting those balls. He isn't playing break points
for you. When a player's winning, it's, 'Oh, you changed your backhand. You worked so hard.' How come you're not thanking the
coach then?"

Blake credits Barker for helping rid him of the bratlike tendencies
few knew he had. "I remember I won a tournament in New England
when I was twelve," Blake said, "and I came back to the tennis club
and sat down with Brian for an hour and talked about it. He said,
'Look around this room. You just won that tournament. Do you
think anyone here cares?' No one did. No one cared that I won because I was a brat then."

At thirteen Blake faced a different kind of challenge, one physical
and emotional. He was diagnosed with scoliosis, a spinal ailment that
forced him to wear a back brace eighteen hours a day.

In 1997 he followed his older brother to Harvard, where both became All-Americans and Ivy League Players of the Year. Thomas
graduated with a degree in economics. James left for the pro circuit
after a sophomore year that ended with him being ranked No. 1 in
the country despite losing in the NCAA singles final to Jeff Morrison
of the University of Florida. But Blake and the agents eager to sign
him had first to convince his parents that leaving school early made
financial sense. "We had to show that he could generate enough income from tennis and endorsements," agent Carlos Fleming said, "to
put money in the bank to pay his Harvard tuition if he got hurt and
couldn't play tennis anymore."

Fleming, an agent for International Management Group, the
world's largest sports management agency, signed Blake in June
1999. As an African-American agent in tennis, Fleming is even rarer

than an African-American player such as Blake. Thirty-five, he grew up in Cleveland and played tennis at Kansas University. Although he achieved All-America status in doubles, he watched such American players as Pete Sampras, Andre Agassi, Michael Chang, Jim Courier, and Todd Martin win important tournaments and reasoned that he would never be able to play at that level. "I had an epiphany one day while working out at the gym," he recalled. "I decided to write on the back of an envelope all the jobs in sports I would like to pursue." He listed three hundred, with sports agent at No. 1. He returned to Cleveland, where IMG has its world headquarters, and began working there as an intern in 1996 while also pursuing Plan B, a master's of business administration and doctorate of law curriculum at Case Western University. The lure of being an agent proved strong enough for Fleming to abandon Plan B. "An agent has to always be there for his client," he said. "They may ask you to do something they could just as easily do for themselves, but you're in this business to get big-time clients and keep them, so you have to do what you can to satisfy them."

Fleming has satisfied Blake by getting him endorsement deals with Nike, Prince racquets, Evian spring water, and the video-game companies Sega and Indie Built. Blake was Fleming's second client. The first was Alexandra Stevenson, a black woman who made a splash at Wimbledon 1999 but has made few ripples since. Stevenson grew up in southern California and played against Venus Williams in tournaments when she was nine and ten. At La Jolla Country Day School, Stevenson's classmates voted her Best Athlete and Most Likely to Be Famous. On stage she acted and sang in high school productions of *Grease*, *Bye Bye Birdie*, and *The Pajama Game*. Her tennis game was built around a big serve and stinging ground strokes, including a classic one-handed backhand. She charmed Wimbledon, singing on the British Broadcasting Company telecast during a rain delay and performing a graceful curtsy and bow to spectators after her victories. And there were more victories than anyone could have predicted. She made the main draw only after winning three qualifying-round matches. She then became the first woman qualifier to advance to a

Wimbledon semifinal, saving a match point to oust Lisa Raymond in the quarterfinals in the process. People clamored to know more about the 6-1 gatecrasher. When her mother, Samantha Stevenson, a veteran sportswriter, coyly suggested to reporters that Alexandra had a famous father and would say no more, the media went into overdrive. On the eve of the biggest match of Alexandra's month-old professional career, the *Fort Lauderdale Sun Sentinel* and *Orlando Sentinel* newspapers in Florida broke the story that her father was basketball Hall of Famer Julius Erving.

Erving, an Orlando resident, initially denied being the father. Married with children, he would have had to admit to an affair with a white woman who covered his Philadelphia 76ers teams in the 1970s and 1980s. Eventually he confirmed his paternity and said he had had only minimal contact with Alexandra since she was a child. The outing of Erving became an international story, and the verve Alexandra had shown in earlier rounds deserted her in the semifinals. She was crushed by Lindsay Davenport, the eventual champion, 6-1, 6-1.

It has been widely assumed that Stevenson was never again a successful player after Wimbledon 1999. But in fact she rose to a career-high ranking of No. 18 in 2002, when she reached WTA finals in Memphis and Linz, Austria, and teamed with Serena Williams to win a doubles title in Leipzig, Germany. Since 2003 Stevenson has been plagued by recurring injuries to her right shoulder. She underwent surgery in September 2004 but continues to struggle. She lost in the first round of the 2006 U.S. Open qualifying event and ended the year ranked No. 394 in the world. With her tennis star fading, the road back to prominence for Stevenson will be much harder than it was for Blake. Wild cards into the qualifying rounds of WTA events are the best she can hope for at the age of twenty-six, eight years removed from her star turn at Wimbledon.

"When she was only eighteen and facing all that scrutiny at Wimbledon, Alexandra handled the entire episode remarkably well," said Fleming, who no longer represents her. His tennis clients are now Venus and Serena; Tatiana Golovin, a Top 20 player from France;

Mark Philippoussis, a two-time Grand Slam finalist from Australia; and Blake, who has a chance to write the most successful story by a black man in tennis since Ashe.

Blake has already surpassed the likes of Roger Smith; Chip Hooper, the world's seventeenth-ranked player in 1982, when he reached the Final 16 at the French Open and lost to Jimmy Connors; Marcel Freeman, ranked No. 46 in 1986; Todd Nelson, who reached No. 58 in 1986; Steve Campbell, No. 78 in 1998; Bruce Foxworth, No. 146 in 1979; Martin Blackman, No. 158 in 1994; and Datus Murray of Jamaica; Phil Williamson; Eric Riley; Troy Collins; Arthur Carrington; and African-born players Nduka Odizor of Nigeria, Paul Wekesa of Kenya, and Yahiya Doumbia of Senegal.

Another African player, Younes El Aynaoui of Morocco, reached the U.S. Open quarterfinals in 2002 and 2003 and the Australian Open quarters in 2000 and 2003. His highest ranking was No. 14 in 2003. Blake's ranking stood ten places higher when the 2007 season began. All his story lacks is the climactic scene of him hoisting a champion's trophy at a Grand Slam event. "I can't say he's a great player," said MaliVai Washington, the last African-American man to reach a Grand Slam final, at Wimbledon in 1996. "A great player is someone who wins a major. But I think he's right there. He's one of those players who on any given day can beat anyone."

Earlier in his career Blake lost matches on any given day because of a suspect backhand. But he has improved that stroke considerably. He has also become one of the fittest players on tour. He has defeated every marquee name in the sport except Federer, against whom he was winless in five matches at the close of 2006. Federer, who won nine Grand Slam titles in his first eight years on the tour, five shy of Pete Sampras's all-time record, looms as every player's greatest hurdle. Another obstacle for Blake is his 0-9 record in five-set matches. Boris Becker, the Hall of Famer from Germany, once said a fifth set is not about tennis; it is about mental toughness and heart. While no one would suggest that Blake, who has overcome many personal challenges to join tennis's elite, is lacking heart, he has yet to silence the critics who point to his failures in five-set matches.

At Wimbledon in 2006, Blake led Russian Max Mirnyi in the third round two sets to one and then won just one game in the final two sets. His stunning collapse epitomized the worst Wimbledon since 1911 for American players: none of them made it past the fourth round. "Blake to me is the big disappointment," John McEnroe said during NBC's coverage at Wimbledon. "He's the one who should have been in the semifinal [against Federer]." Blake lost a five-set match to Gael Monfils, a rangy twenty-year-old black Frenchman, in the third round of the French Open. And he lost a five-set affair to Fernando Gonzalez of Chile in the quarterfinals of the Davis Cup.

"It's a statistical anomaly," Blake said when asked about his difficulty in fifth sets. "I'm definitely in good shape. I don't have the problems with cramps that I had earlier in my career in five-set matches. I'm not out there throwing up on the court anymore like I did in the [2001] Hewitt match. I just think the record is a fluke. I won fourteen straight semifinal matches [in 2005 and 2006]. Does that mean the next time I get to the semifinals that I'm automatically going to the final? No. I still have to play the match. For whatever reason, I wasn't ready to win those five-set matches. But that doesn't mean I won't win the next one."

Blake could have put the issue of five-set losses to bed in the wee hours of September 8, 2005. He was two points from defeating Agassi in a riveting U.S. Open quarterfinal that had begun the night before and extended into a fifth set past the one o'clock hour in New York City. Agassi at thirty-five, in his penultimate U.S. Open, was the crowd's sentimental favorite. But in the first two sets Blake hit forehands with authority and played superbly aggressive tennis to take a commanding lead, 6-3, 6-3. He then appeared to cease applying pressure, which let Agassi back into the match. "Andre really picked up his game," Blake insisted. But Agassi, always a precise ball-striker, had a fraction more time to set up his winning ground strokes because Blake allowed it. He stayed back rather than go on the attack as he had in sets one and two. Agassi captured the next two sets, 6-3, 6-3.

With the night crowd roaring as though attending a heavyweight fight, Blake went ahead after breaking Agassi's serve in the fifth. Back came Agassi to draw even and pull ahead by 5-3 before Blake rallied to send the set to a tiebreak. Blake nudged ahead, and a forehand winner left him two points from victory. Agassi recovered to tie the score, taking advantage of the diminished velocity of Blake's serves and ground strokes. As Agassi put it, "I thought he was losing a little legs on his serve." In the end, Agassi showed a bit more tenacity and had more in reserve. He won the tiebreak 8-6 and the match. "I never feel great after a loss," Blake said, "but I guess it's about as good as I could feel. I fought my heart out. I did everything I could."

As the crowd showered both players with a lengthy standing ovation, Blake looked to some too satisfied about losing a match he led by two sets to none, and by one service break in the final set, and by one service break in the tiebreak. He said he had merely done his best to mask the pain. "My heart dropped a little bit," he said. "Obviously, you want to win. But you feel it in your stomach, once you realize it's over. You got to just walk up there and congratulate Andre. That's all I could do—think about how proud I am of him and, you know, move on. Think about anything that could have gone my way, anything that I did wrong, anything technically I could have done better. Or was it just execution? That's what I thought about. And then I just thought, you know, he played a great match, he's a champion, he deserves it, and I'm glad the crowd had a good time."

Blake's sportsmanship is laudable and in short supply in an era of loquacious braggarts commandeering the headlines in professional sports these days. But the Agassi match raised the question, and still does: Is Blake too nice to be No. 1?

"I think you can be a nice guy and be No. 1," he said. "Roger Federer is No. 1, and he's as nice a guy as you could ever meet. I think he proves that you can be nice to people, and respect other people, and have friends in the sport, and still be No. 1."

Can he do the same?

"I hope I have that ability," Blake said. "That's what I'm trying to do. Every time I play against Roger or anybody else, I'm trying to win. I always go out there trying to be the best."

If Blake were unbeatable, there would be no drama in his story. If he did not have vulnerabilities, if he did not have to deal with adversity, he would not be nearly as interesting to watch. Dealing successfully with adversity is something Blake has learned to do by necessity—like the tennis trio from Texas who learned they were more potent together than apart.

CHAPTER SEVEN

"It was as if God handed these two young girls to me"

• • • • • • • • • • •

H ouston, Texas, came out in force to honor him, including George
H. W. Bush, the forty-first president. His prized pupils, Zina
Garrison and Lori McNeil, the first two African-American women to
be ranked in the world Top 10 in the open era, were there. So were
WTA tour veteran Mashona Washington and Willis Thomas, Jr., a
former protégé who is president of the ATA. Videotaped tributes
came from Jeanne Moutoussamy Ashe and Billie Jean King, and
statements from Houston's mayor and other local dignitaries.

They all came to the Hilton Hotel in Houston on October 28,
2006, to honor John Wilkerson, a self-taught player who has since
taught so many others about winning in tennis and in life. Back in
1973, six months after he started a public tennis program in Houston's MacGregor Park, in the shadow of Texas Southern University, he
met Zina and Lori, and in the 1980s and 1990s he turned them into
world-class players. Zina became the first black woman since Althea
Gibson to compete for a Grand Slam singles championship. Zina and
Lori filled a void in the hearts of black tennis fans yearning to root for
two of their own in tennis's premier events. Those fans were on a first-

name basis with Zina and Lori, as if they both lived around the corner. But not nearly enough has been said about Wilkerson. He should have been on a first-name basis with African-American tennis followers as well. He's a humble man who habitually answers his phone not with "Hello" but with "What can I do for you today?" or "God bless you." That is why the October 2006 tribute to him was fitting, albeit long overdue.

"That was such a great event because I didn't know so many people would have so much to say about me," Wilkerson said with a laugh. "I felt so truly honored." Wilkerson, born in San Antonio, Texas, sixty-seven years ago, picked cotton, as many Southern blacks did then to make money. He found tennis at the relatively late age of eighteen but worked hard at it, so hard that after a five-year stint in the army he became the top singles player at Texas Southern, and in 1971 the men's singles champion of the ATA.

"God, I loved the ATA, because it was the best thing around for any young blacks who wanted to play," he said. "It should be the best thing for young blacks even today. We run away from the ATA and want to do things with the USTA. But in the ATA, we competed hard against each other and pushed each other. The ATA helped us grow."

While employed by the Houston Parks Department, he inaugurated his program at MacGregor Park to share all he had learned, to try to create African-American players who could compete for championships in the major tournaments that had been closed to blacks during his youth. He developed two—which is exactly two more than the USTA has lately.

Arthur Ashe once said about Wilkerson, "I don't know of any other teaching pro who has taken two women to Top 10 status. If Wilkerson were white, he would have been swamped with job offers." The USTA has offered him nothing.

"The USTA would not say and has not said, 'Hey, John, what do you need to develop more world-class players like Zina and Lori?'" Wilkerson said without rancor. "Instead they'll say to me, if I have a promising player, 'Send him to us.' They want to look good. They want to look like they're controlling tennis in America. It's a business for them."

Garrison and McNeil did not know each other before they came to Wilkerson's program. Garrison's older brother, Rodney, a baseball player at Texas Southern, told Wilkerson about his tomboy sister who was good enough to compete in fast-pitch softball with teenage girls and in basketball and track. She was ten the first time Wilkerson put a wooden racquet in her hand. "She had a good grip on the racquet, hit the ball well, and was very excited to hit the ball," he recalled. "Those were very good things."

The McNeil family had recently moved to Houston from San Diego, where Lori's dad, Charlie McNeil, was once a cornerback for the National Football League's San Diego Chargers. Her mother, Dorothy, was an avid tennis fan who approached Wilkerson so that she and her daughter could learn to play. Once he put a racquet in Lori's hand, he knew the McNeil girl and the Garrison girl were destined for big things. "It was as if God handed these two young girls to me," he said with a throaty laugh. "They were meant to play tennis."

All of Wilkerson's charges were taught to play all-court tennis in the classic serve-and-volley style with wooden racquets. Graphite racquets, which produce more powerful shots but give a player less touch and control, would not appear until the 1980s.

"It was a highly disciplined program," McNeil said. "We played tennis seven days a week, and we had several coaches. But John was definitely in charge. He emphasized the mental side of the game. You had to be able to think your way through a match and be mentally tough and know how to handle difficult situations."

In describing his program, Wilkerson explained, "We start the kids at age four. From ages four to six we just let them hit the ball and enjoy it. From ages seven to twelve we teach them how to understand themselves and their environment, how past situations dictate who they are and how they're going to respond to whatever happens to them in life. If you're black, you're going to be dealing with some tough situations as a racial minority in this country. And you have to be able to handle those situations."

Garrison, the youngest of seven children, proved particularly adept at handling adversity, before and during her professional career. Six years after being handed a racquet by Wilkerson, she was the No. 1–ranked junior player in the world—despite competing in USTA events in Texas, not because of it. By the age of eleven Zina was already 5 feet 3 inches and 115 pounds, and white tournament officials routinely demanded to see her birth certificate at events. Neither she nor Wilkerson ever recalled seeing the officials ask a white girl who was tall for her age—and there were more than a few—to produce such evidence.

In a Texas sectional tournament that Zina, Lori, and other blacks from Wilkerson's program entered, Zina heard one official say, "Throw the niggers in the same bracket." That way, two black players could not meet each other for the championship. And forget about seeing anyone who was not black rooting for the black players at those events.

Regardless, Zina went undefeated in Texas junior matches for five years running, and she performed just as well in national and international events thanks to her family's sacrifices. Her father, Ulysses, a postal worker, died at forty-three when Zina was only five months old. Her mother, Mary Elizabeth, worked as a nurse's aide. A grandmother, Julia Walls, also lived with the family. The Garrisons sold barbecue dinners and desserts to raise the money to send Zina to ATA tournaments. She won the ATA girls' singles title at ages fourteen, sixteen, and eighteen. In 1977 and 1978 she won the ATA women's crown. Her first international title came at the JAL Cup, a December 1977 tournament in Japan in which she competed only because her siblings went without Christmas gifts to pay for her round-trip ticket. Zina was playing, and winning, for her whole family. Some neighborhood friends who used to ignore her success would ask, "Why are you playing that sissy sport?" But Zina was playing, and winning, for them too. She was showing them all what a black girl could do in a sport once closed to them at the highest levels.

Ignoring the skepticism in the neighborhood was easier for Zina because of the level of support she had at home and in the African-American tennis community. In 1979, when she was fifteen, she was invited to join pros Leslie Allen, Kim Sands, Renee Blount, and Andrea Buchanan for a week of tennis instruction and sisterly bonding with Althea Gibson at the Sportsmen's Tennis Club in Boston. "She told me time and time again that nothing was going to be given to me," Garrison said, "and that I would always have to work harder than the white girls on the tour. She said I had to be far better than everyone else, and even then I'd probably find myself in a situation where being the best wasn't good enough."

Althea's advice proved prescient after Zina became the first black girl to win the Wimbledon junior championship and the USTA responded by putting her on a list of alternates for the U.S. Open juniors. The USTA placed five white girls ahead of her, even though Zina was ranked No. 2 in the world at the time. That meant Zina could compete at the Open only if another American girl dropped out. "John was really hot about it," Garrison said. "The experience also reinforced what Althea repeatedly had warned." Fortunately for Zina, an American player did withdraw, allowing her admission, and she won the U.S. Open junior title. No other black player has ever won the Wimbledon and U.S. Open junior events in the same year. That she had almost been unjustly kept out still irritates Garrison.

"That was my first real brush with USTA racism at the highest level," she wrote in her autobiography. "That kind of thing still happens to blacks in the USTA across the board. It got in the way of Chanda Rubin when she was advancing. It bit MaliVai Washington, Lori McNeil, [former pro] Katrina Adams, and every other black player. We were often pushed back from getting into an event, receiving an award, or just being properly recognized when it was obvious that recognition was deserved."

In 1981 the ATA still had enough clout that the men's and women's singles champions each got a wild card from the USTA into the qualifying round of the U.S. Open. Garrison, having won the ATA title in each of the previous two years in Atlanta, was going for a "three-peat" at the finals in Detroit. She had already qualified for that year's Open because she played for the U.S. team in the Wightman Cup, an annual women's competition against Great Britain. But

McNeil, Garrison's final-round opponent, had not yet qualified for the Open. Garrison had never before lost a match to McNeil. Not until that day . . . on purpose. McNeil accepted the largesse, went to the Open's qualifying rounds, and played her way into the main draw. Two young black women from Houston, childhood friends from the same public parks program, were in the U.S. Open main draw for the first time. All because Garrison intentionally lost or, as tennis players would say, "tanked the match" in the ATA final. "The fact that I tanked isn't something Lori or I feel good about," she said, "but it shows what we were sometimes pushed to do for equal access."

ATA champions no longer receive a wild card from the USTA into the U.S. Open qualifying round. Nor do the NCAA champions. The USTA changed its policy, it said, because so many foreign-born players came to America to play college tennis, win in the NCAAs, and get automatic berths into the Open. The USTA would prefer to give those berths to American players. Since the USTA took the wild cards away from the NCAA champions, it reasoned, taking them away from the ATA champions was a fair thing to do. But Garrison believes the USTA took away the ATA wild cards when greater prize money came into the sport in the 1980s. A first-round loser in the U.S. Open then was assured of $10,000. At the 2006 U.S. Open, a first-round loser received $16,500 from a total prize purse of more than $12.1 million. Given the USTA's long-standing insensitivity to black people in tennis, Garrison's argument is much easier to believe.

For a time on the pro tour, Garrison and McNeil were so close that many thought they were blood relatives. Rarely did anyone see one without the other. They practiced together, socialized together, and acted as each other's emotional anchor on an international tennis circuit that was at times inhospitable and sometimes downright offensive to the few blacks involved.

"At the beginning of my career," McNeil said, "I would play at some exclusive club and somebody white would look at me and tell me to go get them something, as if I was there to wait on them. I would have to tell them I was there to play tennis. That would happen to the black players then. People didn't see your racquet, they just saw your color."

Black tennis fans looked at the women from Houston and saw both. They saw in McNeil and Garrison athletic reflections of themselves, inner-city girls trained by a black man to succeed in the tennis world. While neither McNeil nor Garrison won nearly as many tournaments or had the worldwide impact of Venus and Serena Williams, they gave black people—black women in particular—sportswomen to emulate, sportswomen from whom to draw inspiration.

"They both had great careers," said Ahsha Rolle, a twenty-one-year-old pro. "They were both out there competing in the big tournaments, winning championships, and competing hard as two of the best players in the world."

And they always seemed to be there for each other. When McNeil's father committed suicide—the former Chargers star having found it difficult to adjust to a post-football life—Garrison took the long-distance call from Houston during the Australian Open and told McNeil to call home.

"Not many days go by when I don't think about my dad," McNeil said. "It's so sad to lose a parent, and you never really get over it. The suddenness of it was the shock. But I guess that's part of life also."

Zina and Lori, born thirty-two days apart in 1963, were a team. As a team they won three doubles titles—Indianapolis in 1986, and New Orleans and Canada in 1987—and were ranked No. 3 in the world. All told, Garrison won fourteen singles titles, twenty doubles crowns, and three Grand Slam mixed doubles titles. She won at Wimbledon with Sherwood Stewart in 1988, taking the advice of Wilkerson to partner with the then thirty-two-year-old Texan, whom she considered too old. She won the Australian Open with Stewart in 1989, and Wimbledon with Rick Leach in 1990. She was a Grand Slam finalist in mixed doubles on three other occasions. Yet it was not until 1988 in Seoul, South Korea, when she partnered with Pam Shriver to win the Olympic gold medal in doubles, that people who did not follow tennis recognized her as a celebrity.

McNeil captured ten titles in singles, thirty-two in doubles, and the 1988 French Open mixed doubles title with Jorge Lozano of Mexico. Her first legitimate win over Garrison came in Tampa, Florida, in 1986, 2-6, 7-5, 6-2. It marked the first time two black women faced each other in a WTA Tour final. McNeil ended up winning seven of her eleven pro matches against Garrison.

Both reached the rarefied level of Top 10 in the world, McNeil rising as high as No. 9 in 1989, Garrison a career-best No. 4 in 1990. And despite being the only African Americans in the world Top 10 in the late 1980s, neither one had an endorsement deal.

In 1984 Garrison had a three-year endorsement deal with Pony, a sportswear and tennis shoe company, for $125,000 and a racquet deal with Wilson for $75,000 annually. But Pony did not renew her contract, deciding instead to build an advertising campaign around Anne White, a blonde-haired, blue-eyed American whose tennis claim to quasi-fame was the white lycra body suit she wore at Wimbledon in 1982. When Pony dumped Garrison, she was ranked No. 7 in the world; White was No. 46.

Wilkerson at the time was not sifting through a stack of lucrative job enticements, either. He didn't get any, despite being the world's only tennis coach with two Top 10 players. He soon brought in Willis Thomas, Jr., to help him with the two stars. By 1988 Wilkerson would have only one. "Zina just thought it was time for a change," he said simply. "That's why I stopped coaching her."

Soon Thomas was replaced as coach by Sherwood Stewart, Garrison's mixed doubles partner. "This is not to knock John or Willis," she said, "but they never played on the tour; Sherwood did. I felt that he could relate better to what I was feeling because he'd been there."

McNeil continued to work with Wilkerson, but the Garrison-McNeil partnership ended too. Both women had signed with different agents—McNeil was represented by IMG, Garrison by Octagon. Although it had never mattered to their black fan base whether they were billed as "Lori and Zina" or "Zina and Lori," it would soon matter to the players that they were not billed separately.

Shortly after McNeil reached the 1987 U.S. Open semifinals and lost a three-set match to world No. 1 Steffi Graf, McNeil signed an IMG contract that included an annual $30,000 payment if she played doubles with Betsy Nagelsen, the wife of IMG founder and president Mark McCormack.

"It was divide and conquer," Wilkerson fumed. "The whole management group issue broke up Zina and Lori. The people around them starting telling them that one should be better than the other. When one lost to the other, the people would say, 'How could you lose to her?' IMG didn't want Zina and Lori, the way the press always talked about them. IMG wanted to market Lori on her own. But if the management groups had only used their imaginations, they could have marketed the friendship, the bond between two young black women, from the same city, the same tennis program, who grew up to be Top 10 players."

Instead the management wizards created a split. There could have indeed been national endorsement deals appearing first in such black media outlets as *Essence*, *Ebony*, *Jet*, *Black Enterprise*, Black Entertainment Television, black radio, and black newspapers with the winning partnership of Garrison and McNeil, on court and off, as the prevailing theme. Perhaps McNeil-Garrison joint endorsements would not have had crossover appeal in the late 1980s to early 1990s because tennis was not yet considered hip. Consumers of all hues responded in the late 1990s to the Williams sisters as endorsers because Venus and Serena were the first black female sports stars of the hip-hop generation, and each of them won Grand Slam singles titles on their own, something neither Garrison nor McNeil could do. Still, it was unfortunate that the marketing potential of Garrison and McNeil, together or separately, was never realized. And a successful tennis partnership and friendship was allowed to cleave.

"What the people around them said they shouldn't do is what made them stronger," Wilkerson said, taking aim at the agents. "They relied on each other, supported each other. It can be lonely on the tennis circuit. But Zina and Lori had each other. They didn't have to worry about somebody else learning too much about their games because they had each other to hit with. That's what helped the Williams sisters so much. They had each other to play doubles with. How much is that worth? Nowadays, players have to pay a friend to travel with them. You have to pay somebody now to be your hitting partner. Zina and Lori already had that in each other."

Garrison and McNeil soldiered on and won doubles crowns with other partners, though they never displayed the same chemistry with others that they had shared together. McNeil won three doubles titles and Garrison won seven playing alongside Katrina Adams, a black Chicago native and Northwestern University graduate.

At age six Adams followed her older brothers, Myron and Maurice, to a Boys and Girls Club where tennis on a hardwood gymnasium floor was among the activities. After two weeks of begging the local pro who ran the program, she was allowed to play. The speed of tennis on hardwood helped her develop as a volleyer. She won an NCAA doubles championship at Northwestern and twenty professional doubles titles. "I was the put-away player at the net," said Adams, now thirty-eight. "Zina and I worked better together because she was the set-up player. Lori and I played a similar style."

Adams achieved career-high rankings of No. 67 in singles and No. 8 in doubles (both in 1989), and retired from the tour in 1999. She coached in the USTA player development system for a while before putting her Northwestern degree to better use. A communications major, she is the only black full-time tennis commentator on television. She does up to fifteen tournaments a year on the Tennis Channel. She is also executive director of the Harlem Junior Tennis Program, where James Blake learned the game.

For Adams, her most memorable match occurred at Wimbledon in 1988, her first year on the circuit. She led Chris Evert 7-5, 3-1 in a Round of 16 match on Court 2, known as "the Graveyard of Champions" because so many former titleholders have been defeated there. Evert might have joined the list, but, as Adams recalled, "I let the occasion get to me a little bit. I looked at the scoreboard and realized I was about to beat Chris Evert." Adams recalled no one rooting for her on Court 2 that day, not because of race, she said, but because Evert was immensely popular and married to Britain's John Lloyd at the time. Evert won the last eleven games and prevailed, 5-7, 6-3, 6-0.

Giving a postmatch rationalization that would have made Althea Gibson cringe, Adams said that going into the interview room after the match was not that bad because "I played Chris Evert. I was supposed to lose. I reached the Round of 16. I was supposed to lose in the first round."

Why? Because you didn't believe you deserved to beat anyone at Wimbledon? Wilkerson posits the argument that black players, always a distinct minority in tennis, have not won more major championships because too many of them believe deep down that they don't belong in the sport. "If you take a Roger Federer or a John McEnroe, they would have been mad as hell if they had lost a match like that," he said. "It's not enough to get close. White folks, they want us to play well and lose. You can't buy into that. The Williams girls don't buy into that. They were brought up by their parents not to feel good about losing. They were brought up to win. You give me the player who loves to win and hates to lose. That's a champion."

Garrison and McNeil both came close to becoming a Grand Slam singles champion at Wimbledon. McNeil as an unseeded player stormed into the semifinals in 1994. But in retrospect she wishes she had given herself a better opportunity to go farther. At that time in tennis, the major tournaments seeded only sixteen players (now thirty-two are seeded). McNeil was the No. 17–ranked player in 1994 and drew what seemed the shortest straw; she faced top seed and defending champion Steffi Graf in the first round. But McNeil had beaten Graf before, indoors at Madison Square Garden, and had confidence against the hard-hitting German. "She had just come off a loss in the French Open semis to Mary Pierce," McNeil recalled, "and she usually wasn't good in her first match after a loss because she's such a front-runner."

In a match delayed twice by rain, McNeil ousted Graf in three sets, marking the first time in Grand Slam history that a player lost in the opening round after winning the tournament the year before.

The 5-7 McNeil carried her momentum into the semifinals against Conchita Martinez of Spain. McNeil was playing the best tennis of her life. Unfortunately she was playing too much of it. She was still alive in the doubles with Renee Stubbs and in the mixed doubles with T. J. Middleton. Her unexpected run to the final four in singles gave her body little time to rest.

"I was totally exhausted," she said. "I think about that tournament from time to time. I tried to play three events at the age of thirty. I wasn't nineteen any more. I probably should have withdrawn from the doubles or mixed doubles. My right knee was a little sore. Basically, I ran out of gas, mentally more than physically."

But not before putting up a fight against Martinez, the No. 3 seed. They split the first two sets and played a marathon final set. "Trying to win my first Grand Slam," McNeil said, "took a lot of emotional as well as physical energy. I felt drained. I just didn't see a way to close out the match, even though I kept going ahead, 6-5, 7-6, 8-7."

The battle-tested champions in women's tennis history—names such as Navratilova, Evert, King, Graf, Court, Connolly, Gibson, Venus, Serena—find a way to win that kind of match. McNeil could not. She lost the next three games and the decision, 3-6, 6-2, 10-8. A similar fate befell her in the 1987 U.S. Open semifinals. Up one set against Graf, she succumbed, 4-6, 6-2, 6-4. It should be pointed out that McNeil and Middleton advanced to the 1994 Wimbledon mixed doubles final and lost to Todd Woodbridge and Helena Sukova. McNeil and Stubbs were eliminated in the quarterfinals.

Garrison made her strongest run at Wimbledon in 1990. As the No. 5 seed, she defeated No. 10 Helena Sukova in the Round of 16, 6-3, 6-3, and Monica Seles, the No. 3 seed, in the quarterfinals, 3-6, 6-3, 9-7. The win over Seles settled a five-year-old score. Garrison was offended when Seles offered her flowers on court before thrashing her, 6-3, 6-2, in a French Open third-round match. And Garrison was annoyed to learn that before Seles signed a contract to work with fitness coach Bob Kersee (the husband of Olympic gold medalist Jackie Joyner-Kersee), she insisted that Kersee not work with another female tennis player ranked in the Top 20, as Garrison was at the time. After subduing Seles, Garrison won an intense semifinal-round match against the No. 1 seed Graf, two years after Graf's "Golden Slam"—victories at the four majors and the Olympics in the same calendar year. Garrison punctuated her 6-3, 3-6, 6-4 victory with an ace down the middle and a triumphant leap.

That Garrison concluded matters with an ace was noteworthy, if not startling, because her serve had long been her Achilles' heel. The girl who stood 5 feet 3 inches at age eleven and had her identification papers scrutinized by skeptical tennis officials in Texas, had grown only one more inch vertically since then. At the same time she had filled out considerably, which would cause her more inner turmoil than anyone could have known. Still, as Garrison put it, "I never allowed the fact that I was short, pigeon-toed, and black stop me from doing anything."

Following her six impressive wins at Wimbledon in 1990, Garrison still had another to play: the championship match against Navratilova, the venerable No. 2 seed. Adding intrigue to the final was the issue of what Garrison would wear. During the fortnight she wore tennis outfits from Navratilova's nascent clothing line—for no money, just to promote it—but Garrison's newfound status as a Grand Slam finalist finally sent the corporate suits running her way. Before taking Centre Court for the final, she signed a three-year endorsement contract with Reebok for clothes and shoes, and deals with Sun-Maid raisins, Budget rental car, and S. Oliver, a German jeans company. Whether or not Navratilova felt snubbed because of Garrison's financially motivated decision to change her attire, the legendary lefty rolled to a 6-4, 6-1 win, her ninth and final Wimbledon title.

Garrison, as a newly minted Wimbledon finalist, received a heroine's welcome upon returning to Houston. She had competed as a married woman at that tournament, having wed Willard Jackson, a Houston businessman, two weeks after the 1989 U.S. Open. That, incidentally, used to be the tournament for which Garrison was best known, because she defeated Evert in the quarterfinals, in the Hall of Famer's final match. "If I had to lose to anybody," Evert said that day, "I'm happy that it was Zina."

Acceptance from a tennis legend is one thing; acceptance of self is infinitely more important. At the time Garrison, alas, lacked that quality. Her marriage, rarely in good health, died in 1997. Cause of death: infidelity. "My husband was telling me," Garrison wrote, "he'd be willing to start a family if I stayed on the tour one more year. In the meantime he was spending my money to have an affair with one of my friends. And for more than a year I listened to that same husband repeatedly tell me he thought I was fat and ugly."

Garrison suffered silently for several years from bulimia. She fell into a pattern of practicing her tennis, playing a match, returning to her room, gorging on junk food, and vomiting. The problem began, she said, during the 1980s when she felt pain in her knee and could not persuade anyone that she was injured. She underwent therapy, and in 1989 she publicly disclosed her problem in an article in *Sports Illustrated*. That admission did not make the problem or her self-esteem issues go away. But it did make her more of a human being to the public—less of a job description (black tennis player) or a label of expectancy ("the next Althea Gibson"). And it did make her accomplishments in an anxiety-filled sport even more commendable. She split with the coach that taught her the game, and split with the best friend with whom she shared so many tennis memories, suffering silently from a negative body image and a failed marriage. Through it all, Garrison persevered. Her career serves as a reminder that it is never just a mastery of tennis strokes that makes a player what she becomes.

"When you're working with young people, especially young ladies, you have to be so aware of what's going on with them from an emotional point of view," Wilkerson observed. "Everybody hits serves, backhands, and forehands. But you have to look at that *fore-head*. Why don't you work on that forehead? Most coaches are afraid to do that."

At times Wilkerson's most celebrated pupils, Garrison and Mc-Neil, found his style too controlling. Yet his approach brought both players to where they were, and to where they are today. Both are coaches. And they are back together as friends.

McNeil lives in Key Biscayne, Florida, where she coaches in the USTA player development program. Ahsha Rolle, who won her first pro title in 2006, and Megan Bradley, the former No. 1 player at the University of Miami, are among her charges. McNeil, who once mentored South African pro Amanda Coetzer, is also the assistant captain for the U.S. Federation Cup team. The appointment was made by Garrison, the captain. Garrison got the top job after serving as Billie Jean King's assistant for Federation Cup matches, and for the 2000 U.S. Olympic team on which Venus Williams won gold in singles and teamed with sister Serena to win gold in doubles.

The reconciliation of Garrison and McNeil warms the heart of Wilkerson about as much as the public outpouring for him that autumn evening in Houston. "I've always believed that the two of them could do so much more together than they could apart," he said. "That's not only true for them. That's true for black folks, period." The patriarch of the family that has produced more black tennis professionals than any other undoubtedly would agree.

CHAPTER EIGHT

"Tennis is a family sport"

• • • • • • • • • • •

William Washington is angry. An African American and the only father ever to guide four of his children into careers as professional tennis players, with one becoming a Wimbledon finalist, Washington is convinced that the USTA is squandering its vast resources and deliberately preventing more black players from succeeding in the sport. "The USTA's attitude is to maintain the status quo," said Washington, who is sixty-seven and lives in Flint, Michigan. "The USTA, the ATP [men's tour], and the WTA [women's tour] are not minority-friendly. Tennis players of color are stonewalled and excluded by design. It's a conspiracy." Washington points to former USTA president Alan Schwartz spending $1.2 million in 2004 to take six hundred staff members and volunteers to a seaside resort for three days, and former USTA president Franklin Johnson spending more than $100,000 in 2006 to take the USTA board to Honolulu to discuss adding Billie Jean King's name to the National Tennis Center as examples of the kind of bureaucratic waste any pork barrel–spending politician would envy.

Rodney Harmon is frustrated by Washington's criticisms. An African American and the director of men's tennis for the USTA,

Harmon has been assigned the task of increasing the number of American men good enough to contend for championships, particularly at the Grand Slam events. Lately his job has been similar to that of Sisyphus, the king in Greek mythology sentenced to forever roll uphill a huge stone that always rolls down again. Since 2002 American tennis has lost to retirement Pete Sampras, Andre Agassi, and Michael Chang, who combined to win twenty-three Grand Slam singles titles (Sampras fourteen, Agassi eight, Chang one) and reach the finals in fourteen other Grand Slam events (Sampras four, Agassi seven, Chang three). No American male has stepped forward to fill the breach. Of the current crop, only Andy Roddick has played in Grand Slam finals, winning the 2003 U.S. Open and losing in the 2006 U.S. Open final and the 2004 and 2005 Wimbledon finals. In 2006 every American man was eliminated from both the French Open and Wimbledon by the third round. And at the U.S. Open, James Blake, the only African-American man in the world's Top 200, was the lone American male to reach the quarterfinals. He lost in that round to the eventual champion, Roger Federer of Switzerland.

"We're trying to do more to bring tennis to more people in the black communities," said Harmon, who is based in Key Biscayne, Florida. "But one of the problems we face is that tennis is only the twenty-sixth most popular sport in the United States, behind bowling and darts. In a lot of other countries, tennis is the second or third most important sport, so they get the second- or third-best athletes. If tennis were the second most important sport here, we would be getting [NBA All-Stars] Dwyane Wade types and LeBron James types, and then you would definitely see more American champions."

Washington is convinced that the system under which tennis operates needs an overhaul, otherwise it will never be sufficiently appealing to blacks to attract the premier athletes who choose other sports. The arbitrary distribution of wild cards by tennis officials is, according to Washington, the biggest deterrent to advancement in the sport by black players. A wild card gets a player into a main draw or into the qualifying rounds of a tournament when that player would not otherwise likely have qualified. "A wild card is an opportunity to play in the main draw and get points and make money," Washington said. "If you're not getting good results and you don't get wild cards, you don't play. And if you don't have the finances to stay up there, you're finished, and the white man knows that."

If injured star players are on the comeback trail, as were Serena Williams and Chanda Rubin at the 2006 U.S. Open, those players are virtually guaranteed a wild card into a major tournament. If a sports management agency such as IMG wants to attract a new client, it will give that player a wild card into a tournament it controls, such as the Pacific Life Open in Indian Wells, California, or the Sony Ericcson Open in Key Biscayne, Florida. Both tournaments are run by IMG. When an agency such as IMG signs a player, that player will have language in his or her contract that guarantees a certain number of wild cards into the main draws of tournaments. Donald Young, the heralded seventeen-year-old from Chicago who has twice won the U.S. National Hardcourt Championships for players eighteen and under, received ten wild cards into the main draw of men's tournaments from the time he signed with IMG in 2004 through the end of 2006. He did not win a match in any of those tournaments. Wild cards are even bartered among national tennis federations. At the 2006 U.S. Open the USTA gave wild cards to Australians Alicia Molik, a former Top 10 player, and Mark Philippoussis, a former Wimbledon and U.S. Open finalist, in exchange for wild cards into the 2007 Australian Open for the American man and woman who won at a play-in tournament in Florida in December 2006. The USTA decided who got to compete in the play-in tournament.

Sometimes the distribution of wild cards is star-driven rather than race-driven. Serena Williams and Chanda Rubin, both former Top 10 players who are black, received wild cards into the 2006 U.S. Open. James Blake, a charismatic player whose world ranking plunged from No. 23 to No. 210 because of injuries, got eleven wild cards in 2005—the most ever given to a black player in one year—which smoothed the path for his drive to world Top 10 status.

But at other times, wild cards are handed out in a transparent attempt to *create* a star. Mardy Fish, a white pro since 2000 who has won only one tournament, received twelve wild cards into main draws in 2006. "That's the second time Fish has been recycled that way," said Washington, whose son Mashiska plays on the Challengers circuit. "He got the same free ride before in his career. But they do white players that way. They don't do that for black folk. That's what people who watch tennis don't understand, or don't want to understand. The media, they're talking about 'Mardy Fish, the comeback kid.' Well, hell, when they put you in twelve straight tournaments with wild cards, all you have to do is win a couple of rounds because you're already getting ranking points and you're getting money. Your computer ranking is going to go way up. Give [black players] Scoville Jenkins, Marcus Fugate, Mashiska the wild-card breaks that Mardy Fish got, and the black players will make it too."

According to the USTA, Mashiska Washington has received six wild cards in his career: one into the U.S. Open main draw in 1999 and five into the U.S. Open qualifying tournaments in 1994, 1995, 1996, 1997, and 2000. Further, the USTA said, Mashona Washington, Mashiska's sister, has received five wild cards in her career: one into the U.S. Open main draw and four into the qualifying round. But neither Mashona nor Mashiska has been given anything close to the wild card help afforded to Fish.

William Washington sends e-mails to journalists and tennis organizations denouncing the USTA, the ATP, and the WTA as obstacles to black progress in tennis. "These white people really don't believe a black man can play tennis," he said. "So when a black man comes on the scene, they're not going to invest in him. They think he's not going to make it. He might hang out there for a year or so before they help him. A white player, they'll support him from jumpstreet [the start]." He refers to Harmon as "the USTA's house slave." He dismisses David Dinkins, the black former New York City mayor who sits on the USTA board, as "just a politician. He doesn't know anything about tennis."

"I seem to be Lucifer as far as Mr. Washington is concerned," Harmon said in an exasperated tone. "When he has asked to meet with the USTA to discuss his concerns, he has asked that I not be in the room. I'm sure he knows that I could refute every point he wants to make. So when the USTA doesn't agree to his terms, he cancels the meeting. When I started at the USTA, we didn't have a multi-cultural grant program to help kids at the local level to play in national events. We provide funding for that now. We spend $300,000 to try to help kids around the country."

Phillip Simmonds, who made his Grand Slam debut at the 2006 U.S. Open, is one of those young players. He lost his first-round match at the Open to France's Richard Gasquet and ended 2006 ranked No. 256 in the world. The twenty-year-old son of Jamaican immigrants, Simmonds grew up in Reston, Virginia, where his father taught him tennis. After Simmonds showed promise in local and regional events, the USTA supplied grant money to further his development. "You really have to show your stuff when you play those tournaments in your hometown," he said. "That's how you can catch the USTA's eyes. I was able to get grants to play in some national junior tournaments that would have been very difficult to pay for otherwise. Basically, if the USTA likes your game and your potential, they'll give you a little help."

A little help is not enough for all the talented youngsters who could use it. The U.S. Open, a two-week event, generates $190 million in income each year. That makes a $300,000 outlay for the USTA's multi-cultural grant program, or a $1.2 million tab for a three-day junket for six hundred staffers at a seaside resort, a relative drop in the bucket. Harmon estimates that revenue from the U.S. Open is divided as follows: 70 percent for community tennis programs, 15 to 20 percent to the USTA, and the rest for player development. At the Australian Open, conversely, one-third of the money generated from that annual event goes to player development programs Down Under, one-third goes to the Australian Tennis Federation, and one-third goes to community tennis programs.

Given the USTA's current distribution formula, an American has a better chance of seeing Aunt Betty become a weekend hacker than seeing a return to American preeminence in international tennis. The slip has been showing for a while. American players traditionally struggle on the red clay at the French Open, so it was hardly a surprise in 2006 when no American man or woman qualified for the final sixteen spots in singles. But at Wimbledon, where Americans traditionally shine, only one player, Shenay Perry, reached the final sixteen. In the 2006 Davis Cup an American team led by Blake and Roddick lost to Russia in the semifinals. America has won the Davis Cup thirty-one times, more than any other country, but not since 1995.

Largely because of the inactivity of Venus and Serena Williams, American women have also floundered lately in major tournaments. In 2006 no American woman played in any of the four Grand Slam finals. That had not happened since 1937, three decades before the advent of professional tennis, thirteen years before a black player was allowed to compete in a Grand Slam event. Before 2006 at least one Williams sister appeared in a Grand Slam final in every year since 1999. At the 2006 U.S. Open, Serena was the last American woman standing; she fell in the fourth round. Eighteen American women competed in the main draw of 128 women. But Russia, a considerably smaller country, had 19 women qualify for the main draw. Of those 19, three went through the qualifying rounds—where a player must win at least three matches—to reach the main draw. Conversely, 19 American women competed in the qualifying rounds; none of the 19 reached the main draw.

So while more Americans than ever are playing recreational tennis, fewer Americans are winning on the pro circuit. The USTA's inability to develop world-class players in a country of enormous wealth is the cause of the decline. The problem affects blacks disproportionately because black families tend to have less money than white families to fund a player's tennis ambitions. While it is not unusual for a family of means to spend twenty thousand dollars per summer to get a promising junior into national and international tournaments, and also pay for coaching, few black families can foot such a hefty bill.

"The only black people who are going to get through in this sport are family projects," William Washington said. "My sons and daughters, family projects; the Williams girls, family projects; John Wilkerson with Zina and Lori in Houston, that was like a family project; Chanda Rubin, a family project. If these jokers at the USTA had any sense, they would give every family coach in this country a grant to coach their own kids. The USTA commits nothing to family tennis projects for coaching, lodging, per diem, travel, equipment. Nothing. Yet only black family units have produced quality pro players in America. We have to do it all ourselves."

The problem with that argument, Harmon said, is that there is no way of knowing which tennis families, however dedicated, will produce a world-class player. Today's star in junior tennis could easily become tomorrow's bust in the pros. Thus it is highly unlikely that the USTA would give money to parents merely for wanting to coach their own progeny. Until now the USTA has been content to sit back and let tennis parents fend for themselves, offering help in the form of grant money—for travel to a tournament, for example—only if the junior has already achieved impressive results. Now, Harmon said, the USTA will follow a model that has succeeded outside the United States.

"Other countries have tennis development programs," he said, "They fund those programs with tax dollars, and they have academies. For example, the French have fifty full-time coaches, a main academy at Roland Garros [the site of the French Open], and regional academies. Here we'll have our first academy in 2007—we'd never been allowed to have one before—and we'll have eighteen full-time coaches. France fifty, America eighteen. How much bigger is our country than theirs?"

In the past, private tennis camps expressed concern about being put out of business by a USTA-run tennis academy. But with America no longer dominating the sport, the national academy concept will come to fruition. The USTA academy will be on the site of the Chris Evert Tennis Academy in Boca Raton, Florida. Promising young players will be housed there and receive daily tennis instruction while attending school. That's the way it is now done in France, Belgium, Russia, China, Switzerland, and any other smaller country you care to name that is beating the pants off America in international competition. There are, however, critics of the academy system as it relates to black youth. Washington, not surprisingly, is one of them.

"Tennis is a family sport," he said firmly. "Your support system is your family. You don't take a black child away from his family and familiar surroundings and put him in an environment where he's the only black child, or one of the very few, around all these white people, so the child is made to feel different and uncomfortable. The USTA will take a promising black player and assign just anybody to coach that kid. Black kids taken out of their family structure and turned over to the USTA are not going to make it."

John Wilkerson, who developed two world Top 10 players from his public parks program in Houston, also believes the tennis-academy concept is anathema to young black players. "These academies kill our people," he said. "You bring people together from different backgrounds and teach them the same thing? They are not the same people. The individuality is lost. That black child's sense of who he is or who she is, the cultural identity is lost. The way I see it, the USTA is a tree. It hasn't produced any apples lately. So why would you want to get anything from that tree?"

The Washington family tree, headed by William, a retired General Motors worker, and his wife Christine, who works for the global company that owns GM, decided early on to use their resources to get their children into tennis. Why tennis? "That's what we wanted to do," he said matter-of-factly. "We weren't into softball or basketball. Our thing was tennis."

The six Washington children all have names beginning with M, again because that's what the parents wanted to do. They are, in order of birth, Mikoyan, Michaela, MaliVai, Masanja, Mashiska, and Mashona. Michaela and Mashona are females. Mikoyan died in a boating accident at age sixteen. Before that tragedy, all six children used to play tennis together. "My dad was there, giving us drills and having us practice hitting against each other," said Mashona, who began playing at age four. "My mom usually wasn't there. She was home preparing meals or taking us to practice or picking us up after practice. By the time I was able to play, my older brothers and sisters were going to college or starting their careers." At one time William Washington traveled and coached each of his four tennis-playing children. Michaela played on the pro circuit for two years, reaching a career-high ranking of No. 103 in 1984. "She didn't like tennis," her dad said. "But she was very good." Masanja did not turn pro. Mashiska, thirty-two, continues to play on the Challengers circuit. He ended 2006 ranked No. 658 in the world.

Mashona, the baby of the family at thirty, plays the kind of well-rounded game that can give an opponent fits. She had three match points against Maria Sharapova in a first-round match at the 2006 French Open, but a two-minute delay caused by pigeons on Suzanne Lenglen Court seemed to rattle her. After Sharapova escaped with a three-set victory, the Russian glamour girl told reporters, "Pigeons are my best friends." Mashona beat Sharapova in a tournament at Yale University in August 2004, a month after Sharapova won Wimbledon. But as has happened often in her twelve-year pro career, Mashona looked flat in her next match and lost to Russia's Elena Bovina in straight sets. She has been very good in many matches, but not consistently good in enough tournaments.

"Sometimes I get upset with myself because I'm out there thinking, 'You should have done this. You could have done that,'" the Houston resident said. "I always think there's something I can improve on. That's what drives me to keep playing." In 1992, as a junior, she won the U.S. Indoor eighteen-and-under Nationals. Her best result in a WTA tournament came at the Pan Pacific Open in Tokyo in January 2004: she lost in the singles final (to Sharapova) and in the doubles final (with partner Jennifer Hopkins). Mashona, now coached by Lillian Rios, achieved her career-high ranking of No. 50 in 2004 and played on the U.S. Federation Cup team in 2005. But her ranking plummeted to No. 231 at the end of 2006 after a knee injury suffered in June.

The most successful of the tennis-playing Washingtons has been MaliVai, the No. 1–ranked college player in the country after his sophomore year at the University of Michigan. He turned pro that year and became a force on the ATP tour a year later when he defeated Ivan Lendl in straight sets in the second round of a tournament in New Haven. Had Lendl won the match, he would have regained the world No. 1 ranking he had lost the week before. Once MaliVai (pronounced mal-a-VEE-ah) reached a career-high ranking of No. 11 in 1992, he began to face media questions whether he was "the next Arthur Ashe."

"Certain players would have been crushed by that kind of pressure," said Tim Mayotte, a former pro once ranked No. 7 in the world, "—to be constantly compared to a great player and be expected to live up to what Arthur accomplished on and off the court. But Mal handled it well. He was one of the guys on tour who always conducted himself with class."

MaliVai won four ATP tour titles—Memphis and Charlotte in 1992; Ostrava, Czech Republic, in 1994; and Bermuda in 1996—and was a finalist in nine others. But injuries prevented him from having a longer, more successful run in the sport. He retired in 1999 at the age of thirty. He played Davis Cup for the U.S. and teamed with Andre Agassi in doubles at the 1996 Olympic Games in Atlanta. Yet his career highlight occurred earlier that summer at Wimbledon. In the semifinals MaliVai rallied after being down two sets to one and down 1-5 in the final set to defeat Todd Martin, 5-7, 6-4, 6-7, 6-3, 10-8, in one of the great comebacks in Grand Slam history. But in the final he faced Richard Krajicek of the Netherlands, whose bullet serves were at their most formidable on Wimbledon grass. As MaliVai's relatives gathered at a family reunion in Michigan to watch the men's final at 9 a.m. local time, he succumbed, 6-3, 6-4, 6-3. Still, he joined Arthur Ashe as the only African-American men ever to reach a Grand Slam final.

"There's great joy with it, but there's also disappointment with it," MaliVai said during the 2006 U.S. Open, where he competed in a tournament of former tour champions. "One of my goals was to win a major. I wasn't one of those players reaching the finals of majors year in and year out. That was my one opportunity to win a major, and I failed. I failed at that one goal. I realize there are thousands of players out there who would love to reach the finals of a major and never will, or never did. Still, the competitive person in me wanted that title."

After retirement, the perspicacious MaliVai became a frequent presence on ESPN as a courtside reporter and postmatch interviewer on tennis telecasts. But in the last two years his air time has dwindled. He didn't work on ESPN at all in 2005, and in 2006 he broadcast only the NCAA championships. He used to appear on the network's marquee tennis events: the Australian Open, French Open, Wimbledon, and almost a dozen other events. His diminished role invites speculation as to whether his father's scathing letters denouncing the ATP and WTA and powerful sports management agencies IMG and Octagon led someone to tell ESPN to remove MaliVai from a high-profile job. "He has not told me that," William Washington said. "I have not asked him that, and no one else has told me that. It's a white system, though. The McEnroes are white. That's the way it goes." William Washington alluded to the McEnroes because John McEnroe and his younger brother Patrick appear as network television commentators on all four Grand Slam events and virtually every men's event broadcast on ESPN, CBS, NBC, or USA.

MaliVai, however, insists that he wanted to get off the road to spend more time with his wife and two kids, and devote more time to his real estate company and an eponymous kids' foundation that began in 1994 and since 1997 has been based in Jacksonville, Florida. "Our original mission was to introduce tennis to a lot of youth who didn't have the opportunity," he said. "We were going to cater to a lot of inner-city youth from underprivileged backgrounds. But we changed the focus and used tennis as a platform to get the youth to concentrate more on their education, to conduct themselves in a positive way, and to become responsible human beings." MaliVai, in a partnership with the City of Jacksonville, has broken ground on a new facility, a 9,200-square-foot complex that will include nine tennis courts, a basketball court, and an academic building. In March 2006, Bill Cosby, donating his time and talent, performed at a fund-raiser in Jacksonville that netted $400,000 for the foundation.

"Mr. Cosby did a great job putting a spotlight on the kids," MaliVai said. "Our after-school program now has 125 kids, five days a week. We partner with other organizations and provide just tennis to another 200 kids on a weekly basis. But I'll be honest with you: for every kid we help, there are another 100 or 500 kids who could benefit from the same type of program, and those kids aren't being reached now."

Once the MaliVai Washington Kids Foundation builds its new facility, a black family in northern Florida whose children show promise in tennis will have the option of letting them cultivate their talent there, in a black community, or enrolling them in a predominantly white USTA academy.

Rodney Harmon does not frown on tennis academies for black youngsters. He came out of one. After showing promise in ATA junior events, Arthur Ashe helped him get a scholarship to the Bolletieri Academy when he was seventeen. "If that had not happened, I don't believe the rest of my career would have been possible," he said. "That was the first time I was able to go somewhere and train and play tennis for three to four hours a day against good players like [future pros] Aaron Krickstein and Jimmy Arias." Harmon went to the University of Tennessee on a tennis scholarship, was a three-time NCAA All-American with the Volunteers, and teamed with Mel Purcell to win an NCAA doubles championship. When Tennessee's head coach left, Harmon took Arthur's advice and transferred to SMU where Ashe's former Davis Cup teammate, Dennis Ralston, was head coach.

"Arthur was a reference when I got my first coaching job with the USTA in 1988," said Harmon, who later coached men's tennis at the University of Miami from 1995 to 1997. But between college and coaching, Harmon had a playing career during which he faced the same burdensome questions as MaliVai Washington, questions about being "the next Arthur Ashe." Although Harmon never reached a

Grand Slam final like MaliVai, the Ashe questions were unavoidable; both he and Arthur come from Richmond, Virginia.

"I never felt much pressure because of the comparisons," Harmon said, "because I wasn't the only black guy out there. Yannick Noah was also playing, and so was Chip Hooper." Hooper, a tall serve-and-volley player from San Diego, was ranked No. 17 in the world in 1982. Harmon's highest ranking was No. 56 in 1983. But he made his greatest impact at the 1982 U.S. Open when he won a fifth-set tiebreak against Eliot Teltscher to become the first African-American man since Arthur to reach the Open quarterfinals. Alas, Jimmy Connors, the eventual champion, defeated Harmon, 6-1, 6-3, 6-4. "In my career, things didn't go the way I wanted them to go," he said. "I got injured a lot. I was never really healthy enough to build on the momentum I had when I reached the quarters at the Open. But whose fault is that? Everyone can say, 'You should have done this or that.' At the end of the day you're responsible for what happens in your life."

Now the married father of three-year-old twin girls, Harmon is also responsible for the future of American men's tennis. He's in constant contact with the nation's young hopefuls, including black players Donald Young, Phillip Simmonds, Scoville Jenkins, and Marcus Fugate, a nineteen-year-old from Rochester, New York. On Harmon's recommendation, Young ended 2006 at the Bolletieri Academy from whence Harmon sprang nearly thirty years earlier.

William Washington, when asked about Young, suggested that the seventeen-year-old is being mishandled. "The USTA and IMG [his management agency] pushed him out there too quickly. My son, MaliVai, was as good as they come at Donald Young's age, but I sent him to college for two years. You have to be physically, mentally, and emotionally ready to compete against these pros. If Donald Young's parents, who are first-generation tennis people, had asked me for advice, I would have told them to make sure Nike gives you the money that IMG got for you, but keep him in the juniors until he's eighteen or nineteen. He's not ready to play the pros. They're going to ruin that kid."

Ultimately Young's performance will determine who is correct in the latest difference of opinion between Washington and Harmon. Both want fervently to see African Americans excel on the court, but they have markedly different ideas on how to achieve it. Sometimes, though, for African Americans to continue to make progress in tennis, they must air their concerns in a different court.

CHAPTER NINE

"You niggers gotta get off the court"

• • • • • • • • • •

Thereere is an adage in tennis that applies as well to other sports:
When you don't notice the umpire (or referee), that's when you
know he's done a good job. Yet that does not mean a tennis referee
should never be noticed. Surely the United States Tennis Association,
which runs the U.S. Open, would prefer that players, fans, and media pay no attention at all to who maintains the position of authority in the umpire's chair during the most important tennis matches in
America. The USTA and the International Tennis Federation, the
group that supervises umpires in the international tournaments,
would prefer that it not be known they were sued by two African-
American umpires, Cecil Hollins of New York City and Sande French
of California, alleging systemic discrimination based on sex, gender,
and age. Since French continued to work as a linesperson and umpire
at men's and women's tournaments in the United States, attorneys ad-
vised her not to speak publicly about the suit. And as an ITF member she is bound by the organization's code of conduct, which
prohibits her from making public comments.

Regardless, her change in professional status in the past fourteen years speaks volumes. On Saturday, September 11, 1993, French served as the chair umpire for the U.S. Open women's singles final in which world No. 1 Steffi Graf of Germany defeated Helena Sukova of the Czech Republic, the No. 12 seed, 6-3, 6-3. Nothing out of the ordinary occurred during the match. No controversial rulings were made. The American and international media said virtually nothing about French's role in the match. That was unfortunate, because she made history that day. Never before had an African-American umpire, male or female, worked a championship match at a Grand Slam tournament. It was bad enough that no African American had had such an opportunity before 1993. It is unconscionable that it has not occurred again since.

"For thirteen years the USTA has kept Sande in the minor leagues," said Hollins, the co-plaintiff, who resigned from tennis after filing the suit. "In 1994, the year after she worked the Open final, she was assigned to work only the lines at the matches. She didn't get to sit in the umpire's chair. She went in to complain to Rich Kaufman, who had just replaced Jay Snyder as the chief of umpires. She asked, 'How come I've been demoted from chair umpire to the lines?' And Kaufman told her, 'You didn't deserve to do that women's final last year.' That's outright racism. Sande is still the only woman to work a Grand Slam final who has not been promoted by the USTA or the ITF."

A chair umpire in tennis, like a plate umpire in baseball or a referee in football, presides over the match. The chair umpire announces the score after every point, keeps track of the official score, controls the players, controls the crowd, settles disputes, stops play when deemed necessary, makes sure new balls are put in play at the appropriate time, makes note of the three crews of linespeople who rotate on and off court during a match, overrules a line umpire's call, and has the power to default a player for egregious conduct. The line umpires—those you see standing behind the players or sitting in a chair on the service line and calling balls in or out—are rotated at least three times during a match. But the chair umpire works the entire match from an elevated chair, often with a canopy attached to prevent sunburn or to lessen the effect of wind. Having the umpire in an elevated position makes a player approaching the chair appear similar to an attorney approaching the bench in a judicial court. That helps explain why the job of chair umpire appealed so much to Hollins, a graduate of Pace University Law School in New York City. "As a litigator, I was a tough person to win an argument against," he says with a laugh.

Always an avid tennis fan and a recreational player, Hollins attended the 1991 U.S. Open and rooted hard for his favorite player, Jimmy Connors, the left-handed bomber from Belleville, Illinois, who made an improbable though crowd-pleasing run to the semifinals that year at age thirty-nine. "I loved the way Jimmy played the game—the passion, the intensity," said Hollins, who is fifty-five. "I was at his fourth-round match on Labor Day against Aaron Krickstein, and I had great seats. Close enough to notice that the chair umpire and linespeople were missing a lot of calls. Since I'm in New York City, I'm yelling at the umpires just like everyone else. I'll never forget the chair umpire, David Littlefield, overruling a call that took a point away from Connors. The place went nuts! Connors went nuts! He goes to the chair and yells, "I'm thirty-nine years old and I'm out here busting my butt and you're pulling some crap like that? You're a bum! Get out! You! Out!"

Players, of course, lack the authority to eject an umpire. But since Connors already had the capacity crowd of twenty thousand at Louis Armstrong Stadium, then the main court at the U.S. Open, in the palm of his hand, he decided to try some umpire intimidation. Littlefield stayed put, despite Connors yelling at him later in the contentious match, "You're an abortion!"

Hollins too continued to hoot and holler from the stands. Actually, he had done more yelling than Connors during the Open fortnight. "One of the umpires, Tommy Jenkins, finally said to me, 'If you think you can do better, why don't you become an umpire?'" Hollins recalled.

Working at the time as an assistant to an attorney in the New York County court system, Hollins approached USTA official Jay

Snyder about joining the umpire ranks. He found there are finishing schools for umpires, and different color-coded designations for umpires based more on ability than experience. Upon learning the basics of umpiring, one gets a white badge; the next highest level is bronze, followed by silver and gold. Here is what professional tennis umpires are allowed to do based on the color of their badges, according to ITF rules in 2006:

Gold badge: can work any match anywhere in the world.

Silver badge: can work any match anywhere, except a Davis Cup final.

Bronze badge: can work any match anywhere, up to a quarterfinal at a Grand Slam event, and not a Davis Cup final.

White badge: can work matches, but not in the main draw of a Grand Slam event.

French held a bronze badge at the time she worked Graf vs. Sukova in 1993, so according to the ITF rules now in place she would not have a chance to officiate another Grand Slam final from the umpire's chair. But the lawsuit against the USTA alleges that other umpires besides French had worked Grand Slam finals while holding a bronze badge, and the decisions that have kept her from earning a higher badge have been arbitrary, punitive, and racially discriminatory.

While French was kept in tennis-umpire limbo, Hollins progressed rapidly through the ranks—too rapidly for some. In April 1993 he completed training at a white-badge umpiring school in Florida and then was assigned to work as a chair umpire at tournaments in Tampa, Florida; Hilton Head Island, South Carolina; and Washington, D.C. To work evening matches at the Legg Mason Classic in Washington that August, he drove five hours from New York after his day job and five hours back from D.C. to be in court the next morning. Based on glowing reviews from Bill Barber, the chief of umpires for the Association of Tennis Professionals, Hollins got to officiate matches at the U.S. Open.

"I'd done only twenty professional matches by then, but I loved doing it, I felt comfortable doing it, and people were telling me I was a natural," Hollins said. "I'd have ITF officials in the locker room giving me advice—'You might want to watch the server's foot before he serves to make sure he doesn't step on the line'—and I'd say, 'Thanks. Who are you?'"

After serving as a chair umpire at the 1993 U.S. Open, much to the delight of family and friends in the New York City borough of Queens, Hollins attended a bronze-badge school in London, moving to the next level in October 1993. By December he had become a member of the ITF team of officials, which enabled him to work matches abroad. The ITF travel department provided first-class airline tickets and hotel accommodations and reimbursed him for all other expenses. Now a full-time professional umpire, his passport soon bore the official seals of Spain, Costa Rica, El Salvador, Guatemala, Guadaloupe, Martinique, Trinidad and Tobago, Jamaica, St. Lucia, Venezuela, Australia, France, and Great Britain. He was the only African-American chair umpire in 1994 to work tennis's most prestigious event, Wimbledon.

"I remember having Cecil work some of my matches, and he did an excellent job," said Roger Smith, a former Davis Cup captain from the Bahamas. "He stayed on top of things, he was very decisive, and he was an umpire you could talk to. Some umpires act like they're above talking to players. He was never like that."

Considering all the money there is for players in tennis—the 2006 U.S. Open men's and women's champions each took home $1.2 million—it is rather surprising that the top chair umpires in tennis, those with the coveted gold badges who can work any match, any time, anywhere in the world, are paid, according to Hollins, roughly $60,000 a year. There is no shortage of people who would love to have the job, so the powers-that-be in tennis evidently see no need to pay anyone more. Hollins, who made infinitely more money each year in law, worked as an umpire because he loved it.

Often he used humor to break the tension of a tight match. A 1995 U.S. Open quarterfinal between American rivals Jim Courier and Michael Chang was a case in point. Before a capacity crowd at Armstrong Stadium, both players approached the chair frequently in hopes of gaining some sort of edge. Each player seemed to believe that if he sat back and let the other do the talking on court, maybe the next crucial call, a game-deciding call, would go his opponent's way.

"When Courier objected to a call I made," Hollins said, "he looked at me and said, 'coño.' In Spanish, coño means pussy. So I said into the courtside microphone, 'Code violation. Audible obscenity. Warning: Mr. Courier.' I found out later that John McEnroe was doing the commentary of the match on USA Network and he said, 'Well, obviously, the chair umpire, Cecil Hollins, knows exactly what that word means.' But Courier was steamed. He came to the chair and said, 'What did I say? All I said was con-you—with you.' I said, 'Nooooo. "With you" in Spanish would be comigo.' There I was giving Courier a Spanish lesson at the U.S. Open on national TV! Courier said, 'So what did I say?' One of the first things you learn as a chair umpire is to cover the microphone when you think something bad is going to go out over the air. So I put my hand over the microphone and mouthed the word 'pussy.' And Courier starts laughing. He says, 'You want to say that louder into your microphone?' It was such a tense match, and the episode seemed to have a calming effect on him."

Courier went on to win, 7-6, 7-6, 7-5.

Every umpire has a list of players whose matches he cannot officiate because of a previous run-in with that player. David Littlefield, still an active gold-badge umpire, has Jimmy Connors on his list because of that volatile U.S. Open match on Labor Day 1991. Hollins had only one player on his list, an American named David Witt. Witt never made it onto the main tour. Hollins's problem with him occurred in 1993 while working a match on the Challengers circuit. "I had to default Witt because he hit a ball while I was in the chair that happened to hit me in the chest," he said. "His aim was a lot better than his game."

Asked if he ever thought a player had a problem with him because he's black, Hollins said no. Indeed, he said proudly, the ITF used to assign him to work John McEnroe matches on the Seniors Tour because he could handle the Bad Boy of Tennis. If you think McEnroe, now forty-eight, has mellowed since being nicknamed "Superbrat" in the late 1970s, think again. Hollins worked a McEnroe vs. Connors Seniors match in Dallas during which Connors walked off the court because McEnroe accused him of cheating. Before Connors's unscheduled exit, McEnroe snapped at Hollins in the chair:

"Why are you here?"

"They told me to come because nobody else wanted to do your match."

Hollins found himself in the chair again for a Seniors match between Hall of Famers McEnroe and Sweden's Mats Wilander at Stanford University. McEnroe, livid after an errant shot, kicked a courtside scoreboard to the ground. "Sparks are flying, and the crowd's booing," Hollins said, "and I announced, 'Code violation. Unsportsmanlike conduct. Warning: Mr. McEnroe.' The crowd's going nuts. The workers come out and repair the scoreboard. To try to lighten the mood, I tell the crowd, 'Ladies and gentlemen, the scoreboards at both ends of the court were installed improperly. They were built to withstand a kick from John McEnroe. Because they were installed improperly, I have to rescind the code violation penalty to Mr. McEnroe.' Now, McEnroe and Wilander both start kicking the scoreboards. The crowd is applauding like wild. Both players are laughing. It was a priceless moment."

On the cross-country flight back to New York, Hollins and McEnroe ended up together in first class, and they talked all the way home. "John would still question my calls," Hollins said, "still argue with me as he would with any other umpire, but I had his respect."

Hollins admits to being somewhat disappointed that McEnroe, who has a forum on national television during three of the four Grand Slam events—the French Open and Wimbledon on NBC and the U.S. Open on CBS and the USA network—has not mentioned on the air how things turned sour for Hollins and other black umpires. "I'm sure John likes the position he has now and doesn't want to say anything that might jeopardize that," he said, choosing his words carefully.

By the time the first ball was struck at Wimbledon in 1994, Hollins was the only African-American umpire in the world with a gold badge. And he rose to the highest level faster than any other umpire in the sport's history. In the back of his mind he knew jealousy would soon manifest itself, but he prided himself on an ability to choose the right friends and take nothing for granted. "Other umpires would try to sabotage you by leaving messages on your answering machine like, 'You have the third match after eleven o'clock tomorrow'—when you actually had the eleven o'clock match," he said. "If you don't show up early enough to check the schedule yourself, you'd miss your match, which is a major offense for an umpire. Or a linesperson would give an unsighted call (one hand over the eyes) indicating he didn't see whether the ball was in or out, which meant that I had to make the call. You're supposed to give the unsighted call only if someone is blocking your vision. I used to get unsighted calls when nobody was blocking anybody. Or if I'm discussing something with a player during a changeover, when the linespeople are supposed to change balls, and they don't change balls. You had to watch out for things like that."

Hollins said there were people behind the scenes determined to undermine him, people who openly predicted in the umpires' locker room that he would "crash and burn" when faced with an especially difficult high-profile match. He passed a big test in Chang vs. Courier and had managed to come as close as anyone to mollifying John McEnroe. But for Hollins, the acid test came on September 5, 1996, in the U.S. Open quarterfinal match between defending champion Pete Sampras and Spain's Alex Corretja at Armstrong Stadium. An ailing Sampras appeared on the verge of defaulting on several occasions, often wandering about the court like a prizefighter out on his feet. As the grueling match moved into a decisive fifth set under an unforgiving sun, Sampras staggered to the back of the court and vomited. Since Corretja was ready to play, Hollins felt he had no choice but to penalize Sampras for delay of game. "Everyone's booing me," Hollins said with a laugh. "I look across the court at my dad sitting at courtside, and he's booing me. 'Don't you know that's Pete Sampras?' people are yelling. But an umpire's got to be fair to both players." Sampras pulled himself together and somehow summoned the strength to win the final set in a tiebreak, 9-7. Afterward, Hollins said, ITF and USTA officials only grudgingly complimented his handling of a challenging match.

Hollins felt certain that the next year, 1997, he would finally get his chance to work the U.S. Open men's final. He had already done Davis Cup matches and important tournament finals elsewhere. But to sit in the umpire's chair for the U.S. Open men's final, in his hometown of New York City, with family and friends at courtside would be the highlight of his career. Little did he know that an incident at the 1997 Open would mark the beginning of the end of his career.

His morning began as many others had at the National Tennis Center, with a friendly game of tennis against another black umpire, Al Pendleton, on one of the tournament's courts. It is one of the perks allowed umpires who come to the center before the real matches start at 11 a.m. On the adjoining courts, other umpires, all white, were playing tennis as well.

Hollins and Pendleton were not playing on a court closest to a fence. There were courts to the left and right of theirs. "But this white groundskeeper made a beeline right for our court," Hollins recalled. "He didn't talk to anyone else. He came right over to Al and me. 'We gotta get this court ready,' he said to us. 'You niggers gotta get off the court.'

"Now, I'm just stunned. Al's stunned. It's that feeling you get when you hear something that you're not sure you actually heard. Al and I are looking at each other, and the guy is looking at us as if to say, 'Yeah, I said it.' So I asked him, 'What did you just say?' He said, 'You niggers gotta get off the court.' I had my umpire's badge around my neck. I took it off and actually gave it to the guy. I said, 'You hold this. I'll be right back.'"

Hollins said he and Pendleton went to the office of Rich Kaufman, the U.S. Open tournament referee, the man who in 1994 explained to French his decision to demote her the year after she worked a championship match by saying, 'You didn't deserve to do that women's final last year.'"

Hollins remembers his all-too-brief conversation with Kaufman this way:

"Al and I were playing tennis and a groundskeeper walks up to us and says, 'You niggers gotta get off the court.'"

"You're both lucky to be working this tournament. When a groundskeeper tells you to get off the court, you get off the court. Don't come in here bothering me with this. Get out of my office."

For Hollins, who had already seen French demoted after being the first—and only—African American to preside over a Grand Slam final (without all hell breaking loose), and had already seen umpires with grey hair feel compelled to dye it for fear of demotion, and had never seen any woman sit in the high chair for a men's Grand Slam final, because over the entire history of big-league tennis it had never happened, the racial slur was the last straw.

"For me to be told, 'You niggers gotta get off the court' didn't shock me," Hollins insists. "The USTA's response is what shocked me. After all, we live in a country where black people in New Orleans were left screaming on rooftops for days hoping that somebody would save their lives after Hurricane Katrina. Nothing that happens in this country shocks me."

He said he was not shocked after the 2001 U.S. Open incident between American James Blake and Lleyton Hewitt of Australia, when Hewitt insinuated that Blake had received a favorable call from a black linesperson because of race, when Hewitt was not reprimanded by tennis officials. He was not shocked when the USTA's response was the antithesis of what tennis fans and the sports media, who had almost unanimously condemned Hewitt, would have expected: the USTA rotated three all-white officiating crews and assigned a white chair umpire to Hewitt's next match. Twenty-two officials worked the match without a black person in the chair or on the lines. "The USTA had a chance to show Hewitt and everyone watching the U.S. Open that black linespeople are representative of the USTA and American officiating, and they chose to exclude us," Hollins said. "When an African-American official brought it to the USTA's attention that it had used three all-white crews for the Hewitt match, the

USTA said, 'Oh, it must have been a mistake that came out of the computer.'"

Hollins, who left tennis in 2003, says his status was downgraded to silver from gold shortly after he filed the lawsuit. He was further downgraded to bronze after he left the circuit to have arthroscopic surgery on his right knee; the ITF would not give him an injury waiver. "They told me they needed the silver badges for umpires who were traveling full time," he said, "but I know of white umpires who have missed time because of surgery without having to lose their status."

The USTA declined to comment on the lawsuit or on any of the plaintiffs' allegations. The ITF, which is based in London, also declined comment.

"The ITF has wanted Sande French to go away for quite some time," Hollins said. "The ITF has discriminated against other women who then quit rather than stay and fight it out. Me, I'm an attorney. They say, 'Take us to court.' I say, 'Okay, let's go to court.'"

Hollins realized, however, that in labor law it was difficult to make an employer rehire someone who was not wanted. Courts generally don't try to force an employer's hand in such matters.

"Can we win this thing in court?" he asked. "Yes, because everything we're saying is true. But then, what do I win? Do I go back to being an umpire? Do I get my U.S. Open final? How do you compensate Sande, who is now a part-time linesperson, part-time chair umpire when she should have been umpiring many major finals instead of just one?

"I'm fighting a bully," Hollins continued, his voice rising in anger. "And the bully is winning hands down right now. The tennis officials' code of conduct effectively silences the other umpires who could otherwise come to our aid. I never thought we would have to fight this battle alone."

Fortunately for the plaintiffs, in 2005 they also contacted the office of New York State Attorney General Eliot Spitzer. The United States Tennis Association is not a private club, like the Augusta National Country Club which plays host to The Masters golf tournament every April and has refused to admit women as members. The

USTA is a public entity that stages the U.S. Open on public grounds, supported by taxpayer dollars. As a result of an investigation by Spitzer's office that began in late 2005 into USTA hiring and promotion practices, the USTA announced four days after the 2006 U.S. Open that it would increase the number of women and nonwhite men working as chair umpires at its tournament.

The investigation by Spitzer—who in November 2006 was elected governor of New York—found that while women served as chair umpires for approximately half of the U.S. Open women's matches between 2003 and 2005, only five women were assigned to preside over the 567 men's matches during that span. Further, the USTA assigned no woman to officiate a men's U.S. Open match beyond the quarterfinal round while men officiated 20 percent of the women's U.S. Open matches after the quarterfinal round. And the investigation affirmed Hollins's and French's contention that black umpires had been barred from the umpire's chair at America's Grand Slam tournament. As a result of the former attorney general's arm-twisting, the USTA agreed to assign more women as chair umpires of men's matches, implement anti-discrimination measures to ensure that all umpires have an equal opportunity to work major matches, and hire a consulting firm to develop a program to increase the number of nonwhite and female umpires.

"The matter was resolved amicably," French wrote. She worked sixteen matches as a chair umpire at the 2006 U.S. Open, but not a major singles final, and nine matches as a linesperson. The lawsuit has been dropped.

Hollins today works as an administrative law judge in the New York City Department of Housing, hearing cases involving residential disputes. Occasionally he'll hear from a tennis fan in his courtroom who thinks he still sits in the chair of authority at U.S. Open matches or on televised matches—much the way Judge Mills Lane used to work in a Nevada courtroom by day and referee world championship boxing matches at night. "The people are upset to hear that I'm not doing tennis anymore, especially black people," Judge Hollins said. "That's because black people take a lot of pride in seeing one of their own in a position they've never seen him in before. I achieved a kind of celebrity status. I was the one black umpire [with a gold badge]."

Tony Nimmons of Dallas now holds a silver badge. Nimmons officiated the 2000 U.S. Open men's semifinal between eventual champion Marat Safin of Russia and Todd Martin, though he has yet to serve as a chair umpire for a men's Grand Slam final. Since 1993 African-American chair umpires have worked eleven Grand Slam doubles finals and one Grand Slam singles final (Graf vs. Sukova). Peter Kasavage, a white umpire who like Nimmons holds a silver badge, has been a chair umpire for a men's Grand Slam singles final. "The next logical step for Tony after the 2000 semis would have been to let him do a final," Judge Hollins said. "They just wouldn't let him do it. It's their tournament. They just wouldn't let him do it."

Since the lawsuit and Spitzer's investigation, the USTA and ITF have taken constructive steps. At Wimbledon in 2006, for example, Sandra de Jenken, a white umpire from France, took the chair for a men's semifinal match—the first time a woman had presided over a men's Grand Slam match beyond the quarterfinal round, even though men have worked women's Grand Slam finals for decades. She also worked the 2007 Australian Open final between Roger Federer and Chile's Fernando Gonzalez. And de Jenken worked a Davis Cup final in 2006, another first for a woman. On September 10, Carlos Bernardes, Jr., a brown-skinned Brazilian, worked the 2006 U.S. Open men's final in which Federer defeated Andy Roddick. Never before had a nonwhite person presided over a men's Grand Slam final. White women are benefiting, and nonblack men are benefiting. It's anyone's guess how long it will take for African-American umpires to benefit from a lawsuit and subsequent investigation sparked by two African Americans. In tennis, racial progress seems to come only at glacial speed.

CHAPTER TEN

"Nobody called me names on the court, but nobody rooted for me either"

• • • • • • • • • • •

Tennis remained a white preserve in the late 1970s, though blacks had made substantial progress in many other walks of life. Because of the Voting Rights Act in 1965, there were no longer legal impediments to blacks' exercising their franchise. Far more blacks were graduating from college and entering the economic middle class. Although still significantly underrepresented, blacks were more of a presence in American politics, business, sports, and entertainment than ever before.

Sprinters Wilma Rudolph, Wyomia Tyus, and Evelyn Ashford were mining Olympic gold, and Luisa Harris of Delta State University in Louisiana was among the first of the dominant tall women to change the face of collegiate basketball. The Women's Professional Basketball League, a first for female athletes, was formed in 1978. Such successes were spurred by the enactment of Title IX of the Educational Amendments Act, which made illegal any acts of discrimination by schools and colleges that received federal funding. Of course it has always been far less expensive to compete in sports such as track and basketball. The same socioeconomic barriers to success in tennis that existed during Althea Gibson's prime in the 1950s—the high cost of instruction, a lack of access to coaches and tennis courts, and a cultural divide between the sport and the black community— had kept a true successor to Gibson from emerging. Still, young women who were introduced to tennis, through the ATA or other means, began to make inroads in the sport.

In May 1979 Jim Smith, who ran the Sportsmen's Tennis Club, an indoor facility in the Dorchester section of Boston, invited Althea to spend a week coaching and giving life lessons to five black women: Leslie Allen, the 1977 ATA women's champion and a graduate of the University of Southern California; Kim Sands, who won the 1976 ATA title before graduating from the University of Miami; Renee Blount of St. Louis, a junior champion in the Missouri Valley region; Andrea Buchanan, a highly regarded player from Los Angeles; and Zina Garrison of Houston, a fifteen-year-old who would become the world's top-ranked junior and a two-time ATA champion. Diane Morrison of Los Angeles, the 1975 ATA champion, missed the event to attend her graduation from Stanford University.

Of this group, only Buchanan did not play long enough to reach her potential. She achieved a career-best ranking of No. 106 in 1981 and played in the main draw at Wimbledon and the U.S. Open. A year later she was shot dead in Los Angeles. She was twenty-six. According to Sands, Buchanan had a male friend who promised to sponsor her tennis career. But he owed money to drug dealers. Buchanan and the friend were killed at his house. Tennis coach Bob Ryland remembers Buchanan as a talented player who ran with the wrong crowd. "She started in tennis late, but she was a strong player," he said. "Problem was she didn't want to leave L.A. I was trying to take her to New York so I could train her."

Each of the four other women invited to Boston played at least ten years on the pro circuit. They described the week with Althea as a life-changing experience. "I was twenty-two years old and meeting an American legend," Sands recalled. "It had a tremendous impact on me."

"It was empowering for us as black women," said Allen, who grew up in Ohio and New York City. "Each of us stayed with black families in the Boston area. Everybody at the club knew who we were. We got to hit with local college players. When we were on the court, we didn't get those strange looks that you would get from people then, because people still weren't really used to seeing black people play tennis. And we got to spend time with a legend, Althea Gibson. The first time I saw her I was eleven at the ATA camp in Lynchburg, Virginia. I just had my head down the whole time she spoke. It was like being in the presence of royalty. But that week [in Boston] she gave us coaching. She told us about her travels, and we sat around telling our stories. I remember talking about wanting to qualify for the French Open and wanting to qualify for other tournaments. Then Althea said, 'Okay, you need to start talking about *winning* tournaments.' That was a light bulb moment for me." Allen went on to qualify for the French Open and win three matches, and her world ranking rose more than 100 points.

Each of the invitees would have a chance as tennis pros to become the answer to the question, "Who was the first African-American woman to win a tennis tournament after Althea Gibson?" Allen, a long-limbed six-footer, earned that distinction. But hers was a circuitous path to success. Her parents both played tennis in the ATA. When she was ten and eleven, Allen spent summers in the ATA's Junior Development Program. But she didn't love the game then. She would not pick up a racquet again until age fourteen. Because her high school did not have a girls' tennis team and she had heard about Title IX, she sued the Ohio school district and won the right to play on the boys' team. "None of us in the district was any good, so it wasn't a big deal," Allen said with a laugh. "I remember playing the white boy who was considered the best player in the district. I beat him."

Allen earned an academic scholarship to Carnegie-Mellon University in Pittsburgh, but a restless spirit took her to the Fashion Institute of Technology in New York and Texas Southern University in Houston before enrolling at USC. She left Texas Southern when the school reneged on a plan to start a women's tennis team. As a walk-on at USC, she was the No. 6 singles player, last on the totem pole. "In college I didn't play doubles because I couldn't volley and I didn't have a good serve," she said. "I never had a junior tennis ranking in my city, state, or region. I played once in a twenty-one-and-under tournament and lost to someone 6-0, 6-0."

But despite being unpolished as a player, Allen had size and athletic ability, and potential. After graduating magna cum laude with a degree in communications, she took Arthur Ashe's advice and competed on a satellite tour of pro hopefuls in Australia. Bill Cosby, a friend of her actress-mother, Sarah, sponsored her for two years on the women's circuit.

In a 1980 tournament in Los Angeles, Allen became the first black woman in the open era (since 1968) to play in the main draw of a professional tournament. Avon served as the chief sponsor of women's tennis then. Allen, still learning her craft, competed in main tour events and on the Avon Futures, a level one notch below the big leagues. Players then, particularly on the minor-league circuit, stayed with host families during a tournament instead of in hotel rooms, to reduce the costs of being on the tour. Usually Allen stayed with a black family that had an ATA connection. Whenever no black family was available, the housing issue often became problematic. "I'd go to a tournament where a family wanted to house the No. 1 seed," she said. "But when that family found out that the No. 1 seed was me, then suddenly the housing disappeared."

Being black and a well-spoken college graduate whose mother appeared in Broadway productions meant that Allen was the subject of newspaper articles in virtually every city in which she played. But that did not make her recognizable to everyone at those tournaments. "If there were five players walking into the tournament together, the four white ones just went through, but the rent-a-cop at the door would always stop me," she said before mimicking the guard. "'Can I see some I.D.? . . . I'm going to have to call my boss before I can let you go through.'"

Following a good showing at the Avon Futures in Montreal, which had a total prize purse of $50,000, Allen qualified for the Avon Championships of Detroit, a big-league event at Cobo Arena in February 1981 with a $150,000 prize purse. In the first round she played a morning match against Ros Fairbank of South Africa. "I was losing, and there was this fat white guy in the stands who clapped every time I made a mistake," Allen said. "Serve a fault, he'd clap. Miss a backhand, he'd clap. So my job in my brain was to not give that guy any more reasons to clap. That's what I focused on, and I rallied to win the match."

Her hitting partner during the tournament was Michael Reese, a college friend from her days at Texas Southern. "He was an urban creature," she said. "He just had a down-to-earth way of giving advice that helped me stay relaxed and confident. I played Mima Jausovec of Yugoslavia in the second round, a player with a name in the sport. But Michael just said, 'That bitch can't hit a second serve. Kill her second serve.' He would put things in such a way that I didn't feel intimidated by the name of the opponent." Allen defeated Jausovec as well as Virginia Ruzici of Romania and Barbara Potter en route to the final.

One day after a practice session with Reese at a suburban club used by the pros that week, a white woman approached Allen with what the player remembered as a sense of astonishment. "She said to me, 'You're good!' I'm thinking, okay. Then she said, 'You should play in some tournaments. You know they're having a tournament downtown at the arena this week, don't you?' It was so early in the existence of black women in tennis that she could not conceive of a black woman actually playing tennis. She didn't ask, 'Are you a pro? Are you playing in the tournament downtown?' Those thoughts never occurred to her."

That woman would have got the message on Sunday, February 9, 1981, the day Allen met Hana Mandlikova, a strong yet graceful player from the former Czechoslovakia, in the championship match. Allen had played creditably in losing to Mandlikova in the Montreal futures tournament, so she felt no trepidation about playing Hana again. But reading about the match in that morning's *Detroit News?* Well, that was a different story.

"At breakfast," she said, "I saw this article saying that if I won I would be the first black woman in the open era to win a professional tournament. I put that paper down because it was making me nervous." Allen's mother was performing in a play in New York and missed the match, but her brother, stepfather, and cousins came up from Ohio and sat at courtside in a section reserved for family and friends. Allen remembers a security guard trying to eject her party because he assumed all those black people at a tennis tournament must be in the wrong seats.

Allen broke Mandlikova, then No. 5 in the world, in the third game and took the first set 6-4. She began the second set with another service break and built a 5-2 lead. Unable to serve out a straight-set victory the first time, Allen got another chance at 5-4. She did not waste it. "What I remember most is that on match point, Hana hit a service return wide down the line," she said. "I turned to look at the linesman. He was a brother. You didn't have many black people calling the lines at tennis matches then. He stuck his arm out, indicating the ball was out. Then I turned to look at the chair umpire who could have overruled the call. The chair umpire nodded. The ball was out. Just at the moment that I won the title, it was good to see a brother make that call."

Not since Althea Gibson's triumph at the 1958 U.S. Open had an African-American woman won a big-league tournament. And something else occurred in tennis that afternoon to make the date even more historic: Yannick Noah defeated Czech star Ivan Lendl by default (leg injury) to win the United Virginia Bank tournament. Never before had a black woman and a black man won professional tennis events on the same day. Noah earned $35,000 for his title, Allen $24,000 for hers. The winner's check represented more than half of Allen's 1980 earnings of $40,513. In her acceptance speech she told the crowd, "This is what happens when people get an opportunity."

Allen's world ranking rose to a career-high No. 17 in 1982. In June that year Mandlikova won the French Open, the first of three Grand Slam titles in a career that culminated in her induction into the International Tennis Hall of Fame. Allen, who was good enough to beat a future Hall of Famer in 1981, did not win another pro tournament. Ryland, a longtime family friend who coached her, said, "She could have won more, but she didn't train the way she should have. If she had practiced more, she could have been a Top 10 player."

Allen sees it differently. "Even as a pro, I used to have a hitch in my serve," she said. "I spent many hours practicing with a volley machine. I learned to play serve-and-volley and construct a game on the pro tour." To hear Allen tell it, she got the most out of her ability considering that between the ages of eleven and fourteen—critical years in the development of a player—she put tennis aside and pursued other interests. She retired from the tour in 1987 at age thirty.

"I really wasn't having a life," she said. "I had been so obsessed with tennis." Allen also longed to spend more time around other blacks, something a pro tennis career has really never allowed. "I used to count the number of blacks in the stands at tournaments," she said. "It was unusual if I got to the second hand. You were so separated from a black culture in tennis. If you went to a city and hoped you might meet somebody—not necessarily somebody you would have a romantic relationship with, but maybe somebody who might come into your life over time—if you hadn't met that person by Wednesday of the tournament, you pretty much knew that you were going on to the next city without meeting him."

Allen married and gave birth to Rachel Selmore, an active daughter she nicknamed "Hurricane." Now twelve and the picture of health, Rachel needed a bone-marrow donor as an infant, a cause that galvanized the tennis community. Allen, the former women's coach at Fordham University, now represents the world's Top 20 players on the Women's Tennis Association board. She is also the executive director of the Win4Life Foundation, which introduces African Americans to tennis and other tennis-related careers such as marketing, management, advertising, and journalism. The foundation's slogan is, "Tennis is more than just hitting the ball." In 2005 she received the USTA Service Bowl Award as "the person who makes the most notable contribution to the sportsmanship, fellowship, and service of tennis."

Like Allen, Kim Sands has gone from serving winners to serving the larger community. She also got a late start in tennis but made up for lost time. She reached a career-high ranking of No. 44 in 1984 and played ten years on the pro circuit. She began playing at fifteen. By that age, most future pros have at least five years of amateur experience on their resumés. But Sands, who was also the leading scorer on the basketball team at Thomas Edison High School, found that her speed, agility, and strength translated well to tennis. "I would've played tennis first, but like a lot of black girls I was not exposed to tennis first," she said. "Seeing Billie Jean King beat Bobby Riggs on TV [in 1973] opened my eyes to the sport." She attended the University of Miami without a tennis scholarship but became the first African American to earn one. She also became the team captain. She was an NCAA finalist in doubles and had the most successful pro career of any UM graduate. Working with Arthur Ashe, then the touring pro at Miami's Doral Resort and Country Club, undoubtedly spurred her development. "I could not have had a better teacher," she said. "I served the way Arthur used to serve."

Five-ten, of athletic build with light brown skin, red hair, and freckles, Sands cut a unique figure on the pro circuit. "Whenever I used to play in Australia, the blacks there, the Aborigines, would come to my court and watch me and pray for me," she said, laughing. "They wouldn't leave until my match was done. It was nice to have some support. You didn't see too many blacks at tennis tournaments back then. I remember at one tournament in Japan, one of the women behind the scenes obviously forgot my name and asked 'Where's the brown lady?'"

When Sands was a tour rookie without an endorsement contract, she showed initiative to stay financially afloat in the sport. After reading an article in *Jet* magazine about Michigan judge Ed Bell, who managed the careers of singer Gladys Knight and former heavyweight boxing champion Leon Spinks, Sands wrote Bell asking if he would sponsor her. The letter prompted Spinks to send her $20,000.

Once Sands turned pro, she befriended the few other black players on the circuit, including Roger Smith, a Davis Cup player from the Bahamas. But she did not find out they were cousins until an aunt of Sands's died in Coconut Grove, Florida, in the mid-1980s, and several Bahamians attended the funeral.

Sands did not win a singles title but won several doubles events while paired with Gigi Fernandez or Lori McNeil. She became a student of the game, which led to her success as a coach. "My coaching technique is a melting pot of what I've been taught and what I've learned from watching other players," she said. "It was great to watch [Hall of Famers] Martina Navratilova, Chris Evert, Billie Jean King, and Stefan Edberg—their volleys, their strokes, their technique. I would stay for the whole tournament at the Grand Slams and watch all the top players. I liked to watch men's matches because I always knew someday I wanted to coach boys and men."

Sands coached at her alma mater before returning to her roots in inner-city Miami to coach people with the same background as hers. Since 1999 she has managed a sports and education center on Thirty-sixth Street and Eighth Avenue, named after Hall of Famers Ashe and Butch Buchholz. Nike recently donated one thousand pairs of sneakers to the center, where one of the courts is named after Althea Gibson. Ashe-Buchholz includes twelve tennis courts, a baseball diamond, and a basketball court. A sign on the door to the center, an oasis on a block otherwise featuring boarded-up storefronts, reads, THIS IS A GAMBLING AND DRUG FREE ZONE. "My mission now is to develop world-class players out of our program," Sands said. "But I want these young people to know that they're human beings first. We already have kids here who have been No. 1 on their tennis teams at schools like Stanford, Miami, Georgia Tech, Howard, Spellman, and Grambling State."

Until that future pro star comes along, Sands's program continues to produce scholars. The center also has a computer room, which accommodates 125 children each day with up to 65 teachers providing academic instruction. For Sands, the phrase "No Child Left Behind" is not just a political campaign slogan; it is her reality. Ashe-Buchholz turns no one away. Serena Williams has visited the center, as have James Blake, Anna Kournikova, and Boris Becker. Indeed, Sands gives tennis lessons to Becker's sons, Elias, six, and Noah, four. Perhaps one or both of the Becker boys will develop into world-class talents under her tutelage.

Renee Blount coaches today in a more bucolic setting, a facility featuring an indoor court and an outdoor court on her farm overlooking the rolling hills in Charlottesville, Virginia. This is where the St. Louis native has settled after ten years on the pro circuit, reaching a career high of No. 63 in 1981. "I needed something more than the country after coming off the women's tour," she said.

Blount, the daughter of a surgeon, was the first successful black junior player since Ashe came out of the ATA in the 1950s. Ashe, Buchholz, and Richard Hudlin were among her first teachers in St. Louis. She also competed successfully in the ATA juniors. After completing her junior year at UCLA, she joined the pro tour. There are no Grand Slam titles in singles or doubles on her resumé, no commercial advertisements featuring her brown visage, but that is hardly the only measure of success in a tennis life. Blount worked hard at her craft—sometimes up to ten hours a day—and her strength in withstanding acts of racism smoothed the path somewhat for black players who followed.

As an amateur, Blount traveled to the national twelve-and-under tournament in Little Rock, Arkansas, and, after being reluctantly allowed to compete in the event, was told not to attend any of the social functions. Instead she was given money to go to a movie by herself. At her father's insistence, she attended the social functions anyway. She was then told that the tournament itself would be moved to another city if she didn't stay away. When she qualified again the following year, the organizers moved the event rather than accept her.

As a pro she endured an episode similar to Arthur Ashe being asked by a Russian coach if he could touch a black man's hair. As Blount recalls, "Most of the foreign players had not seen many black people before, and I can remember the Czech players just wanted to touch my hair because they were very curious. I didn't mind at all."

What troubled her most about the tour, she said, was the tacit pressure on players to maintain a high ranking, because winning is the lifeblood of tennis. That the other players did not speak to her until she had "proven herself" by taking a set off Chris Evert is something she attributes more to the dog-eat-dog world of the tour than to any racial motive. What she enjoyed most about the tour was the travel: the Grand Slam tournaments alone ensured two weeks every year in Melbourne, Paris, London, and New York City. Blount found enough time to see the sights. "It's very exciting because you see a part of the world that you thought you would only read about in books," she said. "Each country tries to show you the best things they have to offer, things that you wouldn't necessarily be exposed to if you were a tourist. That makes it exciting. . . . I don't think I would be the same kind of person I am today if I had not had a job that allowed me to travel as tennis did." Blount played her final pro tournament in 1987.

That Diane Morrison would miss the week of tennis hitting and giggling in Boston to walk down the aisle in a cardinal and white Stanford cap and gown at her graduation came as no surprise to those who know her best. Today she is known professionally as Dr. Diane Shropshire. "When I went to Stanford, women's pro tennis was not yet on the rise," she said. "The thought of being a pro athlete was not in the forefront of my mind. My mother was a teacher, and my father was a professor in biomedical engineering, so I was more academically oriented."

Nevertheless her success in tennis at Stanford, becoming the No. 2 singles player after being No. 5 as a freshman in 1975, and winning an NCAA doubles title with Susan Hagey, compelled her to give the pro game a shot. Always a talented player, she won the ATA women's title in San Diego in 1975. In her first year as a pro, she reached her career-best ranking of No. 50 and won a Wimbledon tuneup event called the Trophee Pernod, in West Worthing, England, defeating among others a future network television sportscaster named Mary Carillo. "That was a big victory for me," she recalled. "I didn't win a tournament on the main tour. I lost to [Hall of Famer] Virginia Wade at the U.S. Open, but you always remember the victories more fondly than the defeats."

As she traveled the pro circuit, competing in Grand Slam tournaments and the Avon-sponsored main tour events and satellite events, "There were racial undertones everywhere I played. Nobody called me names on the court, but nobody rooted for me either. When you'd go to tennis clubs, you'd get strange looks. And it was always trickier finding housing for the black players. I tried to tune out the issues and just focus on the tennis."

Yet the unspoken but persistent vibe that you are not welcome, that others would be happier if you went away, a vibe that black tennis players have sensed on the main tour for decades, makes it difficult to find the rhythm and comfort zone needed to perform at your best. What made the tennis life even more challenging for Shropshire were the high expectations of journalists who presumed that a player who cracked the world's Top 50 as a rookie would become "the next Althea Gibson."

"When I zipped up to No. 50, that was the natural thing people would say," she said. "I remember it coming more from the black press, because everybody was always looking for the next black champion, the next great one. But I didn't worry about that. I certainly wasn't calling myself 'the next Althea Gibson.'"

The tennis tour in the early 1980s could be a lonely place, particularly for a young black woman traveling abroad before the big money came into the sport. Back then, a European trip could last up to two months, and the only other black people you might see aside from the few on the circuit were the skycaps at the airport. Shropshire, more of an academic than a jock, gave the tour three years and then moved on.

"I was playing consistently well, but if you didn't have a coach who was traveling with you then—and I didn't—it was difficult to stay in the Top 50," she observed. "In the early 1970s the players could just travel around and play. But when I came in, tennis was becoming more of a business. Also, I liked winning so much that when I was no longer able to continue to win and rise in the ranks, tennis wasn't as much fun for me. I knew by the end of 1981 that I wasn't going to be No. 1, so I went to medical school."

She graduated from the UCLA School of Medicine and is now an anesthesiologist at Pennsylvania Hospital in Philadelphia. She married Ken Shropshire, an attorney and professor of legal studies and business ethics at the Wharton School of Business at the University of Pennsylvania. She has two children, Theresa, thirteen, and Sam, eleven. And she has become a tennis mom. Sam plays in USTA-sanctioned twelve-and-under events in Philadelphia. "It's funny that Sam now has a coach and practices so often," Dr. Shropshire said. "I used to get one tennis lesson a week and have to figure out the rest for myself."

While the son figures out how far he wishes to go in the game, the mother figured out long ago a truism once spoken by a tennis player named Ashe: "You can certainly become a doctor. You may or may not get to the Top 10 in the world. That's not up to you. But you can become a doctor. That *is* up to you."

It is remarkable how far a tennis life can take someone. For Evonne Goolagong, tennis took her from an impoverished existence in the Australian outback to her continent's largest city, to the pinnacle of her sport, and then, finally, back to Australia with a recognition of what it truly means to be home.

Goolagong, the third daughter of a poor Aborigine sheep-shearer in the town of Barellan—the wheat and sheep country in New South

Wales—burst onto the international sports scene in 1971 through a rare tennis feat: winning the French Open on clay and Wimbledon on grass within a two-month span. For her to accomplish this double at the age of nineteen was remarkable. For her to do it as a black woman—the first black female Grand Slam winner since Althea Gibson—was particularly significant. It would have been more significant to other blacks around the world but for her reluctance to publicly identify with her ethnic roots at that time. Blacks in America, for instance, did not readily cheer Goolagong as one of their own, because they generally did not know. And that was fine with Goolagong's tennis mentor, if not Goolagong herself.

Goolagong was the first Aborigine woman to star in any international sport. Aborigines, the first Australians, are distinguished by brown skin, straight hair, thin lips, and wide noses. They were colonized when British Lt. James Cook arrived on the continent in 1770. As of 2001, the last year for which a population estimate is available, according to the Australian Bureau of Statistics the total Aborigine population numbered approximately 450,000.

As one of eight children reared in a shack with a dirt floor, Goolagong would have found tennis beyond her socioeconomic means if not for a local resident named Bill Kurtzman, who invited the curious preteen into the local club to learn to play. At age nine she displayed hints of the exceptional grace and fluidity of movement and shot-making that would define her tennis excellence. Vic Edwards, a renowned tennis coach, was summoned from Sydney to see Evonne in action. Edwards convinced her parents to let her accompany him at age thirteen to learn at his school and live with his family. Edwards became her coach, mentor, manager, and surrogate father.

Acceptance of Evonne outside the Edwardses' household did not come readily. As a teenager Evonne heard "nigger" for the first time after partnering with Tricia Edwards, the coach's daughter, to win a club league match in Sydney. During the handshake at the net, one of the women said, "That's the first time I've ever lost to a little nigger." When a tearful Tricia said she was crying because her sister's feelings had been hurt, the same woman snapped, "She's not your sister."

"In those days Vic Edwards steered Evonne away from the racial and political stuff," said Bud Collins, who collaborated with Goolagong on her 1975 autobiography. "There was a civil rights movement among Aborigines at the time, not very successful, and they wanted help from her, and he forbade all that." After Goolagong's 1970 Wimbledon debut, a first-round loss to Jane "Peaches" Bartkowicz, Collins recalled the international media wanted to talk about race, but Goolagong did not. "People asked her if she could understand what Arthur Ashe had been through. She'd never met Arthur Ashe."

In those days Collins kiddingly referred to Goolagong in the *Boston Globe* as "The Great Dark Hope" and "the girl from the bush." But she bristled at such race-specific references, as did Edwards. Following his advice, she traveled to South Africa in 1971 and became the first nonwhite to play in a tennis tournament there. That decision annoyed Aboriginal activists. One said, "It was an insult to her people to play for those racists. But living with the Edwardses has made Evonne more white than Aboriginal. The whole arrangement is paternalism at its worst."

Goolagong, however, never objected to putting tennis first. Her star ascended after she defeated Britain's Helen Gourlay, 6-3, 7-5, in the 1971 French final and then trounced fellow Aussie Margaret Court, 6-4, 6-1, in the Wimbledon final. Goolagong was named Associated Press Female Athlete of the Year and Australian of the Year, and was ranked No. 1 in the world. Throughout the 1970s she became as familiar a name in women's tennis's winning circle as those of Evert, King, and Navratilova. She won the Australian Open title four times, Wimbledon twice, and the French Open once. She never won the U.S. Open, losing four straight finals (to Court in 1973, King in 1974, and Evert in 1975 and 1976). In 1974 she became the highest-paid player in World Team Tennis, signing a five-year contract worth one million dollars with the Pittsburgh Triangles. Her feline style of play, combined with great hands and quick reflexes, captivated many, including a future tennis champion from Houston.

"When I was a young junior player, I remember watching Evonne on television and realizing that, even though she was Australian, her skin was dark like mine," Zina Garrison wrote in her 2001 autobiography. "Sometimes at the park, we'd try to hit a topspin lob or a slice backhand, have a little twist in our walk or sit down cute, like Evonne."

The only aspect of Goolagong's game that no one wanted to emulate was the concentration lapses that sometimes plagued her in important matches. It sometimes appeared that she was not on the court at all. In the prime of her career, for example, she lost the 1975 Wimbledon final to Billie Jean King, 6-0, 6-1. Edwards coined a term for Goolagong's disappearing spells: "walkabout." She addressed the term in her 1975 book in a manner that indicated she had not completely sacrificed her racial pride: "Walkabout: fade away, retreat, withdraw, bug out, get away from it all. It can be physical or mental. Or both. In my case, it's almost always mental. I've accepted the expression 'walkabout' for my spells, but the word didn't come from me. It came from Mr. Edwards. Though I know he wasn't being condescending, it's an expression which irritates many Aborigines because it's the white man's word for an Aboriginal trait, and because it's a word that is frequently used derisively to mean shiftless or purposeless. . . . But don't whites lose concentration playing tennis, too?"

Goolagong did not lose her focus throughout the Wimbledon fortnight in 1980. Competing five years after marrying Briton Roger Cawley and three years after the birth of their first child, she ousted No. 2 seed Tracy Austin, 6-3, 0-6, 6-4, in the semifinals, then defeated Evert, the No. 3 seed, 6-1, 7-6, to capture her second Wimbledon title nine years after her first. Goolagong's final Wimbledon appearance came in 1982, a second-round loss to Garrison. She retired in 1983 with fourteen Grand Slam titles (seven in singles, six in doubles, and one in mixed doubles). She won forty-three career titles in singles and nine in doubles. In 1988 she was inducted into the International Tennis Hall of Fame.

Australians of all shades expressed criticism about her decision to live in the United States: first in Naples, Florida, later on Hilton Head Island, South Carolina. But the death of Goolagong's mother,

Melinda, in 1991 brought about a profound change. "She went to the funeral and found black people there," Collins said. "Evonne said to someone, 'Who are all these people?' And the person said, 'Evonne, this is your family.' Well, her husband told me that she went into seclusion after that, until she finally came to terms with her past. Then she became an activist."

Goolagong, fifty-five, now lives in the Australian province of Queensland. She holds tennis clinics for Aborigine youth and since 1997 has been a sports ambassador to the Aboriginal and Torres Strait Islander communities. She also serves on the Australian Sports Commission and is captain of Australia's Federation Cup team. She has come home. "The original Australians have a champion of Australia," she has said of herself. "I hope the first of many." A generation ago Africa celebrated its first world tennis champion to be reared on the continent. Africa, too, hopes he will be the first of many.

CHAPTER ELEVEN

"You could play the French Open and never really see Paris"

• • • • • • • • • • •

In the early 1980s tennis was just beginning to attract the beautiful people: A-list actors and runway models who mingled and partied with the top players. For a New York minute in the eighties, supermodel Cheryl Tiegs even worked as a courtside reporter on tennis matches on ABC. But Yannick Noah, the sport's first star to be born in Europe and reared in Africa, was hardly content to rub tennis elbows with the in crowd; he became part of it.

With an infectious gap-toothed grin and dreadlocks flying, Noah played hard. He partied even harder. One former wife with whom he has two children was a high-fashion model. Another former wife with whom he has two children was crowned Miss Sweden in 1978. Another woman with whom he has a child is a film producer. And Noah today is an international singing star. On court he became one of the great players of his era and one of the most spectacular to watch. Remarkable speed and court coverage, dynamic net-rushing, and the kind of shot-making artistry that fans crave propelled Noah into the upper echelon. His signature shot—a between-the-legs shot on the dead run with his back to the net—is one today's players find impossible to match.

Hall of Fame recognition came relatively late for Noah; his 2005 enshrinement came fifteen years after his final Grand Slam event. Apparently the gatekeepers had to make up their minds about a player who had never advanced past the third round at Wimbledon and made just two quarterfinal-round appearances in eleven U.S. Opens. But his emotional triumph at the 1983 French Open, his impressive 40-12 record at the French Open, his stellar play in France's 1982 Davis Cup finals defeat by the United States, his leadership role for the French team that beat the United States in 1991, and his coaching of the French women's team to its first-ever Federation Cup championship in 1996 are all moments worthy of immortalization.

What Noah represents is important too: an African-reared player who brought to tennis the kind of physique and athletic ability that blacks to this day are more likely to showcase in other sports. The 6-4 Noah did not play professional basketball, soccer, or football, and did not box or pursue Olympic medals on the track, though he might have had he grown up in inner-city America. As an eleven-year-old he was playing a makeshift version of tennis when spotted by Arthur Ashe. Arthur was in Africa playing exhibitions as a part of a State Department tour. He saw Yannick in Yaounde, the capital of Cameroon, hitting tennis balls with a plank, and contacted Philippe Chatrier, president of the French Tennis Federation.

"When I telephoned him one day in 1971 with the news that I had just seen a remarkably gifted eleven-year-old boy playing on a court in Africa, Chatrier responded in his typically generous way," Arthur wrote in his 1993 memoir. The following year, French authorities convinced Yannick's parents, a Cameroonian father, who was a pro soccer star, and a white French mother, that the boy had a unique gift that could be developed fully at a tennis academy in Nice.

"It must have been hard for him to be a twelve-year-old kid having to leave his family in Africa," said Noah's son, Joakim, a seven-footer who led the University of Florida to the 2006 and 2007 NCAA basketball championships.

The Noah family made the sacrifice, and the son left an indelible imprint upon the game. Tennis crowds buzzed whenever Noah took the net and an opponent threw up a lob—a signal that the between-the-legs shot was coming. But he had more than style going for him at the 1983 French Open. He displayed an equal measure of substance, dropping only one set in his first six matches. In the final he faced Sweden's Mats Wilander, who entered the match with a consecutive-match win streak of forty-three on European clay and twenty victories in a row overall. Noah pressed him throughout, utilizing his reach and court quickness to retrieve shots that would have won points against lesser players. He fought off cramps in the third set and, after a Wilander service return sailed long on match point, dropped to his knees in exultation. And few will ever forget the sight of Noah hugging his white-haired father Zacharie at courtside.

After becoming the first Frenchman since Marcel Bernard in 1946 to win the French title, Noah said, "I worked hard, but I did that before. This time I practiced to win. I thought about winning, not only a few matches but the tournament. That was the difference . . . my mind. I was ready to fight to win the tournament."

Noah was ready to join Arthur, whose intervention in 1971 opened new vistas for a Cameroonian boy, as the only black men to win a Grand Slam singles crown. Noah has been enhancing his celebrity status in France ever since, making a successful transition from athlete to musician. His song "Saga Africa" became a national hit upon its release in 1990 and a Francophile anthem in 1991 after the Davis Cup team that he captained danced and performed the song on its way to the victory stand. France has not produced a Grand Slam champion in the men's game since Noah, but perhaps the nation's brightest hope is an exceptionally talented black player who is as at home on the hardwood as he is on a hard court.

Gael Monfils is 6 feet 3 inches with chocolate brown skin, spiked brown hair, and a condor's wingspan. He loves basketball, particularly the Denver Nuggets, the team of his favorite player, Carmelo

Anthony. Once he considered pursuing a career in the NBA, as French hoop stars Tony Parker and Boris Diaw have done. But a gifted black player would hardly stand out in professional basketball. In tennis he does . . . even today. That's why Monfils (pronounced mon-FEES) chose the racquet sport. "I used to like both the same, but now I like tennis more," he said in March 2006 at a tournament in Key Biscayne, Florida. He used an interpreter for the interview, not because he doesn't speak English but because the twenty-year-old does not yet feel comfortable being quoted in a language other than his native French.

Although he was only seven when Arthur Ashe died and never had a chance to meet him, Monfils calls Ashe "my favorite player. I saw a documentary about him on TV, and I know he was a great man." What Monfils learned about Arthur's ability to win on court and battle successfully against adversity and injustice off court inspired him to enter a tennis academy in Paris. According to the French Davis Cup captain Guy Forget, Monfils graded higher on the national federation's athletic tests than any player ever. It is easy to see why—the way he covers every inch of the court from side to side, or rushes the net on a short ball, or leaps to put away an overhead smash. He has a bazookalike forehand, but his two-handed backhand has thus far been his more consistent shot.

Like Noah, Monfils plays with uncommon athleticism. Like Noah, he is the son of a soccer player. His father, Rufin, hails from Guadeloupe; his mother, Sylvette, a nurse, is from Martinique. In 2004 Monfils was the world's No. 1 junior and won three of the four Grand Slam events: the Australian Open, the French Open, and Wimbledon. He went 31-2 in junior events that year before turning pro.

In 2005 he won his first ATP title, a clay-court event in Sopot, Poland, and cracked the world Top 50. He has remained there since. He hovered near the Top 20 in 2006 after beating James Blake in five sets in a thrillingly athletic third-round match at the French Open, featuring full splits and tigerlike roars of emotion from the winner. Monfils had a strong enough summer on the hard courts to prompt ESPN announcer Chris Fowler to predict he would reach the U.S.

Open final. But as the No. 27 seed he had to play two best-of-five-set matches in as many days because of rain delays. The grind took its toll, especially on Monfils's thin legs. He followed a tough four-set victory over Michael Russell with a grueling four-set upset loss to South African Wesley Moodie.

Monfils, who is coached by former French Davis Cupper Thierry Champion, prefers to stay on the baseline and counterpunch. But in time he will be expected to finish more points at the net, where his height and reach would be major assets. Asked what he needs to do to crack the Top 10, he stopped fumbling with his ever-present iPod long enough to say, "Work. Work hard."

While still in the embryonic stage of his tennis development, Monfils may stand his best chance of winning a major tournament at the French Open, where he responds well to the fans' rabid support and where his countryman Noah captured his lone Grand Slam title. "I know Yannick and I admire him," he said. "He gave me some tennis advice, but I don't think it is working." He then grinned broadly, revealing a sense of humor to which sports fans may soon become accustomed. After IMG signed Monfils in 2006, he landed a multi-million-dollar sponsorship deal with Nike.

Another international player with French roots, Ronald Agenor, certainly would not turn his back on a similar offer. At age forty-two, some twenty-four years after his pro debut, Agenor is still playing tournaments on the Challengers circuit while coaching in Atlanta. "I have always enjoyed competing, and it is still in me," he said. "My goal is simply to enjoy myself. I have not been able to participate on the senior tour since I turned thirty-five because of coaching and family commitments, so it's been a little frustrating to be still in good shape and not be able to compete."

Agenor was born in Morocco, the son of a United Nations diplomat and former minister of agriculture in Haiti. By age ten he lived in the Congo in Africa and became acquainted with tennis. Four years later he began playing in junior events in Bordeaux, France. By age eighteen he had won junior titles in France, Belgium, and Monte Carlo; reached the semifinals of the prestigious Easter Bowl Tournament in Miami; and won a gold medal representing Haiti at the Caribbean Games in Havana, Cuba. "I got my award from President Fidel Castro," Agenor said. "He told me, *"Tu es un gran campeon"* ("You are a great champion"). Agenor won his first tour event in Athens in 1989 and invited comparisons to Noah because of his dreadlocks, bandana, multi-colored shirts, and flair for the spectacular shot. "The Haitian Sensation," his fans called him. His highest world ranking was No. 28 in September 1995. Although he never won a major tournament, he had impressive showings in Grand Slam events, reaching the 1989 French Open quarterfinals (where he lost to eventual champion Michael Chang) and the fourth round of the 1988 U.S. Open. A list of players Agenor has defeated reads like a Who's Who in Tennis, 1976–2006 edition: Noah, Jimmy Connors, Andre Agassi, Mats Wilander, Michael Stich, Sergi Bruguera, Brad Gilbert, Pat Cash, Todd Martin. All except Bruguera, Gilbert, and Martin are Hall of Famers or future Hall of Famers.

Tired of life on the road, Agenor left the tour in 1996. He returned two years later and hoped for a wild card into the main draw of the U.S. Open. After all, he had been a world Top 30 player with some impressive wins and a fan following. But he was not offered a wild card. Instead the USTA offered the wild card to Patrick McEnroe, the younger brother of Hall of Famer John. Patrick McEnroe's world ranking at the time was No. 664; Agenor was No. 275. The decision was rather like Radio City Music Hall declining to book a concert with Johnny Mathis in favor of booking Frank Sinatra *Junior*.

"For Ronald Agenor of Haiti, making a comeback on the international professional tennis tour would prove twice as difficult as it would be for Patrick McEnroe of the United States," he wrote in his 2007 autobiography. "Haiti, the poorest country in the Western Hemisphere, does not even host a satellite or Challenger event. It has no presence in the upper echelon of the international tennis hierarchy that is controlled by Americans, Europeans, and Australians. So in crucial moments, such as when decisions have to be made about awarding wild cards, I would be an outsider."

It should be pointed out that McEnroe refused the unjustly offered wild card. Both he and Agenor lost in the qualifying rounds and missed the U.S. Open. Agenor's point is that he, a Haitian, would never be afforded the type of opportunity that Patrick McEnroe and other white players routinely receive.

Agenor, married with two daughters, has since become an American citizen. Asked if he has experienced other racial slights on the tennis circuit, he recalled that a driver at a tournament in Holland refused to drive him back to his hotel. Courtesy cars at tournaments are customary for players, but they are not permitted to drive them. Agenor also recalled a 1991 match against Connors at the French Open in which he believed the on-court officials were biased against him. "Of course, there were other things that happened, but those things are part of daily life and were not related to tennis," he said. "I feel in some way lucky that I did not grow up with the upfront racism that dominates in the United States, as I was able to focus fully on tennis."

Juan Farrow wishes he could have concentrated entirely on tennis. Considered one of the most talented African Americans to compete in junior tennis, Farrow never made it big as a pro. From age ten, some viewed him as a prodigy. He was the last highly touted junior in Dr. R. Walter Johnson's renowned ATA junior development program. Dr. J used to tell anyone within earshot that Farrow in the junior ranks was a better player, with smoother strokes and more raw talent, than Arthur Ashe had been. But Farrow did not follow in the footsteps of Arthur and Althea. He was a three-time NCAA singles champion and a two-time NCAA doubles champion at Division II Southern Illinois University in Edwardsville. And he defeated John McEnroe in junior tennis before Mac became a superstar and Farrow a what-might-have-been.

So what happened? The Virginia native is not entirely clear about it, but he does not take the blame upon himself. He coaches tennis now in Macon, Georgia. "Everybody was saying, 'I'm going to be the next Arthur Ashe,'" Farrow said in a voice as raspy as Harry Belafonte's, though he's more than thirty years younger. Farrow's raspiness results from yelling and screaming while coaching, he said. Others say Farrow smoked as early as age nine, and a pack a day by age twelve, because smoking relaxed him.

Because of the high praise he routinely received from Dr. J, blacks eagerly anticipated Farrow's arrival at ATA events. Whites openly rooted for him to fail at USTA events. When he competed as the only black junior at USTA tournaments in the still-segregated South, he heard racial taunts from the stands, and his on-court errors were applauded. Arthur and Althea were hardly embraced by competitors and spectators under similar circumstances, but they handled it. Their ability to handle it became an integral part of their legend. Whether or not Farrow's smoking was his way of dealing with the pressure of lofty expectations, nicotine was hardly the stuff of champions.

Farrow denies having an addiction, to nicotine or anything else. Instead, he said vaguely, "problems at home" militated against his pursuit of tennis success. Further, he cited a rift that he said existed between Dr. Johnson and son Bobby Johnson over how much time the doctor spent coaching Farrow compared with the son and who would get to play doubles with Farrow in tournaments. When Farrow was twelve and scheduled to compete in an event in Massachusetts, Dr. J died. The ATA junior development program expired with him. But Farrow became the USTA's No. 1–ranked player in the twelve-and-under category, and he continued to rank among America's top juniors in the fourteen-and-under, sixteen-and-under, and eighteen-and-under groups.

With Dr. J gone and the ATA program a memory, Farrow moved to St. Louis to live with college professor Richard Hudlin and finish school, just as Arthur had done as a teenager in the 1950s. Arthur gave Farrow financial support until an incident that occurred while Farrow attended SIU convinced Arthur that Farrow was too undisciplined to become a champion.

"Arthur went into the men's room to check on Farrow and smelled cigarette smoke," tennis coach Bob Ryland said. "Arthur came out and told Hudlin, 'I can't do anything for him.' Arthur cut him off after that. Remember, Arthur was disciplined. He was brought up that way. He was an army man. He knew that boy was smokin' and decided that Farrow wasn't doing anything to help himself."

Farrow said he simply was not Arthur's type of black man. He thinks Arthur saw him as the type who runs around getting high and fomenting trouble. "If Arthur were around today, James Blake would be his boy. That's the kind of player he wanted." Farrow also does not express a glowing opinion of the otherwise revered Dr. J. "Doc ain't know nothin' about tennis," he said. "He knew about football. He'd sit on the sideline and say, 'Juan, listen to the ball or you ain't goin' to the tournament.' He wouldn't let me play tennis unless I rolled the court." But Dr. Johnson made all his juniors perform menial tasks to instill discipline. Farrow chafed. Althea and Arthur did not.

Without financial support or the kind of early success on the pro circuit that might have attracted a sponsor, Farrow was unable to fulfill his potential. His highest ranking was No. 227 in 1985. He remains a mystery to those who remember him as an amateur. "I'm not sure why he didn't make it," said Rodney Harmon, a Virginia native and former pro. "He was a heck of a talent, though. I played him a couple of times on the satellite tour. In Winston-Salem, North Carolina, I beat him in three sets. That was my biggest win at the time because he was a guy I grew up watching and he was really good."

Once good enough to beat John McEnroe. Once considered a better prospect than Arthur Ashe.

"Lots of things happen to throw a player off track," Harmon said. "You can have injuries, family problems, personal problems, and this sport is so competitive at the professional level that if your game goes off kilter, it's really hard to put it back on track."

Farrow's career ambitions careened so far off track, according to Ryland, that he moved to New York City with the intention of becoming a pimp. But after an acquaintance was shot, Farrow returned to the South and became a tennis coach. However successful he may become as a coach, Farrow will always provoke head-scratching for those who thought he would be the Next Big Thing.

Being labeled as someone who fell short of expectations is, of course, relative. In Arthur's day the top Australian players said he would not become world No. 1 in the pros, as they believed he could have, because he was "too conscious of his celebrity." Yet Arthur had an outstanding career. During Noah's fourteen-year career, people often said he had the tools to be world No. 1 and win more than the one Grand Slam title. Still, he won twenty-three singles titles, sixteen doubles titles, and was ranked as high as No. 3 (in July 1986).

Farrow said of Noah, "He told the world, 'Yeah, I'm up all night partyin'. I ain't tryin' to be No. 1 in the world. I make good money. I'm doin' my thing.'" Phil Williamson, another former pro, regards Noah this way: "He said basically, 'I could be No. 1, but I don't want to make that commitment. I don't want to work that hard.' Being in the Top 5 and enjoying life was fine by him."

Williamson signed his first pro contract at Arthur Ashe's Westchester County home, because Williamson's manager at the time was big on symbolism. Every black player then was compared in some way to Arthur, whether the player invited the comparison or not. Williamson didn't; he just wanted to play tennis. He recalls having two particularly awkward conversations with Arthur, one before and one after his first appearance in the U.S. Open main draw: a first-round loss to Australian John Fitzgerald in 1987. Of the first chat, Williamson said, "I was 22 and just graduated from Columbia University and was playing in my first professional tournament. I was expecting some words of wisdom that would provide instantaneous help, but all Arthur said was, 'Do you realize that you are the only player in a draw of 128 professionals to come out of nowhere?'" Sometime after the loss, Williamson recalled, "We just sat there in a room together. I'm waiting for him to say something, and he clearly wasn't sure of what to say. I could only guess that he wasn't all that impressed with my game. He didn't say that. He didn't really say anything, and I was kind of hoping to hear something."

A 5-8 lefthander, Williamson was similar in stature to Michael Chang, the tenacious 1989 French Open champion. Speed was Williamson's asset, a relative lack of size his drawback. He began playing in Mount Vernon, New York, after a local teaching pro spotted him hitting a tennis ball against a wall. As a ten-year-old he got to hit with Arthur, and a few years later he made his mark in junior tournaments. The son of Jamaican immigrants, Williamson comes from a family of engineers. His brother, Richard, graduated from the Massachusetts Institute of Technology. Phil enrolled in Columbia, where he was the No. 1 singles player, the top-ranked collegiate player in the East, and the Ivy League Player of the Year—a distinction he shares with Harvard brothers James Blake and Thomas Blake.

Williamson holds another distinction: in 1987 he became the only ATA champion in the open era (since 1968) to get a wild card into the U.S. Open qualifying rounds and then qualify for the tournament. Williamson won the ATA men's singles title in 1985, 1987, 1991, and 1997. Three times he played in the U.S. Open's main draw, losing in the first round each time: in 1987 to Fitzgerald, for which he received two computer ranking points and $2,000; in 1991 to Australia's Wally Masur; and in 1993 to Agenor. In five other years he played in the Open qualifying rounds. Tennis also took him to all four Grand Slam events and to the Pan American Games and the Davis Cup, in which he represented Antigua (his grandfather's birthplace).

But like most every black player on the tour in the 1980s and 1990s, Williamson found it difficult to cobble together the funds to stay on the pro circuit. At the 1987 U.S. Open he remembered meeting with a black businessman named Tom Skinner who said he wanted to sponsor the careers of more than a half-dozen black pros, including Williamson, Agenor, Smith, Bryan Shelton, Todd Nelson, Martin Blackman, Paul Wekesa, Yahiya Doumbia, and Malcolm Allen, a San Francisco–based player who once beat Pete Sampras, 6-0, 6-4, in a Challengers event. A meeting was scheduled during the tournament. But the proposal fell through because only two players showed up. "I could only guess," Williamson said, "that the other guys had heard so many times from people saying they would sponsor them, and then nothing would happen."

In 1991 DIS Research, a company based in Westchester County, New York, eager to sponsor the best player from the county, invested in Williamson's career. He hired a coach, Jobe Davis, and began playing the best tennis of his life. "When I started on the pro tour, I was missing some vital information," he said. "I was working too hard physically to get the job done. My coach changed my entire game, opened up my stroke rotation so I wasn't using my arm so much to hit the ball." But when DIS Research went public in 1993 and decided to eliminate what it considered unnecessary expenses, Williamson lost his funding and could no longer pay his coach. "It was so frustrating," he said, "to be at my peak performance and not have the money to go out and play the tournaments."

Williamson reached a career-best singles ranking of No. 294 and career-high in doubles of No. 133. He ran ATA tournaments in New York for nine years and is now the senior teaching pro at the Grand Slam Tennis Center, owned by Hall of Famer Ivan Lendl, in Bedford, New York. He did not become "the next Arthur Ashe." Nor will anyone else. But that won't convince others to stop burdening other young African Americans in the sport, all of whom are works in progress, with high expectations. The latest to face that burden is a teenage southpaw from Chicago who may have become too good too soon.

CHAPTER TWELVE

"It's nice not to have to be a fly in milk"

• • • • • • • • • • •

The kid sure knows how to make an entrance. Onto the court he strode wearing a white Nike cap tilted to the left side with the bill curved, a fluorescent lime green shirt with diagonal stripes in the front and a V-shaped design in the back, black cotton pants with white stripes down the side, snap-off gym pants that an NBA player would wear, blue Nike tennis shoes with white socks that he allowed to droop, and a gold earring in each lobe. He carried a black, orange, and white tennis bag bearing the logo of Head racquets and, before taking his chair to unpack his gear, he nodded slightly toward the spectators applauding him wildly on Court One. "There he is," cried a white female fan, "The Donald!"

Only sixteen years old, handsome and brown-skinned with the hint of a mustache, the kid already had a nickname. And the hyperbolic label of "the future of American men's tennis." And multi-million-dollar endorsement deals with Nike and Head. And his own publicist. The only thing he did not have was a man's game.

The major problem with the scene on the morning of March 22, 2006, in the first round of the NASDAQ-100 Open tournament in

Key Biscayne, Florida, was that Donald Young actually had to play a match. He couldn't just take his bows and walk away. He couldn't tell the crowd he would be back in two years as an adult with a legitimate chance to compete against other men, a legitimate chance to be America's next great tennis champion, a legitimate chance to be the magnet that draws more African-American males to tennis, as Venus and Serena Williams had done for females. Instead Donald played a match against a twenty-three-year-old Argentine named Carlos Berlocq, who was 0-7 as a professional. Berlocq was essentially handpicked for Donald by IMG, the sports management agency that represents him and runs the tournament. IMG gave Donald a wild card into the main draw. If Donald, a boy, could look good against any man in the main draw, it would be Berlocq. So went the company line.

Donald lost, 6-0, 6-0. Man against boy.

Lest you think Donald just had a bad day, consider that in Berlocq's next match, against James Blake, the Argentine lost 6-0, 6-0. Never before in the history of the ATP, which dates to 1972, had a player won a match 6-0, 6-0, only to lose his next match 6-0, 6-0.

Donald got into a position to be plucked before ripeness because, while growing up in Chicago, he dominated the competition, locally and nationally, in twelve-and-under, fourteen-and-under, and sixteen-and-under junior events. The tennis establishment knew about him before 2005, the year he won the Australian Open junior championship and the U.S. National Hardcourts in Kalamazoo, Michigan, and was ranked No. 1 in the world. IMG, enthralled by his potential, signed him in 2004, at age fifteen.

Had IMG not signed him, there is little doubt that Octagon or SFX, the two other major management agencies of tennis players, would have. When Donald won the U.S. Hardcourts again in 2006 after his final-round opponent, Jesse Levine, came down with food poisoning, he had a more impressive junior-tennis resumé than any major American pro star of the past two decades, a list that includes Pete Sampras, Andre Agassi, Jim Courier, and Michael Chang. But winning the U.S. Hardcourts twice is not a passport to success in professional ranks. Chang is the only player in the last twenty years to win the U.S. Hardcourts and then enjoy a stellar pro career.

Donald Young has talent. No one would argue otherwise. He displays fine hands, a soft touch, quick feet, and good instincts on court. He grew to 5 feet 11 inches in 2006, an ideal height for the sport, and his size 13 feet may indicate that the seventeen-year-old has more growing to do. He is the only child of tennis coaches Donald Sr. and Ilona, and the protégé of the Indian-born Suhel Malhotra, a highly respected coach in Chicago. But the decision to rush Donald into the spotlight of major men's tournaments has many observers shaking their heads. Still, his parents say, "We know what we're doing."

"He's always been playing a level above [his age], and this is no different," Donald Young, Sr., said. "I don't think there's anyone out there that wouldn't take these opportunities if they were offered." The opportunity for a son to become a multi-millionaire before he is old enough to vote. The opportunity to have his racquets and strings and every stitch of his tennis wardrobe paid for by a multi-national corporation. The opportunity to have people rave about his potential. The opportunity to have his stylish hat handed to him whenever he tries to step up in class.

Donald ended 2006 with a 0-10 record in ATP men's events. He had not won a set in an ATP match until he took the first set against Novak Djokovic of Serbia, 6-4, in the first round of the 2006 U.S. Open. But Donald faded badly in that match, which he attributed to cramps in his left arm, and lost, 4-6, 6-3, 6-0, 6-1.

"I need to work on my game," Donald said afterward. He speaks softly and without much emotion in interviews, but those close to him say he is effusive and outgoing around other teenagers. "I need to hit a lot of serves [in practice], work on forehands, backhands, volleys. Everything. Just work on my game."

Even the USTA, which is in dire need of new American champions, has been critical of the handling of Donald's career. The USTA does not see his signing a pro contract as the major problem, but rather his being exposed to the major leagues before he is truly ready to compete. In tennis players usually go through the Juniors circuit, the Futures circuit, the Challengers circuit, and finally the main draw of the ATP or WTA Tour.

"We would have preferred to see Donald play Futures events," said Rodney Harmon, the USTA director of men's tennis. "After he won at that level, he could move up and play the Challengers, win at that level, and then move up. When a player skips a level, that's when problems develop. Roger Federer, Rafael Nadal, David Nalbandian, three of the best players in the world—those players didn't skip levels. Donald hasn't put on the performance we think he's capable of producing. But the USTA is not in charge of his schedule. His schedule is done by IMG."

Donald's agent is Gary Swain, whose only other full-time tennis client is John McEnroe. Asked about Young, he said simply, "We're monitoring him and being flexible with his schedule."

The flexibility included canceling a proposed exhibition match against Sampras in Houston after the Key Biscayne debacle. The flexibility included having Donald play in the main draw—as a wild card—and the junior event at Wimbledon and the U.S. Open in 2006. But he not only failed to win a match anywhere against men, he also failed to get past the quarterfinal round in either of the major junior events. In 2006 he began to lose to players at his own experience level, players he used to defeat.

"It's a tricky situation," Harmon said, "because Donald is being offered these opportunities by tournament directors to play in main draws. Other players his age don't get those opportunities."

"They're messing up that boy's head," veteran tennis coach John Wilkerson said. "They're telling him he's already great. Man, he ain't done nothing. As he keeps losing, there's going to be more and more pressure on him to start winning. Those sponsors won't sign him again if he doesn't start winning."

Usually for a black tennis player, finding a sponsor in the first place is the problem. Despite his not experiencing success yet on the men's tour, Donald is the most trumpeted of today's crop of black players—the first generation of blacks in tennis not to have seen Arthur Ashe play in person or on television, or to have met him at all.

As for Althea Gibson, the sport's first black tennis idol, today's players have seen her only on a stamp or in a thirty-second commercial during Black History Month.

While Donald attempts to prove that having so much so soon will not cause the ruination of a potentially fine career, other young blacks in the game are just trying to get noticed.

"Nick Monroe: Profile of a Champion" is the title of a DVD created by the father of a player who could become a star. In 2006 Monroe improved his world singles ranking from No. 571 to No. 297 and his doubles ranking from No. 270 to No. 240. He was ranked No. 1 in the country as a fourteen-year-old, and in the Top 20 nationally in the sixteen-and-under and eighteen-and-under divisions. During his junior career a Phoenix businessman, Dennis Ernst, sponsored him. But the relationship ended when Monroe went to college.

When the current tennis season began, Monroe, a 2004 graduate of the University of North Carolina where he played No. 1 singles, was still searching for a new sponsor. Hence the DVD showing highlights of his career and emphasizing the Good Sportsmanship Award he won at UNC. "You need sixty to seventy thousand dollars a year to stay on the tour if you're going to be an international player," he said. "You pretty much have to be able to play international tournaments to make it in tennis. Three of the four Slams [Wimbledon, Australian Open, French Open] are outside the United States, and so are most of the clay-court tournaments."

Monroe, a slender 5-11, spent much of 2006 playing far from his hometown of Olathe, Kansas. He won Challengers tournaments in Costa Rica, Nigeria, Benin City, India, and San Jose, and reached the finals of events in New Delhi. He also spent the summer playing for the Springfield Lasers of World Team Tennis, the highlight of which was losing a match in a tiebreak to the otherwise retired Sampras. "Just being able to look across the net and see that I'm playing Pete Sampras gave me a taste of what big-time tennis is about," said Monroe, twenty-four. "That's what I'm trying to experience more of."

When Monroe travels, which is most of the time, he is coached by the man who taught him the game at age four, his dad, Ben Monroe, a veritable tennis evangelist. "I'll go to a McDonald's and see some young black kids sitting there, and I'll just walk over and say, 'You all should be playing tennis,'" said Ben Monroe, a full-time coach in Olathe. "Black people simply haven't been exposed to tennis. Give me the third-string players on the bench in boys' and girls' basketball—not the second-string players because they all think they should be playing first-string—and those third-string players would become good in tennis. It's not as expensive a game to learn as people think: racquets, shoes, strings, court. That's it."

Yet tennis is an expensive career.

During a 1998 WTA tournament in Oklahoma City, Ben Monroe drove five hours from Olathe hoping to meet Richard Williams and his daughter Venus, who entered the tournament, to get some advice on how to rear a tennis champion. He waited in the hotel lobby, eventually struck up a conversation with Mr. Williams, and got Nick the job of practice partner for Venus, who won her first professional title at the event.

That begged the question: Has Richard Williams, the father of two daughters who have earned a combined $32 million in prize money, not to mention tens of millions of additional dollars from endorsements, offered to sponsor Nick for a year or two? Have you asked?

"Well, Mr. Williams hasn't seen me or Nick since Oklahoma City," Ben Monroe said. "That's why we came here." Here was the 2006 U.S. Open, where Ben Monroe hoped to meet again with Mr. Williams—he did not—and Nick hoped to slip into the main draw.

Players eligible to receive a wild card into the U.S. Open qualifying rounds had to have a world ranking of No. 285 or lower. Nick Monroe's world ranking at the time was No. 299. Still, he came and hoped that someone would drop out of the quallies, opening a spot for him. No one did. Instead, his credential as a pro player gave him access to the locker room, players' lounge, and practice courts, where he hit with several of the competitors. This, the Monroes believed, was preferable, and cheaper, than spending a week in Ecuador, where Nick would have been the No. 1 seed at a Challengers event. The decision proved wise. At the Open, Nick landed a new racquets deal with Prince. But he is still in search of a major sponsorship.

Scoville Jenkins ended the 2006 season with a world ranking fifty-five points below Nick Monroe's. But Jenkins gets noticed. He won the 2004 U.S. Nationals junior event, earning an automatic wild card into the U.S. Open's main draw and, as luck would have it, a nationally televised match against defending champion Andy Roddick. Even though Roddick rolled to a straight-set win, slamming a 152-mph ace in the process, Jenkins did not quit. The 6-3 Atlanta native with braided hair, tiny sparkling earrings, and a muscular game won himself a following. His fan base expanded at the 2005 Open, where he won a first-round match and took a set off French Open champion Rafael Nadal in a nationally televised second-round match.

"It's really funny to be at a major tournament and hear people whispering, 'Oh my God, that's Scoville Jenkins,' or people will just run up to him with a camera phone and snap his picture or ask him for an autograph," said his father, Scoville D. Jenkins. (The son is Scoville A. Jenkins.) "Tennis hasn't seen anybody yet with the size, power, and athletic ability he brings to the game. He wanted to play basketball at first, but I thought he'd have a better chance of getting to the top if he played tennis. There are a million guys with his kind of athletic ability in basketball."

Scoville Jenkins, only twenty, is still finding his game. His forehand is definitely a weapon. His serve, though inconsistent, could become one. He tends to go for too big a shot during rallies. But in a first-round loss at the 2006 U.S. Open to Swedish veteran Jonas Bjorkman, 7-5, 6-4, 6-4, he offered enough flashes of excellence to give himself and his fans hope. "The guys in the Top 10 have something mentally over everyone else," he said. "The difference is in how you play the big points. With experience, you get a better understanding of what to do. I feel like I definitely belong in this atmosphere. I want to be the next great tennis player from America."

It helped Scoville to grow up in Atlanta, where tennis courts are as conspicuous as basketball courts are in other cities where blacks are in the majority. His parents are avid players. His mother, Carol, a hair stylist, competes in the Atlanta Lawn Tennis Association, the country's largest recreational tennis league with eighty thousand dues-paying members. After Donald Young turned pro, his family moved to Atlanta and his parents opened a tennis center, where he and Scoville can play a friendly match whenever their schedules allow.

Jenkins's potential and name recognition in the United States got him a wild card into the 2006 Open. But his father, a former producer at the Weather Channel who travels with Scoville full time, said the sport is not ready for his son. "They're not used to Scoville coming into the locker room with the braids and the earrings; change is hard," the father said. "When we go to Europe, they all look at black Americans the way they see us in films and on TV. They expect him to be pulling out a gun or some [marijuana]. They expect him to walk around sayin', 'What's up, motherfucker?' There's no fan reaction to Scoville when he plays abroad. They know who he is, but there's no reaction."

In 2007 Jenkins will stay on the Challengers circuit until he gets his ranking high enough to compete in the main draw of ATP tournaments. Already he has reached a level where he gets paid to wear Nike clothes and shoes, use Wilson racquets, and pay someone to string his racquets. That is the same level his friend, Lesley Joseph, is trying to reach.

A three-year player at the University of Georgia, Joseph joined the pro tour full time in 2004. A solidly built left-hander, he has been ranked as high as No. 240 in the world thanks to a string of good results in Challengers events, mostly in South America and Australia. But the son of Haitian immigrants has struggled on the circuit since parting with his coach, former Haitian Davis Cupper Ronald Agenor, for financial reasons. Joseph ended 2006 ranked No. 431.

"Lesley did not get the financial support he deserved at a critical time of his career," Agenor said. "I would coach Lesley again on the condition that he gets the necessary financial support to sustain the cost of coaching, traveling, and everything else that comes with it."

Joseph, twenty-five, grew up in Rock Hill, South Carolina, where his parents, Phebe and Samuel, migrated after living in Haiti, Florida, and New York. His parents have taken out loans and scrimped and saved to support their son's tennis ambitions, and Joseph himself pours virtually every dollar he earns back into his tennis. Playing almost exclusively on the Challengers tour, he has found staying afloat to be his biggest challenge. He has endorsement deals in the low five figures with Volkl racquets, a German company, and Pacific Sportswear. "It's good to get some free stuff to alleviate some of the costs," said Joseph, who buys his own Nike shoes online. "Tennis is expensive enough already."

When plotting his schedule, Joseph invariably selects events marked +H, which means the tournament provides lodging for the players. Food is available for players at the tournament, leaving Joseph responsible for his own airfare. During the 2006 U.S. Open, for which he received a wild card into the qualifying round, he stayed with relatives in Brooklyn. After the Open he hit the Challengers circuit in Brazil, Ecuador, Spain, Mexico, and Australia.

Joseph lost his only match in the Open qualifying rounds, but on one brilliant point he displayed his tenacity: he fell and lost his racquet after hitting a lunging backhand volley at net. His opponent, Ilia Bozoljac of Serbia, rifled a forehand into a seemingly open court only to have Joseph spear an off-balance volley winner. Even Bozoljac applauded. But this highlight point occurred in a match watched by dozens, on an outer court, not inside Arthur Ashe Stadium before an audience of twenty thousand-plus, with millions more watching on television. Joseph could use the kind of break Scoville Jenkins got: a match against a "name" player on national television where he could show his stuff. Meanwhile he continues to grind away.

The women's tour became an emotional grind in 2006 for Angela Haynes, a feisty left-hander who grew up with Venus and Serena Williams in Compton, California. Usually Haynes laughs easily and is one of the better interviews on the tennis tour. A 5-8, 145-pound lefthander, she has the size and athletic ability to become a factor on the circuit. But she was not herself in 2006. Haynes lost her brother, Dontia, a San Diego State tennis player, in a motorcycle accident near the campus on September 23, 2005. He was twenty-three. "I've been injured upstairs," Haynes said after she and her partner, Neha Uberoi, lost a first-round women's doubles match at the 2006 U.S. Open. "It's been tough for me to get my priorities in order. Tennis is definitely second for me. I took some time off."

But in tennis, players who take time off—other than a stoppage of six consecutive months because of an injury—see their world ranking plummet. Haynes said she came back on tour even though she was in no condition to compete mentally, to try to protect her ranking. She played poorly and her ranking dropped anyway—below No. 300. "My brother was my best friend," she said. "My father was like, 'Use your brother to give you strength.' But I couldn't. It was depressing me." Around her neck she wore a gold pendant with a picture of Dontia (pronounced Don-tay). "He goes everywhere with me," she said.

Because of her unease, Haynes has been unable to build on the early successes in her career. She reached the third round of the 2004 U.S. Open, defeating No. 22 seed Magdalena Maleeva of Bulgaria. Her best match came against a supersized Serena in the first round of Wimbledon in 2005. Haynes lost, 6-7, 6-4, 6-2, in a taut two-and-a-half-hour marathon. "If I had won," said Haynes, ranked No. 104 at the time, "it could have changed my whole life. Man, I don't know what would have happened if I had won that match."

She's still wondering. "I'm trying to get back to where I was mentally and physically in that match, because that was my best tennis," she said. "I'm still trying to find that same energy. No matter if I'm playing Serena or the No. 1000 player in the world, I need to play with that same kind of energy."

Haynes began playing at age three after her father, Fred, a former baseball player in the San Francisco Giants organization, bought her a racquet with rainbow-colored strings at Toys "R" Us. As an eight-year-old she was ranked No. 1 among southern California girls under ten. Now twenty-two, Haynes is on a comeback trail. She did not qualify for the main draw in any Grand Slam events in 2006 after qualifying for each of them the year before. She ended the 2006 season ranked No. 175 and with renewed hope because of a stint in World Team Tennis in the summer, where she earned team Most Valuable Player honors with the Delaware Smash. That experience, she hoped, would help her get her tennis groove back in 2007.

Whereas Haynes made headlines in major tournaments in years past, Shenay Perry and Jamea Jackson did so in 2006. Perry, twenty-two, ended the season as the highest-ranking African-American female player, No. 43 in the world (five slots ahead of Venus, fifty-two ahead of Serena). She was also the last American standing at Wimbledon in 2006. She reached the fourth round, her best showing in a Grand Slam event, after Venus, Agassi, Roddick, James Blake, et al., succumbed in the worst U.S. showing at Wimbledon since 1911. The weight of carrying Old Glory proved a bit much for the still-maturing Perry, who lost 6-2, 6-0 to Russia's Elena Dementieva. "I think it got to me a little bit," said Perry, who lives in Coral Springs, Florida. "I think when anyone's thrown into a position for the first time, and being the last American, it is a little nerve-racking."

The home-schooled Perry grew up in Washington, D.C., and learned tennis in a public parks program. "I was pretty much the only girl playing tennis in the neighborhood," she said. "I had a social life, but it was a little bit different because I didn't get to do a lot of other things. I was always playing tennis." The family moved to Florida when Shenay was eleven to develop her tennis game. She trained at the Rick Macci Academy before moving to the Nick Bolletieri Academy. She wavered between wanting a pro tennis career and studying to be a pediatrician. So conflicted was she that she did not take advantage of opportunities to play in international junior tournaments. But in 2000 she turned pro, inspired by a woman with whom many players her age are unfamiliar: Althea Gibson. "She was a great pioneer who I'd heard about from my parents," Perry said. "She opened the door for African-American women in this sport." Perry is in search of her first WTA Tour title, but she is healthy again after a

2005 bout with knee tendonitis. She ended 2006 with her highest ranking ever.

So did Jamea Jackson, at No. 45. Three inches shorter than the 5-7 Perry, Jackson plays a more athletic game. No surprise considering her father is former New Orleans Saints cornerback Ernest Jackson. "It's nice to have someone in the family who understands what I'm going through and how hard it is," said Jackson, who grew up in Atlanta. "I used to be really bad-tempered when I started playing at ten. Every time I threw my racquet on the court, my parents sat me down for a week. They didn't allow any misconduct on court. I got it out of my system at a young age."

That doesn't mean Jackson isn't a fighter on court. The 20-year-old staged an impressive comeback from 2-5 down in the final set to beat Ashley Harkleroad in a three-and-a-half-hour match at the 2006 NASDAQ-100 Open. She credits her Brazilian coach Rodrigo Nascimento with improving her fitness and mental toughness. "We do a lot of physical work," she said, "so I'm really competing on every point, being aggressive, really taking it to my opponent." She has to play that way: her listed weight of 113 pounds, which makes her among the smallest women on tour, appears to be accurate.

Jackson showed a strong will in May 2006, leading a depleted U.S. Federation Cup team (without injured stars Venus, Serena, and Lindsay Davenport) to a 3-2 first-round win over Germany. Jackson went 2-0, winning her matches against Anna-Lena Groenefeld and Martina Muller. In June 2006 she reached her first WTA Tour final in Birmingham, England, playing the role of giant killer. She defeated No. 10 seed Klara Koukalova of the Czech Republic, No. 8 Jelena Jankovic of Serbia, No. 4 Elena Likhovtseva of Russia, and No. 1 seed Maria Sharapova before losing to No. 2 seed Vera Zvonareva of Russia, 7-6, 7-6. Jackson had four set points in the first set and rallied from a 0-4 deficit to push Zvonareva in the second set.

With Serena and Venus a less frequent presence on the circuit, Jackson said it's good to have other black women like Haynes and Perry to socialize with on the road, especially as the WTA Tour becomes increasingly global with fewer events in the United States (just eleven of fifty-six in 2006). "It always helps to have a support system, someone else who's black around," said Jackson, who lives in Bradenton, Florida. "When you grow up in the South, you're used to being around other black people. So when you go on the road, it's nice not to have to be a fly in milk."

A couple of fly sisters from Miami, Ahsha and Tiya Rolle, joined them on the road in 2007. Ahsha, at twenty-one is a year older and the only palindrome in pro tennis—her first name is spelled the same backward and forward. In her Grand Slam debut at the 2006 U.S. Open, she lost a tough first-round match to Alona Bondarenko of Ukraine, 6-4, 6-4. There were as many spectators on Court 8 talking about Ahsha's fashion sense as about her big serve and classic one-handed backhand. That's because she wore a white top with the Brooklyn Bridge outlined on the back, the creation of a friend who designs outfits for the ABC show *Dancing with the Stars*. Rolle has a former star for a coach in Lori McNeil and two more stars, Venus and Serena, as sources of inspiration. She grew up watching the Williams sisters on television.

Ahsha did quite well after the Open, winning a Challengers event in Albuquerque, New Mexico, and reaching the finals of another Challengers tournament in Troy, Alabama. Ahsha ended the year ranked No. 129 in the world, Tiya No. 737. If Ahsha improves her volleys, she should be able to crack the Top 100 in 2007. "I like tennis," she said, "because I like competing. I like to create new shots and try new things on the court." She also relies on old-school spirituality: she brings a Bible onto the court, which she often reads during changeovers. "I read the Bible every day anyway; it's my favorite book," she said. "I like to put some tennis notes in there, things I remind myself to do during a match. And sometimes I read Psalms 27."

Psalms 27 begins, "The Lord is my light and my salvation—whom shall I fear? The Lord is the stronghold of my life—of whom shall I be afraid?"

CHAPTER THIRTEEN

"We need you out here"

• • • • • • • • • • •

Leslie Allen had just wrapped up a spirited game of tennis on a sun-kissed afternoon in Central Park in New York, a former champion on the pro tour fine-tuning her skills for the 2006 U.S. Open, where she would be entered in the senior doubles competition. That's when a visitor, someone without knowledge of or regard for tennis history, happened by. "The guy was black, kind of a park urchin," Allen said, "and he walked over and said, 'Oh, you're gonna be like Venus and Serena.'"

It has been more than a quarter-century since Allen made history as the first African-American woman to win a tournament in the open era, the Avon Championships of Detroit in February 1981, long before Venus and Serena Williams came along to make tennis hip for blacks. Allen said she recently showed a boy in his preteens a picture of herself in tennis attire on a magazine cover. "Aww, that's not you; that's Photoshop," the boy said, referring to the computer software that can be used to do such things as doctor a photograph or create a phony magazine cover. Because it was not Venus or Serena in tennis mode on the cover, the young boy, just like the grown man in Central Park, could not conceive of the image being real. For those people, tennis did not exist as a subject of interest before the Williams sisters began hoisting glistening trophies on the world's grandest courts.

What will happen if Venus and Serena's impact on the game continues to erode? Neither was a factor in any of the Grand Slam events in 2006. If the sisters continue to spend more time away from the pro tour because of injuries or indifference, will the legions of tennis fans they created disappear as well?

"When they leave, will women's tennis be boring?" asked tour pro Angela Haynes. "I don't know. Once they're gone, it's hard to say how many black fans that started watching ten years ago will continue to watch, because who else is bringing that flash to the game? Who else except [Spanish star Rafael] Nadal? Venus and Serena get the credit for making tennis hip because they were the first ones in this generation to do it. We're always going to be after them."

Will Donald Young have to live up to the monicker "the future of American tennis" and win major championships to sustain black interest in the sport? Will James Blake have to take the next big step—from Top 10 in the world to Grand Slam tournament winner and contender for world No. 1—to captivate black sports fans the way Venus and Serena have for the past decade? It may not even be reasonable to expect any other tennis player to have the kind of cultural, national, and worldwide impact that Serena and Venus have had.

"Venus and Serena brought a whole new TV audience to tennis, and I don't think that audience stays without them," their former coach Dave Rineberg said. "Tennis isn't getting the same TV ratings to watch Clijsters play Henin. They're not drawing the same crowds to watch Dementieva. Venus and Serena are still the most popular players in the United States, and they're still the top draws in the world."

But of late they have not played top-drawer tennis. Neither Venus nor Serena won a tournament in 2006. That had not happened since 1997. At the end of the 2006 season, the world rankings next to Venus's and Serena's names were completely foreign to tennis fans:

Venus: 48
Serena: 95

A peculiar mix of injuries, indifference, and outside interests has ended a tennis dynasty. Whether the dynasty can be rebuilt may not depend entirely on the sisters themselves. A new crop of women pros from Eastern Europe and China—names like Kuznetsova, Myskina, Petrova, Vaidisova, Li, and Zheng—are playing the game with the kind of hunger, determination, and spirit—though not the same degree of athleticism—that Venus and Serena once displayed. Some tennis people don't believe the Williams sisters will ever again be dominant on the WTA Tour, because their success raised the bar to a level they would now find difficult to reach.

"Richard Williams built two champions, but he didn't build two champions with longevity," New York–based coach Phil Williamson said. "He told the world that they weren't going to be the typical tennis players. He was right. They play tennis by the numbers. They're not instinctive players. When players who are not instinctive take a lot of time off the tour, it's harder for them to get it all back. Venus and Serena are superior athletes but moderate tennis players. The edge was their athletic ability. Now the other players are better athletes. It's more about tennis now."

Others believe that Venus at twenty-six and Serena at twenty-five have the requisite tennis skills. They simply need to get away from the paparazzi and get back to work. "They're still young enough and talented enough to play great tennis," former tour pro Rodney Harmon said. "Have fame and fortune defeated them? I would say fame and fortune are like drugs, and the adrenaline rush you get from winning Grand Slam tournaments and being a celebrity has great allure. They still want to be recognized as great tennis players, not as young women who used to be great tennis players. They have a lot of pride. They don't like losing to players they shouldn't lose to."

Perhaps, as Georgia-based coach Juan Farrow has suggested, the Williams sisters have satisfied their hunger for tennis riches. "Tennis-wise, they're not living up to their potential," he said. "But, hey, you've got everything you want in the world. Who says you just have to be a tennis player? Maybe they only want to play once a month."

"They can be No. 1 and No. 2 again," Houston-based coach John Wilkerson said. "But it's up to them. Will they pay the price to do it? Are they willing?"

Are they willing to work at tennis for four hours before lunch and four hours afterward, day after day after day, as they did before achieving fame and fortune? "It's their call," Miami-based coach Kim Sands said. "It's up to those two women." If Venus and Serena find the task too daunting, or no longer interesting, there is at least a pipeline of young talent in tennis through which the next black champions could spring.

"Just wait a few years," said the father of tour pro Scoville Jenkins. "Players like Scoville, Gael Monfils, and Phillip Simmonds are going to dominate this sport because of their athleticism. Young, fast, quick, good hands. They have a flair for the game, like the brothers playing in the NBA."

Jenkins, Monfils, and Simmonds are all above six feet tall, with the lanky and long-limbed strength commonly seen in an NBA arena. All three played nearly as much basketball as tennis during their childhood, but chose courts of clay, carpet, grass, and cement instead of hardwood. "Tennis is better," said Simmonds, "because in tennis I always get to take the last shot. There's no coach telling me I have to pass the ball with the game on the line. Nobody can keep me out of the game or on the bench. There aren't too many variables. Once you're on the court, you control your own destiny."

No one any longer is keeping blacks off the men's or women's tours because of race, as was the case when Althea and Arthur prevailed. Those odious barriers to black progress in tennis have been dismantled. Programs exist today in the United States and around the world aimed at sowing the seeds of young talent, cultivating it, and encouraging it to full flower.

There is indeed a pipeline of black talent in tennis, but it is neither as wide nor as long as it should be. Critics fault the USTA for taking a wait-and-see approach toward young talent in general, black talent in particular, instead of establishing more inner-city tennis programs to attract youngsters who recognize Venus and Serena and are inspired by their example, but have no place to play tennis themselves. "The USTA seems to argue, 'Why spend more money on player development when we don't know the result?'" Williamson said. "The USTA Player Development Program does not really encourage players. The USTA just sits back and waits for the cream to rise to the top. And when those players rise, the USTA will take credit for them."

Still, a black tennis pipeline exists. The Rolle sisters, Ahsha and Tiya, are coming. So are Asia Muhammad, Brittany Augustine, Jewel Peterson, and Megan Bradley. Timothy Nielly is also coming. In 2005 he defeated Donald Young in the Easter Bowl final in Miami—the first time two black teenagers faced each other for a major junior title. Already here are Shenay Perry, Jamea Jackson, and Angela Haynes. Still out there battling are veterans Chanda Rubin, Mashona Washington, and Alexandra Stevenson.

And it so happens that Young is not the only African-American left-handed prodigy from Chicago. Evan King, a fifteen-year-old with smooth strokes and a precocious game, is building a resumé of championships in his age group. He went from teething to tennis at age two, and he is coached by Richie Gray at Chicago's Midtown Tennis Club. Time will tell if King attracts the same level of corporate interest as Young, the same chorus of adult voices Young heard that tell a boy he's ready to compete against men. And if King hears the chorus, time will tell if the boy's parents are protective enough to say, "Thanks, but he's not ready yet."

Or whether King's coach can persuade the parents to say it. Coaches have long been the unsung stars among blacks in tennis, the nurturers, the father or mother figure, the patient yet hard-driving teacher, the strategist. The list of coaches responsible for creating champions, near champions, and lifelong devotees of the sport is voluminous, impossible to record in total. But people such as Gray in Chicago; John Wilkerson in Houston; Ernie Peterson (the father of Jewel Peterson), Branch Curington, and Torrey Hawkins in Atlanta; Willis Thomas, Jr., in Washington, D.C.; Bob Davis, Arvelia Myers, and Bob Ryland in New York City; Ben Monroe in Kansas; Arthur and Lex Carrington in Amherst, Massachusetts; and Bill Johnson in Philadelphia are representative of a much larger group without whom black achievement and progress in tennis would not have been possible.

Johnson, now deceased, was a retired bus driver in Philadelphia who rounded up local youngsters, anyone eager to learn, and drove them to a single court in Fairmount Park, where he taught them the game, eight children per session. Traci Green was among those who emerged from what she called "a low-cost or no-cost program." For Green, now twenty-nine, tennis has been a part of her life ever since.

"Tennis wasn't that cool when I started playing," said Green, who began at age ten. "I went to a predominantly white private school, so I didn't get the questions like, 'Why do you play tennis?' Everyone there played tennis." Just not as well as Green. She dominated in local tournaments and at age twelve received a scholarship to the Arthur Ashe Youth Tennis Center in Philadelphia. The building did not just have Arthur's name on it. He was involved, taking the kids to tennis camps in Florida or to the U.S. Open. He also brought promising black youngsters from around the country to Philadelphia for developmental camps and tennis exhibitions. At one exhibition when Green was fourteen, her family hosted Venus, then eleven, and Serena, then ten.

"I remember being amazed to see them hitting the ball so well," Green said with a chuckle. "They were so good and so young, and they were black. I wasn't used to seeing other black girls playing tennis. I was in national junior tournaments in my age group, and I would be in the group photos with 128 kids. There would be this one black dot in the picture. That was me."

An attractive caramel-skinned woman who wears her hair in dreadlocks, Green was conflicted as a teen about whether to bypass college for the pros. "I decided to go to college because of Arthur Ashe," she said. "He used to stress that education made all the difference in the world." Green played tennis at the University of Florida, winning a national championship in her sophomore year and earning a degree in communications. She competed in every Grand

Slam event on the junior level except Wimbledon and played Challengers events on the pro tour. But academics and coaching became her passions. Following the footsteps of her mother, a professor of kinesiology at Temple University, and the advice of Arthur, Green enrolled in a master's program at Temple and became a volunteer coach of the women's team.

Since then she has earned a master's in sports administration, enrolled in a Ph.D. program in education at Temple, and become the school's head women's tennis coach. "Do I make a conscious effort to recruit African Americans?" Green asked rhetorically. "The good ones. As long as they can excel academically, I can help them improve their tennis." During the 2006–2007 academic year she was one of only four blacks employed as a head tennis coach of a Division I team. The others were Tony Minnis of the Louisiana State University women's team, Mark Riley of the University of Pennsylvania men's team, and Bryan Shelton of the Georgia Tech University women's team. Along with a paucity of black coaches at the Division I level, a problem exists at some historically black colleges and universities where white international players are being recruited to try to win conference titles, reducing the chances for black student-athletes to play.

In the mid-1990s the University of Miami had two black head coaches. Both were former touring pros: Kim Sands for the women, Rodney Harmon for the men. "Even at a lot of the major programs, there's not a lot of pay for head coaches," Harmon said in accounting for the paucity of black tennis coaches. In 2005 Fresno State University, a Division I school, advertised for an assistant tennis coach's position that paid $15,000 per year. Even if the head coach's salary were twice as high, that is considerably less than someone could earn as a coach with the USTA. "I definitely think a black college coach has to be overqualified," Green said. "Look at Bryan Shelton. He was on the pro tour for years and graduated from Georgia Tech, and he still had to fight for his position."

All Shelton has done since returning to his alma mater is turn the women's program around. Seven appearances in the NCAA tournament in his first seven years, compared to zero appearances before he arrived, and two Atlantic Coast Conference championships, compared to none previously. His calm, clearheaded approach to teaching is likely to influence many high school stars to play for him, especially considering that college players are allowed to compete in Challengers events during the summer, and a movement is afoot to allow them for the first time to accept prize money without jeopardizing their amateur status.

Shelton, now forty-one, received a tennis scholarship to Georgia Tech in 1984 after a bittersweet stint in the junior ranks. The Huntsville, Alabama, native enjoyed the ATA experience of meeting other black tennis players his age, but he sometimes got the cold shoulder, or worse, at white-run junior events. "When I was thirteen I won a tournament at the Birmingham [Alabama] Country Club, and the next year I wasn't invited back," he said. "I had another bad experience at the Bellmeade Country Club in Nashville at a national sixteen-and-under tournament. It was just a rude, uncomfortable atmosphere because of most of the competitors and their families." But he persevered in large part because of the encouragement of his parents who so believed in his talent that they sometimes wouldn't pay bills on time to make sure he had money for tennis lessons.

Although the players Shelton now coaches had no contact with Arthur Ashe, they come in direct contact with someone who was profoundly influenced by him. "I kind of patterned my behavior after his," said Shelton, whose calm cadences evoke memories of Ashe. "I used to use his AMF Head Racquet. A lot of what I accomplished in tennis was because of him." Shelton became an All-American with the Yellow Jackets and earned a degree in industrial engineering before hitting the pro circuit. In 1988 he qualified for the first of his six appearances in the Wimbledon main draw. He had the misfortune of drawing Boris Becker, then a two-time champion, in the first round. "I was too nervous to play well, but it was a tremendous boost to my career," he said. The biggest boost occurred at the 1990 U.S. Open, when he took the first set from a thirty-eight-year-old Jimmy Connors in a nationally televised second-round night match. Connors won the match in four sets, but Shelton learned that he could compete well on the tour. "From that point on, there wasn't a stage in the world where I felt in awe," he said.

When Shelton won the 1991 Hall of Fame Championships on the grass in Newport, Rhode Island, he became the first African American since Arthur to win an ATP Tour event. He repeated as the Newport champion in 1992, reached an ATP final in Atlanta in 1993, and won a pair of doubles titles: the 1994 Mexican Open with Francisco Montana and the 1997 Australian Hardcourt with future Hall of Famer Patrick Rafter.

There were enough blacks on the pro circuit at the time that Shelton became part of a support group at the Grand Slam events that included Zina Garrison, Lori McNeil, Katrina Adams, Nduka Odizor, Todd Nelson, and Roger Smith. "When one of us had a match, the others would show up to cheer that player on," he said. "We would go out to dinner together. We would just keep each other going, saying things like, 'We need you out here.'"

Shelton's highest world ranking was No. 55 in 1992. He made his mark on the pro tour and brought pride to black fans seeking a player to support after Arthur's retirement. Still, he believes he could have accomplished more. "I had the talent, but I lacked a little bit of confidence to really get myself into the Top 20 or the Top 10," he said. After he tired of chasing rankings points and prize money on the tour, he coached MaliVai Washington, the 1996 Wimbledon finalist, then became a USTA national coach working with juniors in the Southeast.

The Shelton resumé includes wins over Andre Agassi, Richard Krajicek, Todd Martin, and Thomas Muster, and a 1993 French Open finals appearance in mixed doubles with McNeil, making them the first black pair to play for the championship in Paris. In 1998 Venus and Justin Gimelstob, a white player from New Jersey, won the French Open mixed doubles title.

Back then it seemed as if Venus and Serena would win titles forever. But neither Williams sister won a tournament in 2006. And little was expected from Serena at the 2007 Australian Open. She had entered the year's first Grand Slam event as an unseeded player and ranked No. 81 in the world, having lost to the unheralded Sybille Bammer of Austria the previous week in a tune-up tournament in Tasmania. Nevertheless Serena beat the 34-to-1 odds and won her eighth major title and third Aussie Open championship, proving again that when she is fully committed to tennis she has no peer.

Recapturing her dominant form of 2002 and 2003, Serena overwhelmed top-seeded Maria Sharapova, 6-1, 6-2, in the final. Her lethal returns of second serves forced Sharapova to err more than usual on first serves. With each round during the Australian fortnight, she shed rust and moved with more alacrity and conviction. Her court coverage in the final match played as large a role as her keen shot-making in defusing Sharapova's power game. On championship point, Serena pounded a backhand winner and threw her racquet into the air before falling onto her back on the court. Her two-year absence from the winner's circle was over. "I'm here to stay," Serena said. But she had said much the same about her commitment to tennis after winning the 2005 Aussie Open, only to be sidetracked by outside interests and injuries. With Serena it is always best to wait and see.

Venus missed the 2007 Australian Open because of an injured left wrist. In the trophy presentation Serena lent poignancy to the proceedings by thanking another family member. "Most of all I would like to dedicate this win to my sister, who's not here," Serena said. "Her name is Yetunde. I just love her so much. I said a couple of days ago if I win this it's going to be for her. So thanks, 'Tunde."

For a family as tight-knit and insular as the Williamses, the loss of a relative can be particularly devastating. On September 14, 2003, one week after the U.S. Open, which Venus and Serena missed because of injuries, their half-sister, Yetunde Price, the eldest of Oracene Price's daughters, was shot in the back of the head in Compton while in the passenger seat of an SUV. The driver, her boyfriend, was the intended target, according to the police report. Yetunde Price, mother of three, owner of a hair salon in the neighborhood, a registered nurse, and a personal assistant to Venus and Serena, died at Long

Beach Memorial Medical Center. She was thirty-one. That it took more than two and a half years for anyone to be sentenced in the killing undoubtedly added to the Williams family's trauma.

"The glue that held the family together" is how Venus described Yetunde, a frequent presence at courtside at her sisters' matches. At the 2003 Wimbledon semifinals, Yetunde was credited with leading a family intervention in the players' locker room during a one-hour rain delay, which convinced Venus to continue playing despite an abdominal injury after she had lost the first set to Clijsters. When the match resumed on Centre Court, Venus played through the pain and won, 4-6, 6-3, 6-1.

The divorce of Mr. Williams and Ms. Price on October 29, 2002, also brought pain to the family, though the parents had been separated for eighteen months amid allegations, albeit not publicly confirmed, of spousal abuse. The parents live in Palm Beach Gardens, Florida, but in separate homes. "I was very honest with my children that a reconciliation would not happen," Ms. Price said. "They've accepted our divorce and love us, as we both love them. Richard and I will continue to work together for the good of our girls, and I truly wish him well."

Mr. Williams and Ms. Price remain the coaches of record for Venus and Serena, though both have always been in a supervisory role at practices. Wade Maguire, the hitting coach, is the strategist and tactician. The parents have not sat side by side at a Venus or Serena match in years. The scene in the family box at the 2006 U.S. Open was typical of what has existed since the separation: the Williams/Price women—Oracene; Lyndrea, a singer and actress; Isha, an attorney and singer who has four college degrees; and Venus, who withdrew from the tournament with a right wrist injury—sat beside Kerrie Brooks, Venus's and Serena's athletic trainer, and Keven Davis, their financial adviser. To find Richard during one of Serena's matches, you had to roam the tennis center, as he did. "I don't want to talk about Serena," he said during a changeover in her first-round match. "I don't want to talk about anything."

"The girls have basically taken Oracene's side," Dave Rineberg said. "You never see Richard with the family at courtside. Richard is not really prominent anymore because the public has lost favor with him, and they realize that just about everything he said was basically to manipulate the public. The press won't even interview him anymore. Richard sits by himself in the stands now. Venus and Serena will always respect him: it was his vision, his plan that got them to where they are today. They haven't rejected him. But they've definitely sided with their mother."

Several factors—injuries, family hardship, relative inactivity, and the overall improvement of the other top players—have led to the end of Venus's and Serena's dominance. Justine Henin of Belgium, the winner of five Grand Slam titles, says the success of the Williams sisters spurred her desire to become stronger and fitter. "I lost to Venus in the [2001] Wimbledon final, 6-0 in the third set. She was just in so much better condition than I was at that time. I knew that I needed to be more fit." Listed at 5-5 and 126 pounds, considerably smaller than either Williams sister, Henin hired a personal trainer and added punch to her serves and ground strokes. Each of her five Grand Slam titles has come since her Wimbledon loss to Venus. She reached world No. 1 in the rankings on October 20, 2003.

Amelie Mauresmo, the Frenchwoman who routinely lost to Venus and Serena earlier in her career, made weight training and cardiovascular work more of a priority to close the gap. She rose to world No. 1 on September 20, 2004, and won her first two Grand Slam titles in 2006, the Australian Open and Wimbledon. "I used to be not as confident when I competed against them," she said, referring to the Williams sisters. "They're such great players. But I think as hard as I've worked to get better, I'm more confident now." Her three-set ouster of Serena at the 2006 U.S. Open proved that.

Although both Venus and Serena say they will continue to compete on the pro tour, they also have branched out to form the Williams Sisters Tour, which features an exhibition match between the sisters, musical performances, an appearance at a local school, and a fund-raising effort. Williams Sisters Tour events have been successful in such non-WTA tour cities as Atlanta, Seattle, Denver, and Charlotte.

On December 5, 2006, the sisters visited the New Orleans Arena to raise money for Gulf Coast residents victimized by Hurricane Katrina and to benefit Ronald McDonald House Charities. Before the tennis match, rhythm and blues singers Irma Thomas, a New Orleans native, and Marques Houston performed. The fund-raiser was of vital importance to the sisters, because Richard Williams grew up in Shreveport, and because an inordinate number of those left behind to fend for themselves, or who perished, in the wake of Katrina were African Americans. "It's a disgrace what happened to those people, how they didn't get the help they needed," Serena said. "We just wanted to do something to help."

Oracene Price, meanwhile, had long expressed a desire to see her daughters visit Africa to hold tennis clinics, as Arthur and Althea used to do, and inspire people on that continent in a more tangible way than their pro tennis pursuits have allowed. Oracene and Serena did exactly that, spending ten days in Senegal and Ghana in West Africa in November 2006 (the injured Venus did not go). "I felt that I was finally able to go home; I just felt real comfortable there," said Serena, who gave tennis clinics, took part in an immunization campaign, and visited schools. She was given a plot of land in Senegal by President Abdoulaye Wade, and she promised to pay for the building of a school on that land, a gesture inspired by Oprah Winfrey's funding of a leadership academy for girls in Johannesburg, South Africa, which opened in January 2007. Such a humanitarian gesture, if it comes to pass, would be a crowning example of celebrities using their fame and influence in the right way. Not only would such an act of altruism inspire youth, it could also inspire other professional athletes, particularly black athletes who sometimes seem unsure of what to do with their money and celebrity status, to follow suit. If the Williams sisters, who have already inspired a generation of young African Americans to take up tennis or pay attention to the game, gradually step away from it to take a more active role in humanitarian causes, who could rightly argue against it?

Afterword

I'M EIGHTY-SEVEN YEARS OLD, so I've seen a lot of tennis. I was a champion too. But you probably never heard of me because I'm black, and they didn't let us play in the big leagues during my prime. I played in the ATA—the black league. We had a lot of great players. We could have been champs in the big leagues. I won the ATA singles in 1955 and 1956. When Arthur Ashe was twelve he told me after I won the ATA, "You're my hero. I want to be just like you." In 1959 I was the first black man to play pro tennis, playing against Pancho Gonzales, Bobby Riggs, Don Budge, Frank Parker. Great players.

I was born in Chicago. My parents, Robert Ryland, Sr., and Gussie Gibbs, came from Alabama. They had to leave Alabama because my father was Irish and my mother was black. They went to Chicago because no interracial couple could live in Alabama. Man, you'd get killed for that down there. My mother had tuberculosis and died when I was two. My father sent me to Mobile to live with my grandmother.

When I was eight, my father sent me a racquet. He taught tennis and he wanted me to play. I played in Brooklyn Park, the black park in Mobile. Yeah, there were black parks and white parks. Everything was segregated. But the black park had clay courts. When I was twelve, I went back to Chicago because my father had remarried. I played tennis before school and after school. The other black kids weren't really playing tennis. But I loved it.

I won the Illinois state high school tournament in 1939, the first black kid to do that. I beat Chris Evert's father, Jimmy Evert, in the final. I went into the army and was in special services during World War II, and then went to Wayne State University in Detroit and was one of the first black men to play in the NCAA tournament. In 1945 I lost in the quarterfinals. In '46 I lost in the third round to Bob Falkenburg of USC. Two years later Falkenburg won Wimbledon. Falkenburg could play at Wimbledon. He was white. I wasn't. You could be angry about it, but so what? Anger will kill you.

In 1944 I played in a mixed doubles exhibition in Harlem with another ATA champion, Reggie Weir, and two women from the big leagues, Alice Marble—the world's best female player—and Mary Hardwick. The white players knew how good we were. That's why Alice wrote a letter that helped get Althea Gibson into the U.S. Nationals in 1950. I don't care who you think you are, when you're playing in the big leagues, you're playing for black people. When you lose, we're sad. When you win, we're joyful.

I finally got to play in the U.S. Nationals in 1955. I lost in straight sets. I was thirty-five at the time. I wish they had let me play in that tournament when I was in my prime. Again, what could I do? In 1959 I played on the pro circuit. We would get three hundred dollars for showing up, and the winner would get fifteen hundred.

After I retired from playing, I coached a lot of people: Leslie Allen in the pros, Harold Solomon in the juniors. I gave lessons to Bill Cosby, Dustin Hoffman, Barbra Streisand, and Tony Bennett. I'm sure you've heard of them even if you don't know the tennis names. Richard Williams, the father of Venus and Serena, brought me to Florida to coach the sisters when they were fourteen and thirteen. I could see they were going to be great players. Those girls had a strong support system. That helped them get where they are today.

I still coach in New York City. And still play, three hours every Sunday. We need more places for black people to learn tennis. Everyone doesn't want to play basketball and football, or do boxing and track. We should have a lot more black people in pro tennis today. The opportunity is there. It's up to these kids to take advantage of it.

BOB RYLAND

December 2006

ATA Singles Champions, 1917–2006

Women's Singles

YEAR	LOCATION	WINNER
1917	Baltimore, MD	Lucy Slowe
1918	New York, NY	M. Rae
1919	New York, NY	M. Rae
1920	New York, NY	M. Rae
1921	Washington, DC	Lucy Slowe
1922	Philadelphia, PA	Isadore Channels
1923	Chicago, IL	Isadore Channels
1924	Baltimore, MD	Isadore Channels
1925	Bordentown, NJ	Lulu Ballard
1926	St. Louis, MO	Isadore Channels
1927	Hampton, VA	Lulu Ballard
1928	Bordentown, NJ	Lulu Ballard
1929	Bordentown, NJ	Ora Washington
1930	Indianapolis, IN	Ora Washington
1931	Tuskegee, AL	Ora Washington
1932	Shady Rest, NJ	Ora Washington
1933	Hampton, VA	Ora Washington
1934	Lincoln, PA	Ora Washington
1935	Institute, WV	Ora Washington
1936	Wilberforce, OH	Lulu Ballard
1937	Tuskegee, AL	Ora Washington

*Winners have been identified by their hometown since 2000.

Women's Singles (*continued*)

YEAR	LOCATION	WINNER
1938	Lincoln, PA	Flora Lomax
1939	Hampton, VA	Flora Lomax
1940	Wilberforce, OH	Agnes Lawson
1941	Tuskegee, AL	Flora Lomax
1942	Lincoln, PA	Flora Lomax
1943	not held (World War II)	
1944	New York, NY	Roumania Peters
1945	New York, NY	Kathryn Irvis
1946	Wilberforce, OH	Roumania Peters
1947	Tuskegee, AL	Althea Gibson
1948	Orangeburg, SC	Althea Gibson
1949	Wilberforce, OH	Althea Gibson
1950	Wilberforce, OH	Althea Gibson
1951	Wilberforce, OH	Althea Gibson
1952	Wilberforce, OH	Althea Gibson
1953	Daytona Beach, FL	Althea Gibson
1954	Daytona Beach, FL	Althea Gibson
1955	Wilberforce, OH	Althea Gibson
1956	Wilberforce, OH	Althea Gibson
1957	Wilberforce, OH	Gwendolyn McEvans
1958	Wilberforce, OH	Mary E. Fine
1959	Wilberforce, OH	Gwendolyn McEvans
1960	Hampton, VA	Mimi Kanarek
1961	Hampton, VA	Carolyn Williams
1962	Wilberforce, OH	Carolyn Liquori
1963	Wilberforce, OH	Ginger Pfiefer
1964	Wilberforce, OH	Bonnie Logan
1965	Wilberforce, OH	Bonnie Logan
1966	Wilberforce, OH	Bonnie Logan
1967	Wilberforce, OH	Bonnie Logan
1968	Wilberforce, OH	Bonnie Logan
1969	St. Louis, MO	Bonnie Logan
1970	St. Louis, MO	Bonnie Logan
1971	St. Louis, MO	Bessie Stockard
1972	Boston, MA	Lorraine Bryant
1973	Boston, MA	Mimi Kanarek
1974	Washington, DC	Jean Burnett
1975	San Diego, CA	Diane Morrison
1976	New Orleans, LA	Kim Sands
1977	New Orleans, LA	Leslie Allen

YEAR	LOCATION	WINNER
1978	Princeton, NJ	Joann Jacobs
1979	Atlanta, GA	Zina Garrison
1980	Atlanta, GA	Zina Garrison
1981	Detroit, MI	Lori McNeil
1982	San Diego, CA	Lucy Bacerra
1983	Boston, MA	Lisa DeAngeles
1984	Atlanta, GA	Shandra Livingston
1985	Washington, DC	Kyle Copeland
1986	Chicago, IL	Melissa Brown
1987	Oakland, CA	Iwalani McCalla
1988	Austin, TX	Iwalani McCalla
1989	New Orleans, LA	Iwalani McCalla
1990	New Orleans, LA	Erica Adams
1991	Washington, DC	Iwalani McCalla
1992	Boston, MA	Jeri Ingram
1993	Richmond, VA	Tanya Edwards
1994	Richmond, VA	Erica Adams
1995	Jackson, MS	Jeri Ingram
1996	Memphis, TN	Jeri Ingram
1997	Ft. Lauderdale, FL	Julie Stevens
1998	Birmingham, AL	Victoria Hunt
1999	Not held	
2000	College Park, GA	Jewel Peterson
2001	Atlanta, GA	Erica Adams
2002	Washington, DC	Stephanie Johnson
2003	Brandenton, FL	Alana Devort
2004	Chicago, IL	Tayo Bailey
2005	Chicago, IL	Tayo Bailey
2006	Indianapolis, IN	Cameron Benjamin

Men's Singles

YEAR	LOCATION	WINNER
1917	Baltimore, MD	Tally Holmes
1918	New York, NY	Tally Holmes
1919	New York, NY	Sylvester Smith
1920	New York, NY	B. M. Clark
1921	Washington, DC	Tally Holmes
1922	Philadelphia, PA	Edgar G. Brown
1923	Chicago, IL	Edgar G. Brown
1924	Baltimore, MD	Tally Holmes

Men's Singles (continued)

YEAR	LOCATION	WINNER
1925	Bordentown, NJ	Theodore Thompson
1926	St. Louis, MO	Eyre Saitch
1927	Hampton, VA	Theodore Thompson
1928	Bordentown, NJ	Edgar G. Brown
1929	Bordentown, NJ	Edgar G. Brown
1930	Indianapolis, IN	Douglas Turner
1931	Tuskegee, AL	Reginald Weir
1932	Shady Rest, NJ	Reginald Weir
1933	Hampton, VA	Reginald Weir
1934	Lincoln, PA	Nathaniel Jackson
1935	Institute, WV	Franklin Jackson
1936	Wilberforce, OH	Lloyd Scott
1937	Tuskegee, AL	Reginald Weir
1938	Lincoln, PA	Franklin Jackson
1939	Hampton, VA	Jimmie McDaniel
1940	Wilberforce, OH	Jimmie McDaniel
1941	Tuskegee, AL	Jimmie McDaniel
1942	Lincoln, PA	Reginald Weir
1943	Not held (World War II)	
1944	New York, NY	Lloyd Scott
1945	New York, NY	Lloyd Scott
1946	Wilberforce, OH	Jimmie McDaniel
1947	Tuskegee, AL	George Stewart
1948	Orangeburg, SC	George Stewart
1949	Wilberforce, OH	Finals not played
1950	Wilberforce, OH	Oscar Johnson
1951	Wilberforce, OH	George Stewart
1952	Wilberforce, OH	George Stewart
1953	Daytona Beach, FL	George Stewart
1954	Daytona Beach, FL	Earthna Jacquet
1955	Wilberforce, OH	Robert Ryland
1956	Wilberforce, OH	Robert Ryland
1957	Wilberforce, OH	George Stewart
1958	Wilberforce, OH	Wilbert Davis
1959	Wilberforce, OH	Wilbert Davis
1960	Hampton, VA	Arthur Ashe, Jr.
1961	Hampton, VA	Arthur Ashe, Jr.
1962	Wilberforce, OH	Arthur Ashe, Jr.
1963	Wilberforce, OH	Wilbert Davis
1964	Wilberforce, OH	George Stewart

YEAR	LOCATION	WINNER
1965	Wilberforce, OH	Luis Glass
1966	Wilberforce, OH	Wilbert Davis
1967	Wilberforce, OH	Wilbert Davis
1968	Wilberforce, OH	Robert Binns
1969	St. Louis, MO	Marty Gool
1970	St. Louis, MO	Gene Fluri
1971	St. Louis, MO	John Wilkerson
1972	Boston, MA	Horace Reid
1973	Boston, MA	Arthur Carrington
1974	Washington, DC	Roger Guedes
1975	San Diego, CA	Benny Sims
1976	New Orleans, LA	Terrance Jackson
1977	New Orleans, LA	Terrance Jackson
1978	Princeton, NJ	Rodney Harmon
1979	Atlanta, GA	Warrick Jones
1980	Atlanta, GA	Kelvin Belcher
1981	Detroit, MI	Kelvin Belcher
1982	San Diego, CA	Warrick Jones
1983	Boston, MA	Adrian Clark
1984	Atlanta, GA	Young Kwon
1985	Washington, DC	Phillip Williamson
1986	Chicago, IL	Juan Farrow
1987	Oakland, CA	Phillip Williamson
1988	Austin, TX	Noel Rutherford
1989	New Orleans, LA	Gerard Gbedey
1990	New Orleans, LA	Vincent Mackey
1991	Washington, DC	Phillip Williamson
1992	Boston, MA	Steve Campbell
1993	Richmond, VA	Steve Campbell
1994	Richmond, VA	Billy Ball
1995	Jackson, MS	Vincent Mackey
1996	Memphis, TN	Donovan September
1997	Ft. Lauderdale, FL	Phillip Williamson
1998	Birmingham, AL	Mark Silva
1999	Not held	
2000	Pasadena, CA	Vincent Mackey
2001	Birmingham, AL	Donovan September
2002	Detroit, MI	Steve Campbell
2003	Detroit, MI	Steve Campbell
2004	Washington, DC	H-Cone Thompson
2005	Washington, DC	H-Cone Thompson
2006	Oakland, CA	Phillip Graham

World-Ranked Black
Tennis Players, 1968–2006

Men

NAME	HIGHEST RANKING	YEAR
Ronald Agenor	22	1989
Hicham Arazi	22	2001
Arthur Ashe	2	1976
Bill Ball	1118	1996
Kelvin Belcher	193	1985
Steve Berke	968	2004
Martin Blackman	158	1994
James Blake	4	2006
Thomas Blake	264	2002
Lloyd Bourne	73	1983
Steve Campbell	78	1998
Arthur Carrington	241	1974
Lex Carrington	1096	1993
Bob Davis	793	1984
Yahiya Doumbia	88	1974
Younes El Aynaoui	14	2003
Juan Farrow	227	1985
Bruce Foxworth	146	1983
Marcel Freeman	46	1986
Reid Freeman	662	1979
Marcus Fugate	674	2006
David Hall	265	1994
Rodney Harmon	56	1983

NAME	HIGHEST RANKING	YEAR
Chip Hooper	17	1982
Maurice Hunter	309	1982
J.J. Jackson	602	1995
Scoville Jenkins	236	2006
Jamal Johnson	1297	2000
Robert Johnson	1357	1999
Rick Jones	383	1975
Warrick Jones	429	1984
Lesley Joseph	243	2006
John Lucas, II	579	1979
Vince Mackey	585	1996
Gael Monfils	23	2006
Nick Monroe	288	2006
Todd Nelson	58	1986
Timothy Nielly	1169	2005
Yannick Noah	3	1986
Nduka Odizor	52	1984
Joe Ragland	382	1982
Horace Reid	272	1978
Eric Riley	369	1985
Bryan Shelton	55	1992
Phillip Simmonds	219	2006
Roger Smith	96	1988
Paul Wekesa	100	1995
MaliVai Washington	11	1992
Mashiska Washington	290	1999
Phillip Williamson	297	1992
Donald Young	530	2006

Women

NAME	HIGHEST RANKING	YEAR
Katrina Adams	67	1989
Leslie Allen	17	1981
Louise Allen	226	1993
Melissa Brown	45	1984
Camille Benjamin	27	1984
Renee Blount	63	1981
Megan Bradley	313	2006
Andrea Buchanan	106	1981

Women (*continued*)

NAME	HIGHEST RANKING	YEAR
Kyle Copeland	303	1987
Tonya Evans	638	1993
Zina Garrison	4	1990
Evonne Goolagong Cawley	1	1971
Angela Haynes	95	2005
Jeri Ingram	173	1988
Jamea Jackson	45	2006
Cheryl Jones	250	1987
Shandra Livingston	236	1987
Stacey Martin	58	1989
Lori McNeil	9	1988
Diane Morrison	50	1979
Shenay Perry	43	2006
Jewel Peterson	214	2004
Shadisha Robinson	416	2003
Ahsha Rolle	129	2006
Tiya Rolle	642	2005
Chanda Rubin	6	1996
Kim Sands	44	1984
Alexandra Stevenson	18	2002
Mashona Washington	50	2004
Michaela Washington	81	1984
Serena Williams	1	2002
Venus Williams	1	2002

Bibliography

BOOKS

Ronald Agenor, *Tilted Courts*, ronaldagenor.com, Los Angeles, 2007.

Arthur Ashe, *A Hard Road to Glory*, Vols. 1-3, abridged edition, Amistad, New York, 1993.

Arthur Ashe with Neil Amdur, *Off the Court*, New American Library, New York, 1991.

Arthur Ashe and Arnold Rampersad, *Days of Grace*, Ballantine, New York, 1993.

Association of Tennis Professionals and Women's Tennis Association, *2006 Official Guide to Professional Tennis*, Quebec, Canada, 2006.

Bud Collins, *Bud Collins's Total Tennis*, SportClassic Books, New York, 2003.

Sue Davidson, *Changing the Game: The Stories of Tennis Champions Alice Marble and Althea Gibson*, Seal Press, Emeryville, Calif., 1997.

Sundiata Djata, *Blacks at the Net: Black Achievement in the History of Tennis*, Syracuse University Press, Syracuse, 2006.

Zina Garrison with Doug Smith, *Zina: My Life in Women's Tennis*, Frog Ltd., Berkeley, Calif., 2001.

Althea Gibson, *I Always Wanted to Be Somebody*, Harper and Brothers, New York, 1958.

Evonne Goolagong with Bud Collins, *Evonne! On the Move*, E. P. Dutton, New York, 1975.

Evonne Goolagong and Phil Jarratt, *Home!* Simon and Schuster, New York, 1995.

Frances Clayton Gray and Yanick Rice Lamb, *Born to Win: The Authorized Biography of Althea Gibson*, John Wiley and Sons, Hoboken, N.J., 2004

Richard Lapchick, *Smashing Barriers: Race and Sport in the New Millennium*, Madison Books, New York, 2001.

John McEnroe with James Kaplan, *You Cannot Be Serious*, Berkley Publishing, New York, 2002.

Dave Rineberg, *Venus and Serena: My Seven Years as Hitting Coach for the Williams Sisters*, Frederick Fell Publishers, Hollywood, Fla., 2003.

Edna and Art Rust, Jr., *Art Rust's Illustrated History of the Black Athlete*, Doubleday, New York, 1985.

Bruce Schoenfeld, *The Match: Althea Gibson and Angela Buxton: How Two Outsiders—One Black, One Jewish—Forged a Friendship and Made Sports History*, Amistad, New York, 2004.

Doug Smith, *Whirlwind: The Godfather of Black Tennis*, Blue Eagle Publishing, Washington, D.C., 2004.

Vince Spadea and Dan Markowitz, *Break Point: The Secret Diary of a Pro Tennis Player*, ECW Press, Toronto, 2006.

Venus Williams and Serena Williams with Hilary Beard, *Venus and Serena: Serving from the Hip*, Houghton Mifflin, Boston, 2005.

ARTICLES

Teresa Akersten, "Caught in a Tennis Net: Rosemary Darben Faced Gibson, Ashe and Racism," *Montclair Times*, November 5, 2003.

"Althea Gibson Quits as N.J. Sports Chief," *New York Post*, January 19, 1977.

"Althea Gibson Signs Pro Contract for Nearly $100,000," *New York Times*, October 20, 1959.

"Althea Gibson Tops U.S. Tennis Rankings," *New York Times*, December 16, 1957.

"Althea Trying Court Comeback," *New York Daily News*, December 24, 1968.

Neil Amdur, "Althea Gibson Feature," *New York Times*, August 26, 2002.

Neil Amdur, "Tennis Weathers One Eligibility Crisis over U.S. Open but Another Is Brewing; No Ban on Team Pros; Black Player in Limbo," *New York Times*, August 28, 1973.

Curt Anderson, "Williams Sisters Deny Agreeing to 'Battle of Sexes' Match," Associated Press, December 6, 2005.

Harvey Araton, "Addressing an Attitude Problem," *New York Times*, July 6, 1999.

Harvey Araton, "The Aging Veteran and a Rookie," *New York Times*, July 1, 1999.

Harvey Araton, "Sisters Rise Above, and Emerge on Top," *New York Times*, September 9, 2001.

Harvey Araton, "Talking About the Country Club," *New York Times*, September 9, 1997.

Edith Evans Asbury, "City Pays Tribute to Althea Gibson," *New York Times*, July 12, 1957.

Edith Evans Asbury, "Miss Gibson's Kin Proud of Punch," *New York Times*, July 9, 1957.

"Auss-ome," Associated Press, January 27, 2007.

Marc Berman, "Blake Battles Hard, but Can't Make Swiss Miss," *New York Post*, September 8, 2006.

Marc Berman, "Packed for a Weak," *New York Post*, August 28, 2006.

Marc Berman, "Serena, Your Slip Is Showing," *New York Post*, September 6, 2006.

"Blake Insists U.S. Tennis Not on Decline," msnbc.com, September 29, 2006.

"Blake's Confidence Grows with Ranking," *USA Today*, March 24, 2006.

"Blake's 'Incredible Year' Caps a Return from Loss, Illness," Tennis.com, November 20, 2006.

"Blake's Streak Stalls in Spain," *New York Daily News*, October 19, 2006.

"Blake Tops Ljubicic, Wins Thailand Open," *New York Times*, October 1, 2006.

"Blake Wins Tiebreak in Third to Beat Roddick," espn.com, July 23, 2006.

Filip Bondy, "Just Turn It On? Sister, You Got Another Thing Coming," *New York Daily News*, September 5, 2006.

Charles Bricker, "Arthur Ashe Inspired a Generation of Black Americans," *Fort Lauderdale Sun-Sentinel*, June 22, 2006.

James A. Burchard, "This Could Be Althea's Year for Net Heights," *New York World Telegram*, July 20, 1955.

Christopher Clarey, "Blake Still Finds Five to Be Loneliest Number," *New York Times*, July 1, 2006.

Christopher Clarey, "Williams Is Trying to Recover the Magic," *New York Times*, January 14, 2007.

Christopher Clarey, "Williamses Reprise Wimbledon Final," *New York Times*, July 4, 2003.

Rachel Clarke, "Sister Was 'Rock' Behind Williams Success," BBC News Online, September 16, 2003.

Bobby Clay, "American Tennis Association," *Black Enterprise*, September 1996.

Wayne Coffey, "Last Hope Is Lost with Perry Defeat," *New York Daily News*, July 4, 2006.

Wayne Coffey, "Young Ideas," *New York Daily News*, September 9, 2006.

Bud Collins, "Out for Bear," *Tennis Week*, June 2006.

Bud Collins, "Varied Paths, Same Destination," *Boston Globe*, July 9, 2005.

Bud Collins, "Venus in for Paris Near Miss," msnbc.com, June 5, 2006.

Marion Collins, "Arthur Ashe Quietly Ascends to Hall of Fame," *New York Daily News*, July 28, 1985.

Greg Couch, "For Staying Power, Hingis Has Serena Beat," *Chicago Sun-Times*, May 28, 2006.

Jake Curtis, "Mom Aims for NCAA Tennis Title," *San Francisco Chronicle*, May 21, 2006.

Allison Danzig, "Off the Court There Were Victories Too," *New York Times*, December 7, 1958.

Donald Dell, "Arthur Ashe," *Washington Post*, February 6, 2003.

Bonnie DeSimone, "Young Not Concerned Despite Winless Record," espn.com, March 23, 2006.

Lisa Dillman, "Mauresmo Shows Serena Her Point of Departure," *Los Angeles Times*, September 5, 2006.

"Editorial: Wimbledon Winner," *New York Times*, July 8, 1957.

Richard Evans, "Roddick and Blake Lose, Putting U.S. on Brink of Davis Cup Defeat," September 23, 2006.

Chris Evert, "Dear Serena," *Tennis*, May 2006.

"Father of Tennis' Williams Sisters Becomes Ill," *USA Today*, December 1, 2006.

Robin Finn, "Hingis Dominates, and Then Reconciles," *New York Times*, September 4, 1999.

Robin Finn, "Little Sister Becomes the Stardust Half," *New York Times*, September 12, 1999.

Robin Finn, "Stevenson's Big Shot Pays Off," *New York Times*, July 1, 1999.
"For First Time in Nearly a Century, No Americans in Wimbledon Quarterfinals," Associated Press, July 3, 2006.
Zina Garrison, "Remembering Althea Gibson," 2004 U.S. Open Program, August 2004.
"Gibson Honored in U.S. Open Tribute," msnbc.com, September 8, 2004.
Althea Gibson, "Transcript of Althea Gibson Interview at International Tennis Hall of Fame," July 14, 1979.
Kay Gilman, "Althea Gibson: Still Every Inch a Queen," *New York Daily News*, June 30, 1974.
Leighton Ginn, "Ryland's Seen All the Changes," *Desert Sun*, March 18, 2000.
Jon Gold, "Student Dies in Accident," *Daily Aztec*, September 27, 2005.
Jane Gross, "Noah Captures French Crown," *New York Times*, June 6, 1983.
Milton Gross, "Speaking Out," *New York Post*, July 8, 1958.
Cecily Hall, "Girl Power," geniusinsight.com, May 4, 2006.
Neil Harman, "Nielly Plays Lead Role in Making History," *Times* (London), October 19, 2006.
"Harrell Advances in U.S. Net Event," *New York Times*, August 17, 1938.
Emma Harrison, "Althea, Pride of One West Side, Becomes the Queen of Another," *New York Times*, September 9, 1957.
Sandra Harwitt, "Blake to Meet Federer in Masters Cup Final," *New York Times*, November 19, 2006.
Sandra Harwitt, "For Roddick and Blake, Recovery and Reward," *New York Times*, November 12, 2006.
Sandra Harwitt, "Nadal Advances, and Rival Awaits," *New York Times*, November 18, 2006.
Sandra Harwitt, "Williams a 'Lone Flag Waving Gently in the Wind,'" Associated Press, June 4, 2006.
Christy Helsinger, "Tennis, the Sport of a Lifetime," *Tennis Week*, April 21, 2001.
Mark Hodkinson, "Serena's Career at Point of No Return," *Ottawa Citizen*, April 17, 2006.
Peter Horner, "ATA: The Best Kept Secret in Tennis?" *Tennis USTA*, July 1991.
Johnette Howard, "Serena Still Can Become Old Self," *Newsday*, August 30, 2006.
"The Jack March Story," *Tennis Week*, August 9, 1984.
"James Blake," *ATP Tennis Weekly*, March 20, 2006.
Lee Jenkins, "Serena Williams Savors Her Role as an Underdog," *Tennis*, September 2006.
Mike Jensen, "Joakim Noah Making His Own Racket," *Philadelphia Inquirer*, March 31, 2006.
Julian Johnson, "A Whirlwind Event," blackathlete.net, June 22, 2006.
Pat Jordan, "Daddy's Big Test," *New York Times Magazine*, March 16, 1997.
Dan Kadison, "Line Judges Spur 'Bias' Probe of USTA," *New York Post*, April 10, 2006.
Melanie D. G. Kaplan, "Roddick vs. Blake," *USA Weekend*, August 18–20, 2006.

Robert F. King, "Letter to the Editor on Arthur Ashe," *New York Times*, June 8, 1975.

Matthew Kredell, "Lindsay Davenport and Serena Williams Return with the Hopes of American Tennis Placed on Their Shoulders," *Los Angeles Daily News*, August 8, 2006.

Jose Lambiet, "Serena Scores Love with Longtime Friend," *Palm Beach Post*, November 11, 2005.

Brian Lewis, "Mauresmo Snaps Hex vs. Serena," *New York Post*, September 5, 2006.

Grace Lichtenstein, "Where Is the Next Althea Gibson?" *Ms. Magazine*, December 1973.

Jackie MacMullan, "Winning Lessons in the Game of Life," *Boston Globe*, May 23, 2004.

Dan Markowitz, "Athlete Traces Tennis Success," *New York Times*, August 31, 1977.

Ted McGraw, "Former Pro Tennis Player Teaches Local Students," *Cavalier Daily*, June 15, 2006.

James McKinley, "Tennis Cinderella's Father Has a Name: Julius Erving," *New York Times*, July 3, 1999.

Casey McNerthney, "Williams Sisters Embrace Young; Tennis Superstars Rub Elbows with Awestruck Kids," *Seattle Post-Intelligencer*, November 18, 2005.

"Miss Gibson Gains Best-of-'57 Prize," *New York Times*, January 12, 1958.

"Miss Gibson Keeps Wimbledon Title," *New York Times*, July 6, 1958.

"Mr. Williams Bold to the End," *New York Times*, September 12, 1999.

"Mrs. Peters Is Set Back," *New York Times*, August 19, 1945.

"New York Negro Girl Will Enter National Tennis Championships," *New York Times*, August 23, 1950.

Chris Nicholson, "Making a Splash," *USTA Magazine*, May 2000.

Keith Niebuhr, "Ashe's Wimbledon Win Is Tops in Black History," *St. Petersburg Times*, February 15, 2005.

Richard Pagliaro, "Red, White, Blue & Silver Star," *Tennis Week*, June 2006.

Ted Poston, "The Story of Althea Gibson," *New York Post*, September 1, 1957.

"Promoters Sue Williams Sisters," *New York Times*, November 18, 2006.

"Review of *The Horse Soldiers*," *Hollywood Reporter*, July 9, 1959.

William C. Rhoden, "The Father Really Did Know Best," *New York Times*, September 8, 2001.

William C. Rhoden, "For Sisters, Ambivalence Overshadows Performance," *New York Times*, September 7, 2002.

Liz Robbins, "For Williams, Biggest Changes Are on the Inside," *New York Times*, August 28, 2006.

Selena Roberts, "Serena Williams Wins Match, Then Takes a Shot at Hingis," *New York Times*, September 3, 1999.

Douglas Robson, "Most Top Americans Drop," *USA Today*, March 24, 2006.

Lester Rodney, "Gibson Leads Brough, Rain Stops Play," *Daily Worker*, August 30, 1950.

Lester Rodney, "Meet the Wimbledon Favorite," *Daily Worker*, June 17, 1956.

Lester Rodney, "Miss Gibson Plays at Forest Hills," *Daily Worker*, August 24, 1950.

Ronald McDonald House Charities, "Williams Sisters to Assist Hurricane Katrina Relief Efforts as Part of Third Annual McDonald's Williams Sisters Tour," August 29, 2006.

Gene Roswell, "Althea Hasn't a Thing to Gain in Tennis Now," *New York Post*, September 8, 1958.

Darren Rovell, "Are Venus and Serena Bad for Tennis?" espn.com, February 3, 2003.

"Rubin Wins at Fortis Championships," Associated Press, September 26, 2006.

Holly M. Sanders, "Style Racket: Top Pros Show Fashion Along with Forehands," *New York Post*, August 22, 2006.

"Scott Keeps Net Title; Victor Keeps McDaniel in Negro Final," *New York Times*, August 20, 1945.

"Scott Takes Net Title; Tops Ryland in Negro National Play—Miss Peters Winner," *New York Times*, August 21, 1944.

"Sequera Wins USTA Tennis Classic," Associated Press, October 8, 2006.

"Serena Returns After Mental Break," Associated Press, July 13, 2006.

Doug Smith, "Ashe's 'Hero' Is Still Going Strong," *USA Today*, March 21, 2001.

Doug Smith, "Color Bind: Fair or Not, Gael Monfils Plays for More Than Himself," *Tennis Week*, June 2006.

Lara de Souza, "Kim Sands: Employee of the Month," Miami Parks & Recreation Employee Newsletter, January 2006.

Greg Stoda, "Serena Struggles Past Childhood Neighbor," *Palm Beach Post*, June 22, 2005.

Steve Strunsky, "Wimbledon Champion Gibson Remembered as Pioneer," Associated Press, October 2, 2003.

"Tennis Sportswire: Blake Loses in Davis Cup," *New York Daily News*, April 8, 2006.

"Tennis Title to Stewart," *New York Times*, August 24, 1947.

"That Gibson Girl," *Time*, August 26, 1957.

"Top Americans Roddick, Blake Make Final at Indy," espn.com, July 22, 2006.

Fred Tupper, "Althea Gibson Becomes First Negro to Take Wimbledon Tennis," *New York Times*, July 7, 1957.

Fred Tupper, "Ashe Topples Connors for Crown at Wimbledon," *New York Times*, July 6, 1975.

Fred Tupper, "Mrs. King Wins Her Sixth Wimbledon Singles Title; Mrs. Cawley Is Trounced in 39 Minutes," *New York Times*, July 5, 1975.

"USTA Agrees to Use More Women, Minorities as Chair Umpires," CBS Sportsline, September 14, 2006.

George Vecsey, "Untethered, and Back on Top of Her Game," *New York Times*, July 1, 2005.

George Vecsey, "Where Are Next Gibsons and Ashes?" *New York Times*, August 29, 1997.

"Venus Injures Wrist in Luxembourg Loss," msnbc.com, September 28, 2006.

"Venus Out of Open," *New York Daily News*, August 26, 2006.

"Venus Williams Signs $40 Million Reebok Deal," Associated Press, December 22, 2000.

William Washington, "Nominating Committee Contributes to Death of Tennis in America," e-mailed letter, September 15, 2006.

William Washington, "The Numbers Don't Lie," e-mailed letter, September 12, 2006.

William Washington, "U.S. Open Wild Card Choices and My Analysis," e-mailed letter, September 6, 2006.

William Washington, "You Are Either Part of the Problem or Part of the Solution," e-mailed letter, September 9, 2006.

Frederick Waterman, "Ashe to Enter Hall of Fame," UPI, July 13, 1985.

"Weir Beats Grasing in U.S. Negro Tennis," *New York Times*, August 19, 1944.

L. Jon Wertheim, "World Beater," *Sports Illustrated*, November 27, 2006.

"Williams' Parents Finish Divorce," Associated Press, October 30, 2002.

"Williams Sisters Must Turn Over Tax Returns," Associated Press, September 14, 2006.

"Wimby Flop Drops Venus, Andy in Rankings," *New York Post*, July 11, 2006.

"Yetunde Price, 31, Shot Following 'Confrontation,'" Associated Press, September 14, 2003.

Gene Zaleski, "NAACP to Recognize Top Student Athletes Saturday at Claflin," Orangeburg, S.C., *Times and Democrat*, April 20, 2004.

INTERVIEWS

Katrina Adams, May 31, 2006.

Ronald Agenor, September 29, November 21, 2006.

Leslie Allen, June 20, 2006.

Brittany Augustine, September 3, 2006.

Turhan Berne, March 7, 2006.

James Blake, March 23, March 25, March 27, June 30, August 26, August 30, 2006.

Thomas Blake, September 3, 2006.

Nick Bolletieri, September 3, 2006.

Angela Buxton, September 3, 2006.

Arthur Carrington, December 1, 2006.

Bud Collins, March 27, 2006.

Rosemary Darben, November 27, 2006.

Bob Davis, August 9, 2006.

Wilbert Davis, August 10, 2006.

Cliff Drysdale, September 27, 2006.

Sallie Elam, November 17, 2006.

Juan Farrow, February 21, November 5, 2006.

Carlos Fleming, November 8, 2006.

Marcus Freeman, October 21, 2006.

Virginia Glass, October 16, 2006.

Eric Graves, February 14, 2006.
Frances Clayton Gray, November 15, 2006.
Traci Green, October 18, 2006.
Rodney Harmon, October 18, 2006.
Bronal Harris, October 17, 2006.
Angela Haynes, March 22, August 31, 2006.
Justine Henin, March 23, 2006.
Cecil Hollins, August 8, August 9, 2006.
Eric Jackson, April 17, 2006.
Jamea Jackson, March 22, June 27, August 30, 2006.
Scoville A. Jenkins, August 30, 2006.
Scoville D. Jenkins, August 30, August 31, 2006.
Lesley Joseph, May 18, August 28, 2006.
Phebe Joseph, August 28, 2006.
Billie Jean King, August 28, 2006.
Amelie Mauresmo, March 23, September 4, 2006.
Lori McNeil, June 6, June 26, 2006.
Gael Monfils, March 24, August 31, 2006.
Ben Monroe, September 1, 2006.
Nick Monroe, September 1, 2006.
Ray Moore, October 10, 2006.
Arvelia Myers, November 20, 2006.
Shenay Perry, March 22, July 3, 2006.
Jewel Peterson, March 12, 2007.
Dave Rineberg, August 16, 2006.
Ahsha Rolle, August 30, 2006.
Chanda Rubin, August 28, 2006.
Bob Ryland, January 17, 2006.
Kim Sands, July 22, August 8, November 6, 2006.
Bryan Shelton, October 26, 2006.
Pam Shriver, September 2, 2006.
Dr. Diane Shropshire, November 11, 2006.
Phillip Simmonds, August 28, 2006.
Roger Smith, November 6, 2006.
Vince Spadea, August 30, 2006.
Roger Terry, October 26, 2006.
Tina Tharp, October 17, 2006.
Willis Thomas, Jr., November 22, 2006.
Albert Tucker, August 8, 2006.
MaliVai Washington, September 2, 2006.
Mashona Washington, March 22, 2006.
William Washington, September 6, October 3, 2006.
John Wilkerson, September 4, November 4, 2006.
Serena Williams, August 26, August 30, September 3, September 4, 2006.
Venus Williams, June 25, 2006, June 28, June 29, July 1, 2006.
Phil Williamson, September 25, September 26, 2006.

Vaughn Wilson, October 26, 2006.
Donald Young, March 22, 2006, August 28, 2006.

INTERNET SITES

Altheagibson.com, Frances Clayton Gray biography.
Atptennis.com.
Espn.go.com, "A Legacy of Change and Hope," February 7, 2007.
Findarticles.com, ATA Jr. Development program, ATA 2nd annual Black Enterprise/Pepsi Golf and Tennis Challenges Special Supplement, September 1995.
Forbes.com, Best-paid athletes, March 22, 2006.
Memory.loc.gov, the Library of Congress, 1910–1922.
Midatlantictennisfoundation.com, Arthur Ashe biography, 1991.
Midatlantictennisfoundation.com, Donald Dell biography, 1995.
Montclairtimes.com, "Caught in a Tennis Net," November 5, 2003.
Ramblinwreck.cstv.com, Bryan Shelton biography, September 2006.
Sportsillustrated.cnn.com, Althea Gibson, first African-American Woman to win Wimbledon.
Umkc.edu, African American Firsts.
Usta.com, Black History Month 2004, 2006, and 2007.
Usta.com, "Tennis Legend Margaret Peters Passes Away," November 7, 2004.
Wilberforce.edu, One of the first black universities, where the ATA Championships were held.
Wimbledon.org, "Perry Left Flat as USA Loses Its Fizz," July 3, 2006.
Wm.edu, ITA Tennis Hall of Fame—Lori McNeil: "The Unstoppable Juggernaut."
Wtatour.com.

TELEVISION AND RADIO

ABC News, "Serena Williams: New Cosmetic Line on 'Good Morning America,'" December 8, 2005.
Black Entertainment Television, "The ATA: Yesterday, Today, Tomorrow," December 1996.
British Broadcasting Company, "Ashe vs. Connors: 1975 Wimbledon Gentlemen's Final," July 5, 1975.
CBS Sports, "U.S. Open Women's Final Television Ratings," October 12, 2006.
Harpo Productions, "Venus and Serena Williams Appear on 'The Oprah Winfrey Show,'" November 27, 2002.
NBC Sports, "Analysis by John McEnroe on Wimbledon 2006," July 7, 2006.
WFAN Radio, New York, "Serena Williams on 'Mike & the Mad Dog,'" May 16, 2006.

Index

Aborigines: in sports, 195

Adams, Katrina, 6, 15, 115, 120, 144, 149, 150, 232

Adams, Maurice, 149

Adams, Myron, 149

Agassi, Andre, 36, 79, 115, 134, 137, 138, 156, 204, 212, 221, 232

Agenor, Ronald, 203, 209, 218; career of, 204–205

AIDS, 104

Ali, Laila, 37, 49

Ali, Muhammad, 30, 53, 79, 98

Allen, Leslie, 15, 73, 75, 113, 116, 144, 183, 224, 238; career of, 184, 185, 186, 187; ranking of, 188

Allen, Malcolm, 209

Althea Gibson Community Education and Tennis Center, 75

Althea Gibson Foundation, 49

Althea Gibson Sings (recording), 66

American Heart Association, 118

American Tennis Association (ATA), 3, 4, 6, 53, 54, 73, 77, 93, 108, 115, 116, 123, 237; activities of, 120, 121, 122; challenges facing, 119; founding of, 106, 107; as inclusive, 106, 107

Anthony, Carmelo, 201–202

Apartheid, 81, 85, 86

Arias, Jimmy, 166

Armstrong, Louis, 74

Arthur Ashe Foundation for the Defeat of AIDS, 104

Arthur Ashe Kids' Day, 104

Arthur Ashe Leadership Award, 118

Arthur Ashe Safe Passage Foundation, 78. *See also* Ashe Bolletieri Cities program.

Ashe, Arthur, 5, 31, 42, 71, 74, 75, 105, 106, 113, 114, 120, 123, 125, 130, 141, 164, 166, 167, 189, 190, 191, 192, 194, 196, 200, 201, 205, 208, 214, 227, 229, 230, 232; activism of, 80, 97; apartheid, outrage over, 81; background of, 77, 93; black causes, endorsement of, 98; and Jimmy Connors, 86, 87, 89, 90, 91, 92; criticism of, 83, 101; death of, 104, 202; education of, 95; endorsement deals of, 99; and Juan Farrow, 206, 207; firsts, associated with, 77, 78; heart attack of, 100; illness of, 77, 103, 104; image of, 78, 79; as influence, 231; injuries of, 100; as legend, 6; marriage of, 98; in military, 96; as respected, 96; as role model, vii; as self-assured, 94, 95; social causes,

Ashe, Arthur (*continued*)
  devotion to, 76; in South Africa,
  82, 83, 84, 85; as supportive, 102;
  training of, 94, 95; at Wimbledon,
  88, 92, 93
Ashe, Arthur, Sr., 93, 101
Ashe, Camera, 104
Ashe, Jeanne Moutoussamy, 98, 99,
  104, 140
Ashe, John, 96
Ashe, Mattie, 93
Ashe Bolletieri Cities program, 78.
  See also Arthur Ashe Safe Passage
  Foundation.
Ashford, Evelyn, 182
Association of Tennis Professionals
  (ATP), 78, 88, 92, 155, 158, 172
Astaire, Red, 57
Athletes Against Drugs, 118
Atlanta Lawn Tennis Association, 218
Augusta National Country Club, 179
Augustine, Brittany, 32, 78, 228
Austin, Tracy, 197
Australia, 194, 198
Australian Open, 159
Australian Sports Commission, 198
Australian Tennis Federation, 159

Baker, Bertram, 57
Ballard, Lulu, 109
Bammer, Sybille, 233
Barber, Bill, 172
Barker, Brian, 133
Bartkowicz, Jane "Peaches," 196
Becker, Boris, 136, 191, 231
Bell, Ed, 190
Bengston, Ove, 114
Benjamin, Camille, 115
Bennett, Tony, 238
Berlocq, Carlos, 212
Bernard, Marcel, 201
Bernardes, Carlos, Jr., 181
Betz, Pauline, 70
Bishop Charity Fund, 118

Blackman, Martin, 121, 136, 209
Black Tennis and Sports Foundation,
  78
Blake, Betty, vii, 132
Blake, James, 8, 31, 42, 124, 130,
  135, 139, 149, 156, 157, 160,
  178, 191, 202, 207, 209, 212,
  221, 225; background of, 125;
  coaching of, 133; as
  disappointment, 137; endorsement
  deals of, 134; as fit, 136; following
  of, 128, 129; illness of, 127, 128,
  133; injuries of, 127; as likable,
  126, 128; matinee idol, look of,
  125; and Obama Factor, 129; Q
  rating of, 128; racial identity of,
  131–132; sportsmanship of, 138
Blake, Thomas, vii
Blake, Thomas, Jr., 127, 132, 133,
  209
Blake, Thomas, Sr., vii, 127, 132
Blount, Renee, 15, 115, 144, 183;
  career of, 191, 192
Bolletieri Academy, 120
Bolletieri, Nick, 22, 78
Bondarenko, Alona, 223
Borg, Bjorn, 80, 88
Bovina, Elena, 163
Bozolijac, Ilia, 219
Bradley, Megan, 154, 228
Brooks, Kerrie, 234
Brough, Louise, 56, 57, 58, 60, 61,
  65
Brown, Edgar, 107, 108
Bruguera, Sergi, 204
Buchanan, Andrea, 15, 144, 183
Buchholz, Butch, 190, 191
Budge, Don, 7, 87, 111, 237
Bueno, Maria, 65
Bush, George H. W., 140
Buxton, Angela, 49, 62, 64, 73;
  Althea Gibson, friendship with,
  60, 61
Byrd, Percy, 29

Cameroon, 82
Campbell, Steve, 136
Capriati, Jennifer, 36
Carillo, Mary, 193
Carlos, John, 92
Carrington, Arthur, 72, 101, 113, 114, 136, 228; bad attitude of, 115
Carrington, Lex, 115, 229
Cash, Pat, 204
Cawley, Roger, 197
Central State University, 108
Chaffee, Nancy, 57
Champion, Thierry, 203
Chandra Rubin Foundation, 118
Chanfreau, Jean, 71
Chang, Michael, 134, 156, 173, 176, 204, 209, 212, 213
Channels, Isadore, 109
Charity, Ronald, 93, 94
Chatrier, Philippe, 200
Chavis, Bernard, 122
Chicago (Ill.), 6, 81, 82
China, 161
Chris Evert Tennis Academy, 161
Civil rights movement, 59
Clarke, Carol, 23
Clifton, Nat "Sweetwater," 54
Clijsters, Kim, 27, 28, 34, 35, 38, 234
Coetzer, Amanda, 154
Collins, Bud, 22, 25, 28, 30, 62, 66, 71, 72, 73, 84, 85, 90, 99, 196
Collins, Troy, 136
Compton (Calif.), 19, 20
Connolly, Maureen "Little Mo," 12, 58, 60, 151
Connors, Gloria, 89
Connors, Jimmy, 6, 79, 85, 136, 167, 171, 174, 175, 204, 212, 231; and Arthur Ashe, 88, 89, 90, 91, 92; as brash, 87; as invincible, 86
Cook, James, 195
Cook, Ralph, 107
Cooper, Charles "Tarzan," 54

Corretja, Alex, 176
Cosby, Bill, 165, 166, 185, 238
Cosmopolitan Tennis Club, 51, 55, 111, 121
Courier, Jim, 115, 134, 173, 174, 176, 212
Court, Margaret, 12, 151, 196
Cowans, Russ J., 67
Craybas, Jill, 10
Cronin, Matt, 73
Cunningham, F. Michael, 23
Curington, Branch, 228

Darben, Rosemary, 55
Darben, William, 63, 70, 73, 74
Davenport, Lindsay, 14, 24, 35, 37, 116, 135, 222
Davis, Bill, 69
Davis, Bob, 80, 115, 119, 120, 121, 130, 228
Davis Cup, 160
Davis, Jobe, 210
Davis, Keven, 234
Davis, Nana, 52
Davis, Wilbert, 108, 121
Davydenko, Nikolai, 126
Deford, Frank, 84
De Jenken, Sandra, 181
Dell, Donald, 82, 96
Dementieva, Elena, 34
Democratic National Convention, 81
Dent, Phil, 87
Detroit (Mich.), 19
Diaw, Boris, 202
Dinkins, David, 53, 70, 158
Djokovic, Novak, 213
Dokic, Jelena, 116
Doumbia, Yahiya, 136, 209
Drysdale, Cliff, 34, 79, 80, 96, 97, 103

Eaton, Hubert, 53, 54, 64
Edberg, Stefan, 190
Educational Amendments Act, 182
Edwards, Tricia, 195

Edwards, Vic, 196, 197
Eisenhower, Dwight, 65
Elam, Sallie, 121, 122
El Aynaoui, Younes, 8, 136
Elcock, Walter, 114
Elizabeth II (queen of England), 63
Emerson, Roy, 80
Ernst, Dennis, 215
Erving, Julius, 135
Evert, Chris, 12, 36, 149, 150, 151, 152, 190, 192, 196; Serena Williams, open letter to, 39–40
Evert, Jimmy, 237

Fageros, Karol, 59, 60, 69
Fairbank, Ros, 186
Falkenburg, Bob, 110, 238
Farrow, Juan, 101, 112, 115, 226; and Arthur Ashe, 206, 207; career of, 205–208; potential, as unfulfilled, 207, 208
Federer, Roger, 34, 126, 136, 137, 138, 150, 156, 181, 214
Fernandez, Gigi, 190
Fischer, Lee, 67
Fish, Mardy, 157–158
Fitzgerald, John, 208, 209
Fleming, Carlos, 133, 134, 135
Flint (Mich.), 19
Ford, John, 66
Forget, Guy, 202
Fowler, Chris, 202
Foxworth, Bruce, 115, 136
France, 161
Fraser, Neale, 63, 92
Frazier, Amy, 13
Freeman, Clyde, 113
Freeman, Henry, 107
Freeman, Marcel, 115, 136
French, Sande, 170, 172, 178, 179, 180; discrimination, charges of, 169
Fry, Shirley, 57, 58, 60, 61, 62
Fugate, Marcus, 167

Garrison, Mary Elizabeth, 143
Garrison, Ulysses, 143
Garrison, Zina, viii, 4, 15, 17, 72, 73, 103, 106, 115, 116, 119, 120, 121, 141, 142, 161, 183, 197, 232; career of, 143, 148, 149, 150, 152; endorsement deals of, 147, 152; illness of, 153; marriage of, 152, 153; Lori McNeil, friendship with, 145, 146, 153, 154; ranking of, 140, 144
Gasquet, Richard, 159
Gerulaitis, Vitas, 24
Ghana, 236
Gibbs, Gussie, 237
Gibson, Althea, viii, 12, 33, 42, 46, 75, 88, 97, 101, 102, 106, 107, 109, 110, 111, 113, 114, 116, 120, 123, 144, 151, 183, 190, 195, 205, 215, 221, 227, 238; as actress, 66, 67; background of, 49, 50, 51; as boxer, 49; burden of, 48; Angela Buxton, friendship with, 60, 61; career of, 56, 57, 58, 62, 71, 72; as celebrated, 5; comeback of, 71; criticism of, 67; death of, 73; as formidable, 53; and Harlem Globetrotters, 69; honors of, 48–49; income, sources of, 70; on international circuit, 60; as inspiring, 62; legacy of, 47; as legend, 6, 184; as "name," 66; personality of, 48, 67, 68; as poor, 67, 73; potential of, 55; retirement of, 69; support system of, 54; tactical approach of, 59; as troublesome, 52; as underappreciated, 49, 74; vulnerable side of, 53; at Wimbledon, 62, 63, 64, 65–66
Gibson, Annie, 49, 65
Gibson, Daniel, Jr., 49, 50, 65
Gibson, Daniel, Sr., 49, 50
Gibson, Josh, 52

Gibson, Lillian, 49
Gibson, Millie, 49, 52
Gilbert, Brad, 204
Gimelstob, Justin, 232
Ginepri, Robby, 126, 127
Glass, Luis, 101
Goldstein, Michael J., 31
Golivin, Tatiana, 135
Gonzalez, Fernando, 137, 181
Gonzales, Pancho, 7, 70, 237
Goolagong, Evonne, 6, 12, 198;
    career of, 194–197; concentration
    lapses of, 197; criticism toward,
    197; race-specific references,
    bristling at, 196
Gourlay, Helen, 196
Graebner, Clark, 96, 97
Graf, Steffi, 12, 15, 148, 150, 151,
    152, 170, 172, 181
Grand Slam, 12, 33, 170, 181; and
    black tennis players, 106; and
    black umpires, 180
Gray, Frances, 49, 73
Gray, Richie, 228
Green, Traci, 229, 230
Groenefeld, Anna-Lena, 222

Hagey, Susan, 193
Haiti, 204
Hall, Scottie, 61
Hamer, Fannie Lou, 81
Hampton Institute, 108
Hantuchova, Daniela, 10, 44
Hard, Darlene, 61, 63, 66
Hard Road to Glory, A (Ashe), 77
Hardwick, Mary, 55, 111, 238
Harkleroad, Ashley, 222
Harlem, 51
Harlem Globetrotters, 69
Harmon, Rodney, 41, 102, 115, 120,
    155–156, 158, 159, 161, 168,
    207, 214, 226; career of, 166,
    167; as coach, 230
Harriman, Averill, 65

Harris, Luisa, 182
Hart, Doris, 57, 58, 60
Hawkins, Torrey, 228
Hawton, Mary, 63
Haynes, Angela, 32, 219, 222, 225,
    228; career of, 220, 221
Haynes, Dontia, 220
Henin, Justine, 34, 235
Hewitt, Lleyton, 125, 130, 132; race-
    baiting of, 131, 178
Hingis, Martina, 13, 17, 36, 37
Historically black colleges and
    universities (HBCUs), 107, 108
Hoad, Lew, 64
Hoffman, Dustin, 238
Holden, William, 66
Hollins, Cecil, 170, 171, 174, 177,
    180; career of, 172, 173, 175–176;
    discrimination, charges of, 169;
    lawsuit, filing of, 179; and racial
    slur, 178
Holmes, Tally, 3, 107, 108
Hooper, Chip, 115, 136, 167
Hopkins, Jennifer, 163
Horse Soldiers, The (film), 66
Houston, Marques, 236
Hudlin, Richard, 95, 191, 206, 207
Hurricane Katrina, 178, 236
Hurricane Katrina Disaster Relief
    Fund, 118

I Always Wanted to Be Somebody
    (Gibson), 48, 68
International Tennis Federation
    (ITF), 181; lawsuit against, 169,
    179
International Tennis Hall of Fame,
    100, 119
Irwin, Nina, 51, 107
Ivanovic, Ana, 44
Iverson, Allen, 31

Jack, Hulan, 65
Jackson, Ernest, 222

Jackson, Jamea, 42, 120, 221, 222, 223, 228
Jackson, Willard, 152
Jacobs, Helen, 109
James, LeBron, 156
Jankovic, Jelena, 41, 42, 222
Jausovec, Mima, 186
Jenkins, Carol, 218
Jenkins, Scoville, 42, 158, 167, 217, 219, 227; background of, 218
Jenkins, Scoville D., 217
Jenkins, Tommy, 171
Johannesburg (South Africa), 81, 83
Johnson, Bill, 229
Johnson, Bobby, 94, 206
Johnson, Earvin "Magic," 104
Johnson, Franklin, 155
Johnson, Fred, 51
Johnson, Marion, 130
Johnson, Oscar, 110
Johnson, Robert Walter, 6, 53, 54, 64, 93, 94, 95, 101, 115, 119, 122, 123, 205; as Godfather of Black Tennis, 112; and Junior Development Program, 112, 113
Jones, C. M., 60
Jones, Sam, 46
Joseph, Lesley, 218; background of, 219
Joyner-Kersee, Jackie, 151

Kaffir Boy (Mathabane), 85
Kasavage, Peter, 181
Kaufman, Rich, 170, 178
Kelleher, Robert, 82
Kelly, Gene, 110
Kennedy, Robert F., 80–81
Kenya, 82
Kersee, Bob, 151
King, Billie Jean, 12, 20, 62, 87, 116, 140, 151, 154, 155, 189, 190, 196, 197
King, Evan, 228
King, Martin Luther, Jr., 80, 98

Klum, Heidi, 44
Kournikova, Anna, 13, 191
Knapp, Barbara, 56
Knode, Dorothy, 61
Koukalova, Klara, 222
Krajicek, Richard, 164, 232
Kramer, Jack, 70
Krickstein, Aaron, 166, 171
Kuznetsova, Svetlana, 34

Ladies Professional Golf Association, 70
Lane, Mills, 180
Laver, Rod, 12, 79, 87, 92, 97
Leach, Rick, 146
Lendl, Ivan, 164, 187, 210
Lenglen, Suzanne, 109
Levine, Jesse, 212
Lewis, Oliver, 3
Likhovtseva, Elena, 222
Lincoln University, 108
Lino, Lourdes Dominguez, 42, 43
Littlefield, David, 171, 174
Llewellyn, Sydney, 59, 64, 69, 70, 101
Lloyd, Earl, 54
Lomax, Flora, 109
Long, Thelma, 63
Louis, Joe, 61
Lozano, Jorge, 147
Lucas, John, 112
Lutz, Bob, 96

Macci, Rick, 21, 22
Maguire, Wade, 234
Malcolm X, 115
Maleeva, Katerina, 31, 117
Maleeva, Magdalena, 220
Maleeva, Manuela, 31
Malhotra, Suhel, 213
MaliVai Washington Kids Foundation, 166
Mandela, Nelson, 83, 86
Mandlikova, Hana, 186, 187, 188

Marble, Alice, 54, 109, 111, 112, 238
Martin, Todd, 134, 164, 181, 204, 232
Martinez, Conchita, 151
Masters, The, 179
Masur, Wally, 209
Matera, Don, 84, 85
Mathabane, Mark, 85
Mauresmo, Amelie, 35, 44, 45, 235
Mayotte, Tim, 164
McCard, Harry S., 107
McCormack, Mark, 148
McDaniel, Jimmie, 4, 110, 111
McEnroe, John, 79, 137, 150, 165, 174, 175, 176, 205, 207, 214
McEnroe, Patrick, 165, 204, 205
McGrady, Tracy, 31
McMann, Renville, 59
McNeil, Charlie, 142, 146
McNeil, Dorothy, 142
McNeil, Lori, viii, 4, 15, 103, 106, 115, 116, 119, 120–121, 141, 144, 161, 190, 223, 232; career of, 147, 148, 149, 150, 151; Zina Garrison, friendship with, 145, 146, 153, 154; ranking of, 140; training of, 142
Metreveli, Alex, 96
Middleton, T. J., 151
Miller, Anne, 13
Mills, Mary, 70
Minnis, Tony, 230
Mirnyi, Max, 137
Modern Tennis Club, 115
Molik, Alicia, 157
Monfils, Gael, 8, 42, 201, 227; career of, 202–203
Monroe, Ben, 216, 228
Monroe, Nick, 215, 216, 217
Montana, Francisco, 232
Moodie, Wesley, 203
Moody, Helen Wills, 109
Moore, Ray, 29, 81, 82, 83, 85
Morgan, J. D., 95

Morrison, Diane. *See* Shropshire, Diane Morrison.
Morrison, Jeff, 133
Mortimer, Angela, 60, 65
Muhammad, Asia, 78, 228
Muller, Fay, 62
Muller, Martina, 222
Mulloy, Gardnar, 46
Murphy, Isaac, 3
Murray, Datus, 136
Muster, Thomas, 232
Myers, Arvelia, 228

Nadal, Rafael, 25, 214, 217, 225
Nagelsen, Betsy, 148
Nalbandian, David, 126, 214
Nascimento, Rodrigo, 222
Nastase, Ilie, 80, 99, 130
National Basketball Association (NBA), 18
National Football League (NFL), 18
Navratilova, Martina, 10, 12, 24, 36, 151, 152, 190, 196
Negro Leagues, 4, 52, 54
Nelson, Todd, 136, 209, 232
Newcombe, John, 79
Nielly, Timothy, 228
Nigeria, 82
Nimmons, Tony, 181
Noah, Joakim, 200
Noah, Yannick, viii, 8, 102, 125, 132, 167, 187, 204, 208; career of, 201; signature shot of, 199–200
N.W.A. (Niggaz Wit Attitude), 19

Obama, Barack, 129
Odizor, Nduka, 136, 232
Off the Court (Ashe), 83
Ogner, Joan, 95
Okker, Tom, 80, 85, 97
Olmedo, Alex, 60
Osbourne, Margaret, 56
Owens, Jesse, 69

Paish, John, 114
Palm Beach Gardens (Fla.), 21
Parker, Frank, 237
Parker, Tony, 202
Parks, Rosa, 83
Pasarell, Charles, 96
Pendleton, Al, 177
Perry, Bob, 59
Perry, Fred, 92
Perry, Shenay, 42, 120, 160, 221, 222, 228
Peters, Margaret, 3–4, 109, 110
Peters, Roumania, 3–4, 52, 109, 110
Peterson, Ernie, 228
Peterson, Jewel, 228
Philippoussis, Mark, 136, 157
Pierce, Mary, 34, 150
Player, Gary, 86
Policinski, Gene, 103
Portrait in Motion (Ashe and Deford), 84
Potter, Barbara, 186
Price, Oracene, 17, 20, 21, 22, 25, 29, 35; in Africa, 236; divorce of, 234
Price, Yetunde: death of, 233–234

Racism, 50, 51
Rafter, Patrick, 232
Ralston, Dennis, 96, 101, 166
Ramirez, Raul, 87, 89
Raymond, Lisa, 135
Redondo, Marita, 71
Reese, Michael, 186
Reid, Horace, 101
Renshaw, William and Ernest, 93
Rhetta, B. M., 107
Rhoden, William C., 35
Rhodes, Keith, 23
Richardson, Hamilton, 59, 60
Riessen, Marty, 101
Riggs, Bobby, 7, 24, 70, 189, 237
Riley, Eric, 136
Riley, Mark, 230

Rineberg, Dave, 17, 22, 28, 225, 234
Rios, Lillian, 163
Robinson, Edna Mae, 53
Robinson, Jackie, 5, 48, 56, 58, 68, 76, 77, 111; success of, 54
Robinson, Sugar Ray, 51, 58, 65
Robredo, Tommy, 126
Roche, Tony, 88
Roddick, Andy, 125, 156, 160, 181, 217, 221
Rogers, Ginger, 57
Rolle, Ahsha, 32, 42, 120, 146, 154, 223, 228
Rolle, Tiya, 223, 228
Rose, Mervyn, 63
Rosewall, Ken, 61, 80, 87, 97
Rubin, Bernadette, 118
Rubin, Chandra, 41, 42, 116, 119, 144, 157, 161, 228; background of, 117, 118
Rubin, Edward, 118
Rudolph, Wilma, 182
Russell, Michael, 203
Russia, 160, 161
Ruzici, Virginia, 186
Ryland, Bob, 6, 7, 22, 53, 55, 57, 70, 91, 109, 110, 111, 112, 183, 188, 207, 228; as coach, 238
Ryland, Robert, Sr., 237

Safin, Marat, 181
Saitch, Eyre, 110
Sampras, Pete, 36, 79, 115, 134, 136, 156, 176, 209, 212, 215
Sanchez-Vicario, Arantxa, 22
Sands, Kim, 15, 18, 86, 101, 115, 116, 144, 183, 184, 227; career of, 190, 191; as coach, 190, 230; description of, 189
Saperstein, Abe, 69
Schwartz, Alan, 155
Seeney, Daphne, 62
Segregation, 108
Seles, Monica, 15, 151, 152

Selmore, Rachel, 188
Senegal, 236
Sharapova, Maria, 34, 37, 163, 222, 233
Shelton, Bryan, 125, 209, 230; Arthur Ashe, influence on, 231; career of, 232
Shriver, Pam, 24, 25, 27, 29, 74, 146
Shropshire, Diane Morrison, 7, 15, 183, 192; career of, 193, 194
Shropshire, Ken, 194
Simmonds, Phillip, 42, 159, 167, 227
Sims, Benny, 41, 106
Skinner, Tom, 209
Slowe, Lucy, 107
Smith, Doug, 103
Smith, Jim, 183
Smith, Rhoda, 56
Smith, Roger, 15, 121, 132, 136, 173, 190, 209, 232
Smith, Stan, 80, 82, 96
Smith, Sylvester, 107
Smith, Tommie, 92
Smith, Wendell, 67
Snyder, Jay, 170, 171–172
Solomon, Harold, 238
South Africa, 81, 82, 83, 84, 86
South African Open tournament, 82, 85
South Carolina State University, 108
Soweto (South Africa), 85
Special Olympics, 118
Spirlea, Irina, 14, 15, 16
Spitzer, Eliot, 179, 180
Sportsmen's Tennis Club, 183
Stafford, Shaun, 14, 22
Stevenson, Alexandra, 134, 135, 228
Stevenson, Samantha, 135
Stewart, George, 110
Stewart, Sherwood, 146, 147
Stich, Michael, 204
Stilwell, Graham, 88
St. Louis (Mo.), 19
Streisand, Barbra, 238

Strode, Woody, 54
Stubbs, Renee, 151
Sukova, Helena, 151, 170, 172, 181
Swain, Gary, 214
Switzerland, 161

Tanner, Roscoe, 87
Tanzania, 82
Taromar facility, 121, 122
Teltscher, Eliot, 167
Tennis: African-American culture, lack of in, 18, 188; as all-white sport, 17, 182; black elite, popular with, 107; blacks, lack of exposure to, 216; blacks in, 3, 4, 5, 14, 107, 150, 156, 227, 228; chair-umpires in, 170, 171; coaches of, as unsung, 228; discrimination in, 56; as elitist, 7, 62; as family sport, 162; line umpires in, 170; and national academy concept, 161, 162; racial progress in, 181; racism in, 27, 29, 52, 191, 192, 193, 205; ranking system of, 128; and umpiring, 172; wild cards, distribution of in, 156, 157, 158
Tennis and Education Foundation, 120
Terry, Albert, 63
Terry, Miriam, 63
Terry, Roger, 63, 71, 74
Thomas, Irma, 236
Thomas, Willis, Jr., 106, 112, 119, 120, 140, 147, 228
Thomas, Willis, Sr., 120
Thompson, Ted, 108
Tian Tian Sun, 117
Tiegs, Cheryl, 199
Till, Emmett, 59
Ting Li, 117
Trabert, Tony, 109
Trump, Donald, 24
Tubman, Harriet, 108
Tucker, Albert, 122

Tuskegee Institute, 107, 108
Tyus, Wyomia, 182

Uberoi, Neha, 220
Uganda, 82
Umpiring: and color-coded
   designations, 172
United Negro College Fund, 98, 118
U.S. Open, 169, 180; black female
   tennis players at, 15; and open era,
   15; revenue from, 159
United States Lawn Tennis
   Association (USLTA), 4, 19, 52,
   54, 55, 58, 66, 102, 141; and ATA
   wild cards, 113–114, 145; as
   public entity, 180; racism,
   accusations against, 114, 144;
   status quo, maintaining of, 155
United States Tennis Association
   (USTA), 115, 158, 159, 161, 181,
   213, 227; and black families, 160,
   162; lawsuit against, 169, 172,
   179; and player development, 228;
   racial slur, response to, 178

Vaidisova, Nicole, 118
Venus and Serena: For Real
   (television series), 38
Vietnam War, 81
Vilas, Guillermo, 80
Voting Rights Act, 182

Wade, Abdoulaye, 236
Wade, Dwayne, 156
Wade, Virginia, 71, 193
Walker, Buddy, 50, 51, 64
Walker, W. W., 107
Walls, Julia, 143
Washington, Christine, 162
Washington, Kenny, 54
Washington, MaliVai, viii, 35, 115,
   125, 128, 136, 144, 162, 163,
   164, 165, 166, 167
Washington, Masanja, 163

Washington, Mashiska, 158, 162, 163
Washington, Mashona, 115, 140,
   158, 162, 163, 228
Washington, Michaela, 115, 162, 163
Washington, Mikoyan, 162
Washington, Ora, 3, 109
Washington, William, 19, 128, 155,
   156, 158, 160, 162, 165, 167, 168
Watson, Lillian, 24
Watson, Maud, 24
Wayne, John, 66
Weir, Reginald, 3, 55, 108, 109, 111,
   238
Wekesa, Paul, 136, 209
White, Anne, 147
Wilander, Mats, 175, 201, 204
Wilberforce University, 107
Wilkerson, John, 4, 22, 77, 103, 106,
   116, 119, 142, 147, 148, 150,
   153, 154, 162, 214, 227, 228;
   tribute to, 140, 141
Williams, Julia, 20
Williams, Richard, 3, 17, 19, 20, 21,
   22, 24, 25, 28, 31, 37, 216, 226,
   235, 236, 238; booing of, 27;
   divorce of, 234; as Father of
   Tennis, 30; lawsuit against, 23
Williams, Serena, viii, 3, 6, 8, 9, 10,
   13, 25, 26, 28, 29, 30, 42, 43, 49,
   75, 116, 117, 119, 123, 135, 148,
   149, 151, 154, 157, 160, 161,
   191, 212, 219, 220, 221, 222,
   223, 226, 229, 232; activities of,
   38; as actress, 46; in Africa, 236;
   background of, 19; and "Battle of
   the Sexes" match, 23, 24; birth of,
   20; booing of, 27, 28; and Cat
   Suit, 11; coaching of, 21, 22; as
   different, 32; dominance, end of,
   235; and endorsement deals, 40;
   Chris Evert, open letter from,
   39–40; family, as close-knit, 234;
   and fashion, 32, 44; in gossip
   columns, 41; on Althea Gibson,

47; and Grand Slam, 12, 33, 45; as hip, 224, 225; injuries of, 35, 37, 233; as inspiring, 227–228; as intimidating, 15; lawsuit against, 23; No. 1 ranking of, 35; popularity of, 23, 33; as proud, 15; and racism, 35; as role model, 22, 146; as Sister Act, 31, 33, 34; sister to sister competition, 35, 36, 37; stardom of, 37; superior ability of, 15

Williams Sisters Tour, 235, 236

Williams, Venus, viii, 3, 6, 8, 12, 17, 18, 29, 30, 39, 42, 47, 49, 74, 116, 117, 119, 123, 134, 135, 148, 149, 151, 154, 160, 161, 212, 216, 219, 221, 222, 223, 226, 229, 232; activities of, 38; background of, 19; and "Battle of the Sexes" match, 23, 24; birth of, 20; booing of, 27; and "bump heard 'round the world," 16; coaching of, 21, 22; contempt toward, 14; criticism of, 15; as different, 32; dominance, end of, 235; and endorsement deals, 21, 40; family, as close-knit, 234; in gossip columns, 41; and Grand Slam, 33; as hip, 224, 225; injuries of, 25, 26, 35, 37, 233; as inspiring, 227–228; as intimidating, 15; as introvert, 32; lawsuit against, 23; No. 1 ranking of, 35; popularity of, 23, 33; professional debut of, 13, 22; as proud, 15; and racism, 35; reputation of, as difficult, 27; as

role model, 22, 146; as Sister Act, 31, 33, 34; sister to sister competition, 35, 36, 37; stardom of, 37; superior ability of, 15; as unwelcome, 14

Williamson, Phil, 7, 136, 226, 228; career of, 208, 209, 210

Wimbledon, 173

Win4Life Foundation, 189

Winfrey, Oprah, 236

Wingfield, Walter, 106

Winkfield, Jimmy, 3

Witt, David, 174

Women's Professional Basketball League, 182

Women's Sports Foundation, 118

Women's Tennis Association (WTA), 71, 74, 155, 158; as global, 222–223

Woodbridge, Todd, 151

Woods, Tiger, 34

World Team Tennis league, 87

Wright, William H., 107

Young, Andrew, 82, 98

Young, Donald, Jr., 6, 42, 157, 167, 168, 212, 218, 225, 228; background of, 213; career of, 213; endorsement deals of, 211; trumpeting of, 214

Young, Donald, Sr., 213

Young, Ilona, 213

Zappa, Frank, 82

Zvereva, Natasha, 20

Zvonareva, Vera, 42, 115, 222

A NOTE ON THE AUTHORS

Cecil Harris was born in Brooklyn, New York, and studied at Fordham University. He has written on sports for *Newsday*, the *New York Post*, the *Sporting News*, and *USA Today*, and has covered tennis for the *Indianapolis Star* and for Gannett Suburban Newspapers in New York. His other books include *Breaking the Ice: The Black Experience in Professional Hockey* and *Call the Yankees My Daddy: Reflections on Baseball, Race, and Family*. He lives in Yonkers, New York.

Larryette Kyle-DeBose was born in San Antonio, Texas, and studied at the University of California, Los Angeles, and the University of Southern California. She has worked as a photojournalist in Swaziland, Southern Africa, and as a real estate executive. She is the author of *The African-American Guide to Real Estate Investing*. For twelve years she has been a player-captain in the Atlanta Lawn Tennis Association, the largest local tennis association in the United States. She lives in Stone Mountain, Georgia.